Cargoes of the East

Cargoes
of The East

*The Ports, Trade and Culture of the Arabian Seas
and Western Indian Ocean*

Esmond Bradley Martin
and
Chryssee Perry Martin

Foreword by Elspeth Huxley

ELM TREE BOOKS · LONDON

This book is dedicated
to my father, E.B.M.

opposite title page
A *pattimar*, a type of Indian
dhow, sailing south of Bombay
in 1972. *Source: Cliff Hawkins*

First published in Great Britain 1978
by Elm Tree Books/Hamish Hamilton Ltd
90 Great Russell Street, London WC1B 3PT

Copyright © 1978, E. B. & C. P. Martin
ISBN 0-241-89855-2

Filmset and printed in Great Britain
by BAS Printers Limited, Over Wallop, Hampshire

Contents

Acknowledgements

I have been carrying out research related to this book since 1964, and, therefore, there are literally hundreds of people who have helped me in Britain, the States, East Africa, Arabia, the Gulf, India and Pakistan. I would like to thank all of my friends who have so kindly given me advice, guided me to new areas, introduced me to invaluable contacts, and who also very often came up with creature comforts in unexpected places.

Although it is difficult to single out the special few among many, I would like to take this opportunity to mention by name some people who have been extremely helpful to me in obtaining information for this book and the preparation of the manuscript for publication. Firstly, I would like to thank most sincerely Elspeth Huxley for writing the Foreword to *Cargoes of the East*. Mrs Huxley has composed a stylish, brilliant essay which is consistent with the many excellent novels and non-fiction books she has written on East Africa. Furthermore, her enthusiasm for this book has given me the best encouragement an author could have. Not only has she graciously entertained Chryssee and me in England, she has also kept in touch with me throughout this past year with a series of delightful letters which have helped to keep me inspired with my work right up to moment of submitting the manuscript for publication.

Four people, all experts in their fields, have read all or parts of this book. Dr Terry Ryan, an economist, read every word and was most helpful in his criticisms, especially on matters dealing with economics. Dr James Kirkman, the noted archaeologist and historian of the Indian Ocean, also read the entire manuscript, and his historical insights combined with twenty-four years of field work in East Africa were most helpful to me. Donald Hawley, British

Political Agent in the Trucial States from 1958 to 1961 and Ambassador to Oman, read the sections on the Gulf and made constructive suggestions. James de Vere Allen, a Research Fellow at the Institute of African Studies at the University of Nairobi, made valuable comments on the society of East Africa and helped me to obtain unpublished material on the dhow trade of Lamu. To these four people, I owe a special gratitude.

Several people supplied photographs for this book. Alan Villiers, the world authority on sailing ships and the author of many books and articles on the subject, kindly allowed me to publish for the first time some of his original photographs which he took on his famous voyage from Arabia to East Africa during 1938 and 1939. I am indeed flattered that Captain Villiers has given me permission to publish these historically important pictures. Joy Adamson, one of the most versatile and productive people working in Africa over a long period and a close friend of mine, has generously let me publish some of her unusual photographs dating back to the late 1940s. In addition, I would like to express my gratitude to Cliff Hawkins and the Kenya National Archives for letting me include their photographs. Jilo and Musa Quraishy have processed and developed all the black and white illustrations for this book, and I thank them for the care and attention to quality which characterize their work.

Finally, I would like to express my appreciation to the following people who have been most helpful to me; without them, it would have been extremely difficult, if not impossible, to gather together information relating to the dhow trade: Mohammed Abdulla, Khalil Aldoy, Tom Allfree, Mahmoud Amr, Maampoun Attia, Dr Bashir Datoo, Wolf Dourado, Hatim Abdul Ghani, Sir Wilfrid Havelock, John Jewell, Robert Kukubo, Dr Adolfo Mascarenhas, Crispin Mbapila, Terry Maginn, Thabit Masood, Hamid Mosteani, O. M. Naaman, Dr Christine Nicholls, Zani Nusseibeh, Dr Perez Olindo, Professor Simeon Ominde, Ian Parker, Victor Pereira, Jaffer Raza, Akberali Saleh, Ali Surur, Michael Tomkinson, Manuel Topjian, and Colin Webb.

The author and publishers would also like to thank the following for their kind permission to reproduce material in this volume. Alan Hutchison for the jacket photograph; the National Archives of Kenya, Tanzania and Zanzibar for permission to use photographs and manuscript material; from *China's Discovery of Africa* by J. J. L. Duyvendak by permission of Arthur Probsthain; from articles in *The Daily Nation* by permission of Nation Newspapers Ltd; from *The Portuguese Period in East Africa* by Justus Strandes by permission of The East African Literature Bureau; from *The Trucial States* by Donald Hawley by permission of George Allen & Unwin Ltd and Twayne Publishers Inc.; from *The Travels of Ibn Battuta AD 1325–1354* edited by H. A. R. Gibb by permission of The Hakluyt Society; from *Sons of Sinbad* by Alan Villiers by permission of Hodder & Stoughton Ltd and the author; from *A Description of the Coast of East Africa and Malabar in the Beginning of the Sixteenth Century* by Duarte Barbosa edited by Henry E. Stanley by permission of the Johnson Reprint Corporation; from 'The Pearl Fisheries of the Persian Gulf' by Richard LeBaron Bowen Jr by permission of the *Middle East Journal*; from an interview with the Shah of Iran in *Newsweek* 21 May 1973 by permission of *Newsweek International*; from *The Persian Gulf: An Historical Sketch from the Earliest Times to the Beginning of the Twentieth Century* by Arnold T. Wilson by permission of the Oxford University

Press; from *The East African Coast: Select Documents from the First to the Earlier Nineteenth Century* by G. S. P. Freeman-Grenville © Oxford University Press 1962, by permission of The Oxford University Press; from *The Book of Ser Marco Polo, the Venetian, Concerning the Kingdoms and the Marvels of the East* edited by Yule by permission of Routledge & Kegan Paul.

Every effort has been made to trace the copyright holders of the quoted material. Should there be any omissions in this respect, we apologise and shall be pleased to make the appropriate acknowledgement in future editions.

Foreword

Always, when as a child I visited or passed through Mombasa, I would make for the Old Harbour to look at the dhows. There they would be, dozens of them, wooden side to wooden side, their sails furled, every kind of object—cooking pots, fish, baskets of oranges, goats, fowls, sea-chests, coconut matting, home-made guitars—strewn about in the vessels' waists (for some dhows are deckless). Nut-brown, black-eyed, bearded sailors in dirty robes, sashes and rust or tomato-coloured turbans would be clambering about, and over all would hang a pungent smell, impossible, like all smells, to describe, compounded of tar, groundnut and fish oil, spices, dried fish, unwashed humanity and a bit of town drainage thrown in. If you were lucky, you might see a dhow beating out of the blue sun-drenched harbour, flags fluttering from the rigging, drums rolling, her big patched lateen sail filling with the salt breeze, heading for the monsoon-swept ocean, and India or the Persian Gulf beyond.

All this never failed to send a tingle of excitement down the spine. 'Romance brought up the nine-fifteen' Kipling wrote, making his point that commuters, too, have dreams. Even more did romance (whatever that is) send out these crude little sailing vessels (sewn together, until fairly recently, like a garment, with copra twine) into the stormy Indian Ocean, blown in one direction by the south-west monsoon and in the other by its north-easterly counterpart. With only the skill and experience of their captains to guide them—no charts or sextants—they either sailed some 2,800 miles right across the ocean to Karachi or Bombay; or they passed Cape Gardefui and the island of Socotra to enter the Persian Gulf; or they turned past Aden into the Red Sea; or they pottered up and down the coast of Zinj, as it was formerly known, from Mogadishu in the north down past Lamu, Malindi, Mombasa, Zanzibar, Bagamoyo, Kilwa and south to Mozambique.

Why do these little vessels, with their polyglot, irregular trade, seem so romantic? Perhaps because in itself trade—taking things from one place to another and bringing back something else—seems to give rise to more intriguing sights and scenes than merely producing or consuming the objects concerned. And then dhows carry cargoes which seem to us, though perhaps not to Arabs, Indians or Swahilis, unexpected. Ivory, apes and peacocks—the last two, certainly, would not be found, but the ivory is very much still there. Shall we say: ivory, turtles and *mira'a* (a twig that stimulates when chewed)—more interesting than sulphuric acid, bathroom fittings or plastic toys.

Moreover the ivory is generally smuggled; and smuggling, although in practice normally a squalid affair, still summons images of Cornish caves, brandy casks and mounted excise men. Finally, and above all, dhows are old, old vessels that, until only yesterday, have withstood all change, still fulfilling purposes that sent them out into the oceans when Antony's fleet sailed forth to Actium and disaster, when Phoenicians set out from Tyre to trade with all the peoples of the known western world. Sea-borne trade, strange cargoes, smuggled ivory, tradition and antiquity, little boats manned by adventurous sailors—it is a heady brew and certainly, whatever truth lies behind it, spiced with the flavour of romance.

In Dr Esmond Bradley Martin I have no difficulty in detecting a romantic in the matter of dhows. He tells us that as a post-graduate student writing a thesis on Malindi's trade he became hooked on dhows and resolved to find out all about them—their history, their *raison d'être*, where they went, what they carried, who sailed in them and what their chances of survival were in this most undhow-like world. This quest has taken him thirteen years, partly searching in such archives as exist, and partly travelling up and down the coast of East Africa to the ports of Arabia and Iran, and all round the perimeter of the western Indian Ocean. With a beaver's assiduity he has talked to dhow captains and sailors; sellers of sea-chests and carpets, buyers of shark meat, dates and henna; to customs officers and prostitutes and all manner of men; and he now presents this anatomy of the dhow, past and present, against a rich background of history. It is stiffened by statistics that will constitute its meat to those concerned with economics, and the rest of us may relish the anecdotal and descriptive trimmings.

Many years ago, I watched a dhow being put together—I would not say built—apparently out of worm-eaten old beams and rusty nails (hand-sewing had gone out by then). This was on a beach at Lamu, once famous for its dhows of a kind called *mtepe* (there are many different kinds). I could scarcely believe that anything so ramshackle and apparently (not actually) unseaworthy could really, with her crew of fifteen or twenty piratical looking men, cross that stormy ocean to reach perhaps Karachi, and return. Mangrove poles cut from surrounding swamps would form her main cargo, with a few extras like dried fish, coconuts and a carved bedstead or two. At the bottom would very likely lie concealed a cache of tusks. Without the smuggling of one commodity or another, Dr Martin tells us, the dhow trade would probably disappear altogether. A century or so earlier, these dhows might have carried slaves packed like matches in a box, in tiers, in the waist of the ship, to conceal them from the Royal Navy's anti-slavery patrols. Women encased in black cloth *buibuis* with slits for eyes were, and still are, carried in roughly constructed, unventilated cabins, subject to extremes of sickness, heat and unpleasantness for which discomfort seems too mild a word.

The dhow I saw taking shape on the beach must have been one of Lamu's last. There is no doubt that East African built dhows are dying, but, on the other hand, there has been an upsurge in dhow-building in Iran. By and large the outlook for them is poor. What is surprising is that, with the Concorde overhead, a means of transport that has scarcely changed, except for nails and auxiliary engines, for at least two thousand years should still be in operation. The more rules and regulations that are introduced by governments, the higher go taxes and customs dues, the greater are the dhows' opportunities for smuggling. 'Where there are breakers,' runs a Swahili proverb, 'there is also a gate through the reef.' Dhows are good at finding them. To continue with proverbs, 'When one door shuts, another opens', and in place of slaves there are illegal immigrants, eager to pay handsomely for a passage from impoverished India and Pakistan to Kuwait, Dubai, Qatar and other wealthy shaikhdoms, whose sudden modern cities must seem to be indeed built of gold. And then there is gold itself—gold bars smuggled in the opposite direction from Dubai in dhows with powerful engines provide an extremely lucrative trade. So gold and immigrants, with sidelines like cloves from Zanzibar, coffee, hashish in all directions, have given a fillip to the dhow trade and possibly saved it from extinction.

But Dr Martin thinks extinction is on the way, and his researches were possibly only just in time. In the Machakos district of Kenya, about thirty years ago, I listened to a withered old Kamba chieftainess tell me, in excellent Kiswahili, how she had been captured as a girl by Arab slavers, taken to Mombasa and sold to a merchant. She ran away and, almost by a miracle, found her way across the Taru desert to her home. That must have been in the 1870s or thereabouts. If people like Dr Martin had got busy with their tape-recorders then, so much would have been saved.

However, in my youth, the African past in the interior—the coast, with its Arab-based civilization, was in a different category—was not taken seriously; though perhaps the second Commissioner of the East African Protectorate (a brilliant diplomat and linguist and an authority on the Ottoman Empire and Japan) was going to extremes in describing it, in 1902, as a record of 'blank, uninteresting, brutal barbarism'. But certainly we endorsed a line from a settlers' jingle of the day celebrating the introduction of new forms of agriculture: 'What a glorious change from the era of beads!' Just as owners of early motor cars gladly exchanged them for more advanced, efficient machines, never suspecting how glorious a future lay before the old wreck in the barn (destined one day to become far more valuable than their splendid new, non-vintage acquisition), so we did not suspect that the despised beads, symbol of a primitive culture, together with all those leather snuff-pouches, amulets containing charms, necklaces of coiled copper wire, spears, swords in red-dyed scabbards, and enormous ornaments in distended ear-lobes, would become museum pieces and subjects of research in depth by university lecturers—clues, in fact, to a buried history.

The same with dhows. Their replacement by swift diesel-engine-powered, tidy, relatively comfortable vessels then seemed a distant but desirable dream. To many of us now—though probably not to their owners and crews—it appears as one more nail in the coffin of a past more adventurous, more individualistic, more picturesque, in short, more romantic than our present, which seems increasingly to be breaking its links with tradition and our human roots.

In suggesting that Dr Martin shares the romantic point of view I hope I do not seem to impute any lack of scholarly exactitude in the facts and figures he has collected and analysed so thoroughly. On the contrary, so far as they go these are illuminating and valuable, and he is the first to admit that statistics about smuggling are elusive, to say the least. The conclusions of history, in the end, come down to guesswork; the art lies in the building of a sound foundation and framework on which to rest the guesswork about human motives and activities, aims and failures. For this I am sure we can trust Dr Martin's judgement, and his resolve to leave no stone unturned.

In the last analysis it is love of the subject that inspires the guesswork, and here too we need have no doubts. Esmond Martin loves dhows. For them he has put up with many discomforts and turned a blind eye on the undoubted villainy of many of their crews. I do not know how to describe a romantic; perhaps one could say that he/she (I wish the language had a bisexual pronoun other than it) sees the splendour of the butterfly and ignores the dung on which it feasts, the raw material of its beauty. Similarly those swarthy captains, one-eyed because of syphilis, avaricious, totally indifferent to the suffering of animals and of women, dirty and corrupt, are heirs of Sinbad the Sailor, of all the Captains Courageous, even in part of Frobisher and da Gama, Raleigh and Drake. As for the dhows:

> It was so old a ship—who knows? who knows?
> —And yet so beautiful, I watched in vain
> To see the mast burst open with a rose,
> And the whole deck put on its leaves again.

Elspeth Huxley

Introduction

The dhow trade of the western Indian Ocean is undoubtedly the most fascinating international commerce in the world today. This trade is thousands of years old, and although some modernization of the sailing boats has occurred within the last thirty years, many of the products and ports of call have remained the same for centuries. Thus, the dhow is one of the most traditional means of international transport to be found anywhere. What makes the study of the dhow trade so thrilling is not just the fact that these sailing craft still today navigate huge distances in the Indian Ocean to exotic ports such as Zanzibar, Lamu, Aden, Muscat, Kuwait, Bandar Abbas, Karachi and Bombay, but also that their cargoes are unusual and varied. For example, from East Africa Persian *booms* carry mangrove poles from the insect-infested swamps of the Rufiji Delta of Tanzania to Kuwait, over 3,500 miles away. Dhows from the Hadhramaut carry to Mombasa salt and dried fish, returning to their home ports laden with ghee, lemon juice and grains. From Kuwait cars are transported across the Gulf to a number of Iranian ports where fresh vegetables and fruit are picked up for the return trip.

Another enthralling aspect of the study of the dhow trade is the illicit movement, or to put it more bluntly, the smuggling of exotic and rare commodities and the subterfuge involved. The major gold smuggling in the world originates in Dubai where this precious metal is transported by small but fast dhows to Bombay. Furthermore, almost every night many immigrants are packed up on dhows from poverty-stricken areas of India, Pakistan and Iran and are dumped on the beaches of oil shaikhdoms hoping to find jobs. Also, Indian dhows sail a couple of thousand miles to East Africa with hashish and pick up, illegally, ivory from the Rufiji Delta which they transport back to

India. Some Indian dhows spend almost half the year travelling and trading around various ports in the Indian Ocean. The illegal movement of both hashish and hard drugs, which originate in Pakistan and India, commonly occurs by dhow amongst the Arabian Gulf ports. It is extraordinary that some of the greatest and most nefarious smuggling is carried on by sailing dhows in this era of space travel and the Concorde.

This book is an attempt to chronicle what may well be the last days of the dhow trade in the Indian Ocean. I am interested in describing the curious and surprising commodities involved in this commerce, the exotic ports from which they originate, the kinds of boats, and especially the people who sail on the dhows and who are active in the trading of the various goods. I will not be examining in much detail the actual voyage of a dhow, although I have personally travelled on dhows both in the Gulf and in East Africa; such journeys have already been well described by Alan Villiers, A. H. J. Prins and Marion Kaplan. My major emphasis will be on the reasons why the dhow trade still continues. I want also to give the reader a vicarious chance to see what it is like to live in exotic towns such as Lamu, Mombasa, Zanzibar, Kuwait, Abu Dhabi and Dubai and to appreciate the importance of rather strange commodities in the lives of people who are, in a way, far removed from the sophistication of the modern world. So far almost all the articles and books written on the dhow trade have been by adventurers who have participated on a dhow voyage. An exception to this is Prins who studied the construction of dhows. No one until now has emphasized the commercial side of this traditional trade.

Unfortunately, the long distance dhow trade between the Indian sub-continent and East Africa is dying. I was indeed lucky to have begun my research before this trade had declined so severely, and therefore the data I collected and the interviews I carried out have now become contributions to history. On the other hand, the dhow trade along the East African coast, amongst the ports of Arabia, across the Arab/Persian Gulf, and between India and the Gulf is still flourishing.

The material for this book has arisen from almost continual travelling and collecting data in the Indian Ocean from 1964 to 1976. During this thirteen-year period I have visited at least once, and, in most cases, more often Mozambique, Tanganyika, Zanzibar, Kenya, Ethiopia, Aden, Ras al Khaimah, Sharjah, Ajman, Abu Dhabi, Dubai, Qatar, Bahrain, Kuwait, Pakistan, India, Iran, Mauritius, and the Seychelles. I have carried out extensive fieldwork on mainland Tanzania, in Zanzibar, Kenya, the United Arab Emirates, Qatar, Bahrain, Kuwait, and all the dhow ports in Iran. Because of political difficulties, I was not allowed to do research in Pakistan or India, although I visited these two countries three times. Furthermore, besides the many archives in these countries, I worked in various libraries in Britain, including the Public Record Office, the Royal Geographical Society, and the International African Institute. I have also examined the Archives in the Seychelles and the Essex Institute in Salem, Massachusetts. Most of my archival research was carried out in the Kenya National Archives in Nairobi, the Tanzania National Archives in Dar es Salaam and the Zanzibar Archives; the latter contains much information on the Gulf and Persia.

The major part of the material for this book comes from hundreds of

Different types of dhows, found off Arabia and East Africa in 1850. *Source:*
M. Guillain, Documents sur l'histoire . . . 1856

Different types of dhows, found off Arabia and East Africa in 1850. *Source:*
Guillain

interviews with people directly involved in the dhow trade. I carried out these interviews, usually through interpreters, in the main languages of the western Indian Ocean: Swahili, English, Arabic, Persian, Urdu, Gujarati and Mahrashtri. I talked to people on dhows, in government offices, in shops, and on the beach; I interviewed ministers, professional smugglers, civil servants, sailors, wealthy businessmen, ivory poachers, academics, drug addicts, and simple crewmen on dhows as well as dhow captains and owners.

On occasion, I encountered some personal risk during these years of research. Doing a study of the dhow trade which by nature is partly concerned with smuggling involved dealings with known criminals and low caste people. During the 1971, 1972 and 1973 dhow seasons in Mombasa I had a rather difficult time which was in fact inevitable. I had to study the most lucrative aspects of the dhow trade which I could only learn from the smugglers and criminals themselves who were involved. Often authorities became concerned about me because of my acquaintances: I was called a spy for the Kenya Government, a C.I.A. agent, an Israeli agent and finally was asked to pay Shs. 2,000 for an interview. Eventually, without getting any information about the Somali dhows during the course of two dhow seasons, I broke down and agreed to pay Shs. 50 for an interview with one Somali dhow captain. This was one of the few times I ever paid for information, and though at the time I worried that I might be setting a precedent, it was instead the dhow captain who set a precedent for his peers: other dhow captains seeing that man talk to me at length decided that there was probably no harm in their answering my questions.

Although I had official research clearance (in 1975, I was unique in having research clearance from the Governments of Kenya, Tanzania and Zanzibar all at the same time), government officers and some civilians were suspicious of my work. I was, however, only arrested once. This happened in Bushine, Iran when I took a photograph of a woman smoking a hookah pipe in the market. Government agents have tailed me in several countries and in some places my notebooks have been confiscated and scrutinized by various officials.

The most frightening experience I ever had was in 1964 when the British were fighting rebels from the Yemen. I was driving up to the Yemen from what was then the Southern Arabian Federation when suddenly I noticed planes swarming overhead. These British jets strafed my vehicle with gunfire and unfortunately, after having spent months obtaining a Yemen visa, I had to turn back. Other political contingencies have also wrought havoc with my research plans. A year after the above incident, I was surrounded by a mob of Sudanese outside Khartoum at midnight who wanted to kill me because I had an American passport and they thought I must somehow have been involved in the Congo chaos.

I have also had to cope with health problems as a result of carrying out this research. After my first trip to India in 1968 I was sick for some time in Britain with a strange disease that no doctor could diagnose; and this disease which affected my muscles kept recurring for eighteen months. I was also severely ill after a trip to Pakistan in 1972. I guess on some accounts such hazards were more than likely to occur; after all, I've spent more nights than I care to remember sleeping on beaches on the Indian Ocean, in leaky boats, and under shelters which even euphemistically could hardly be called huts.

The most unforgettable places I worked in were the Rufiji Delta where the mosquitoes and sand flies made conditions so bad at night that I could not sleep at all, and on the Tana River and Lamu hinterland in Kenya where the mosquitoes are the biggest in the Indian Ocean.

In the course of my travels I have also had to spend many nights in repulsive hotels, consume food which a goat might disdain and work in extreme climatic conditions ranging from the rainy season in Lamu to the exhausting temperature of 48°C. in the shade on the island of Hormuz. However, I personally regret none of this. I have enjoyed every minute of my research in the Indian Ocean and I truly hope that other people will continue where I have left off. Regretfully, for the romantics anyway, much now is rapidly changing in the Indian Ocean. Modernization, especially in the Gulf, is standardizing towns, often at the expense of their cultural heritage. Many of the old towns such as Kuwait, Dubai, Lamu and Malindi have changed enormously during the past decade, losing much of their individuality and charm.

I was happiest when I was sailing on a dhow back to Bandar Abbas from Hormuz, exploring the abandoned historical buildings of Zanzibar town at twilight, interviewing Omani sailors aboard their dhows, photographing the ruined town of Lingeh in Iran, watching crew members assemble on the beaches of Bombay, talking to carpenters constructing *booms* in the streets of Bahrain, and watching the arrival of foreign dhows from the battlements of Fort Jesus at early dawn. Intellectually and romantically, such experiences can hardly be equalled, and I look back on these past thirteen years as the most rewarding of my life.

In the sections of the book on East Africa the author has quoted prices in the local currency. At the time of going to press the rates of exchange are as follows:

	£ sterling	$ U.S.
Kenyan Shs.	14.24	8.32
Tanzanian Shs.	14.24	8.32

When dealing with Kuwait, Bahrain, Qatar, Abu Dhabi, Dubai and Iran, prices are quoted in U.S. dollars.

Early Towns and Trade
in East Africa

Some historians say that the Egyptians knew the east coast of Africa and the Phoenicians, following in their wake, went on to circumnavigate the continent. But the land of Punt, from which Queen Hatshepsut imported frankincense and myrrh was just at the tip of the Horn of Africa, and the wall paintings and engravings of Punt in her tomb show humpless cattle and leafy incense trees unlike anything in East Africa.[1] As for the supposed feat of the Phoenicians, Herodotus himself expresses grave doubts when he reports it, and some scholars today are equally dubious.

Nevertheless, for some centuries now East Africa has had contacts with Arabia, southern Persia and India. The ivory, rhinoceros horn and tortoise shell that were readily available attracted the more venturesome captains of sailing vessels and probably upon their return home they realized fantastic profits from these exotic luxuries. Perhaps a few of the Arabs who came to the East African coast found life pleasanter with the ancestors of the Boni tribesmen than at home, and they may have been the first to establish permanent trading communities on this coast.

The earliest information that we have on these communities and their commerce is the *Periplus of the Erythraean Sea*, written by a Greek living in Alexandria about the trade of the Red Sea and the Indian Ocean during the second or third century A.D.[2] In Azania, as the Greeks called the East African coast, the author of the *Periplus* explains that a bottle of wine will help win the hearts of the 'savages' and that a gift of grain will also be welcomed. Also, according to the *Periplus*, the earliest exports from East Africa consisted of ivory, slaves from the Horn of Africa, tortoise shell and rhinoceros horn; while hatchets, daggers, glass vessels, wheat, ghee and cloth were imported from

Egypt, India and Arabia.[3] The goods were transported in boats which were held together not by nails or wooden pegs but by coconut fibre with which the planks were sewn together. The town farthest south in East Africa called 'Rhapta' (somewhere in Tanganyika) in fact means a sewn boat.[4] The mention of these sewn boats in the *Periplus* is the first reference to a dhow in the western Indian Ocean.

East African place names in the *Periplus* are baffling and academics are continually disagreeing among themselves about their exact locations. For example, H. C. Baxter states that Rhapta was probably located at Pangani[5] while Neville Chittick argues that it was in the Rufiji Delta.[6] Disputes on this subject are typical of scholars and unless new archaeological evidence is produced from Tanzania, disagreements will continue indefinitely. However, certain names from the *Periplus* can be identified with modern towns, although this does not mean that these modern towns have been continually inhabited for 2,000 years. Malao was unquestionably Berbera in Somalia, the emporium of Opone was located at Ras Hafun, Nikon was probably Port Durnford, the Pyralaon islands Lamu, and Menouthias island was perhaps Pemba. The detailed description of Menouthias from the *Periplus* is worth recording:

> . . . the island Menouthias . . . [has] rivers and many kinds of birds and the mountain tortoise. There are no wild beasts except the crocodiles; but they do not attack men. In this place there are sewed boats, and canoes hollowed from single logs, which they use for fishing and catching tortoises. In this island they also catch them in a peculiar way, in wicker baskets, which they fasten across the channel-opening between the breakers.[7]

The importance of this quotation lies in the fact that the sewn boat only disappeared from the East African coast within the last fifty years, and the canoes hollowed out of logs, now mostly from mango wood, are still very common in Tanzania and in Kenya. Furthermore, the use of wicker baskets, called *dema* in Swahili, can still be seen everywhere along the East African coast. The fisherman here plies his trade not only as did his grandfather before him but in the same tradition lasting for 2,000 years.

The dhow is a wooden-built sailing vessel found in the Indian Ocean which may or may not have an engine. The word 'dhow' is a general term and does not refer to a specific type of boat. Thus, the sewn boat referred to in the *Periplus* is the earliest known dhow. These sewn boats probably existed all over the western Indian Ocean from the time of Christ to the twentieth century. Marco Polo mentions the sewn boats he saw at mainland Hormuz in the Arabian Gulf at the end of the thirteenth century, but he was not impressed by them:

> These ships are wretched affairs, and many of them get lost, for they have no iron fastenings, and are only stitched together with twine made from the husk of the Indian nut. They beat this husk until it becomes like horse-hair, and from that they spin twine, and with this stitch the planks of the ships together. It keeps well, and is not corroded by the sea-water, but it will not stand well in a storm. The ships are not pitched, but are rubbed with fish-oil. They have one mast, one sail, and one rudder, and have no deck, but only a cover spread over the cargo when loaded. This cover consists of hides, and on top of the hides they put the horses which they take to India for sale. They have no iron to make nails of, and for this reason they use only wooden

trenails in their shipbuilding, and then stitch the planks with twine as I have
told you. Hence 'tis a perilous business to go a voyage in one of these ships,
and many of them are lost in that Sea of India; the storms are often terrible.[8]

At about the same time that the *Periplus* was written the famous geographer
Claudius Ptolemy also mentioned the sewn boats on the East African coast
along with a reference to cannibals:

> Around this Gulf live the Man-Eating Ethiopians, on whose western side lies
> the Mountains of the Moon, from which the Lake of the Nile receives snow
> water . . . Above them are the Ethiopians who make sewn boats.[9]

Commerce and Trade in the Indian Ocean from the Tenth to the Fourteenth Century
From the second century until the tenth century, there is little information
available on trading conditions in East Africa. During this period, Indonesians
settled in Madagascar, bringing with them the banana and a canoe with
outriggers, known as the *ngalawa* in East Africa. Also, Islam was introduced by
the Arabs, but the Persians may have helped in spreading the faith. They were
then trading extensively on the African coast, and the excavations of Manda,
the oldest known town, indicate that the people living there in the ninth
century were wealthy and under the cultural influence of Persia. Interestingly,
they imported by dhow Islamic pottery from the Persian Gulf.[10,11]

In the 940s, one of the best-travelled Arabs of the Middle Ages, al-Mas'udi,
completed his *Meadows of Gold and Mines of Gems*. This geography was
reportedly so named because al-Mas'udi was afraid that without such a
promising title he would not be able to arouse in his readers curiosity about the
countries he had seen: China, Persia, India and Africa. In spite of his jumping
from place to place and topic to topic, the *Meadows*, along with the records of
the great Arab traveller Ibn Battuta, gives the most reliable picture of the East
African littoral prior to the Portuguese era. Azania is now the 'Land of Zinj'.
For al-Mas'udi it is a strange country indeed. Many of the people are black;
some have hanging lips, some sharpen their teeth with files and eat one
another. Al-Mas'udi is the first geographer to go into detail concerning ivory,
one of the most important single exports from East Africa from time
immemorial right up to the present:

> There are many wild elephants but no tame ones. The Zanj do not use them
> for war or anything else, but only hunt and kill them. When they want to
> catch them, they throw down the leaves, bark and branches of a certain tree
> which grows in their country; then they wait in ambush until the elephants
> come to drink. The water burns them and makes them drunk. They fall
> down and cannot get up: their limbs will not articulate. The Zanj rush upon
> them armed with very long spears, and kill them for their ivory. It is from
> this country that come tusks weighing fifty pounds and more.[12]

Al-Mas'udi also tells us that the ivory usually goes by dhow to Oman from
where it is transported to China and India to be carved into luxury items:

> In China the Kings and military and civil officers use ivory palanquins . . .
> They also burn ivory before their idols . . . In India ivory is much sought
> after. It is used for the handles of daggers . . . But the chief use of ivory is
> making chessmen and backgammon pieces.[13]

9

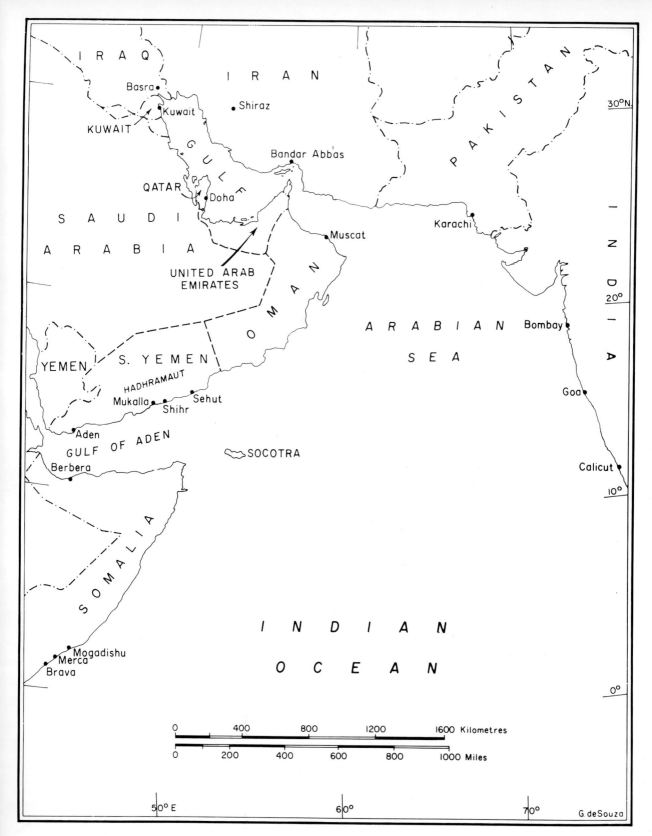

Western Indian Ocean

A curious export from the Land of Zinj mentioned by al-Mas'udi is ambergris.[14] He claims that the ambergris from East Africa is the best in the world, and certainly, from al-Mas'udi's description, it is more attractive than usual, being pale blue and as big as an ostrich egg. A more accurate description of the vile-smelling stuff would make the reader ask how it ever became a valued product. It is still questionable today what exactly ambergris is. Sometimes when sperm whales are harpooned it is found inside their intestines; yet there are occasions when ambergris floats to the shore, having been expelled from the mouth of the whale, so its presence may be due to a sickness. Al-Mas'udi says that Persian chemists have different names for pieces of ambergris depending upon their size and that a great deal of it goes with the ivory to China. There it is popularly known as 'dragon spittle' according to one of al-Mas'udi's contemporaries, Chao Jua-Kua, who also says that it is used (as today) for preserving the scent in perfumes and oil lamps.[15] A line in a poem dating from the Sung Dynasty (960–1280) refers to it: 'At night gilded lamps fed with ambergris shine like pearls'.[16]

The early period of the coast's history probably had its own stories about ambergris, but these have failed to come down to us. I know a recent tale from a former District Commissioner of Lamu, Kenya. He was on safari at Mvundeni when an old Bajun woman brought him an enormous lump of ambergris which he could not even fit into his mess kit but promised to send to Mombasa to be auctioned. When he received the money from its sale he sent word to her to come see him. She did, but was unfortunately accompanied by a string of male relatives. The District Commissioner wanted her to take just ten per cent of the nearly Shs. 3,000 fortune and place the rest in the Post Office Savings Bank, thinking that by so doing she would have enough money to pay off whatever debts she had, give the expected village feast in honour of her extraordinary find, and still have a considerable amount of money for use in the future. She might have been persuaded had it not been for the self-appointed agents who insisted that the entire amount be handed over at that moment, and off they went, in the District Commissioner's words, 'to perpetrate the binge of the century'. Three months later, on his next safari to Mvundeni, he was told that the old woman had drowned herself. Apparently, the hounding of friends and relatives for her money had become too much for her to bear.[17]

Many Arab geographers gave rein to their imagination when they wrote about East Africa because most of them relied on information from the traders who visited the coast. For the most part, such people in the Middle Ages were undistinguished either in the arts or sciences, so their powers of observation were not overly sophisticated. Added to this was an almost limitless credulity prevalent during this period, and the fact that traders to this day are by nature reluctant to disclose precise facts about the origins of their commodities. The following anecdote gives a fair idea of what a scholar is up against when trying to extract reliable reports from the few preserved manuscripts and books.

A biographer, Abu al-Mahasin, wrote in the fifteenth century that monkeys in 1402 were brazen enough to come into the houses of Mogadishu and carry off plates of food. When this happened the master of the house would pursue the thief to try to persuade him by flattery to give back the plate when he had finished eating. Every day in Mogadishu, at this time, the Ministers of

State came before the King's palace. As soon as they were assembled, the King would present himself at a window and the Ministers would immediately fall to their knees to make their obeisance. Once when they afterwards looked up there was a monkey in the king's place.[18]

A good and colourful example of a famous traveller letting his imagination and prejudices run wild is Marco Polo's description of Zanzibar which, unlike Hormuz, he never visited:

> Zanzibar is a great and noble Island . . . [The people] are all black, and go stark naked, with only a little covering for decency. Their hair is as black as pepper, and so frizzly that even with water you can scarcely straighten it. And their mouths are so large, their noses so turned up, their lips so thick, their eyes so big and bloodshot, that they look like very devils; they are in fact so hideously ugly that the world has nothing to show more horrible . . . The women of this Island are the ugliest in the world . . . their breasts too are four times bigger than those of any other women; a very disgusting sight.[19]

The Muslims were good at using the Land of Zinj as the setting for their parables, but nothing quite matches the Greek monk Cosmos Indicopleustes' use of the Sea of Zinj. Because it was so rough when he made a trip to the mouth of the Gulf of Aden in 525, he claimed that the flat world ended there.

During the thirteenth and fourteenth centuries, waves of Muslim expansion in the Indian Ocean led to the development of a number of towns on the East African coast. More and more immigrants came to make their homes here; some because it was politically wise for them to do so, others because they were simple artisans or workers who had become refugees as a result of the Mongol invasions of the eastern part of the Muslim world. Gedi, Kenya's equivalent to Pompeii, was founded at this time; Manda had passed the height of her prosperity; and Kilwa, making up for her rather humble beginnings, was then circulating her own coinage which was made of copper and inscribed with rhymed couplets (Kilwa's coins are the earliest known to be minted in sub-Saharan Africa[20]). Stone buildings in these towns were beginning to replace simple mud dwellings. In some instances, there were even plumbing facilities.

From the time of Christ to the end of the fifteenth century, when the Portuguese first arrived, the East African coast exported ivory, mangrove poles, rhinoceros horn, wild animal skins, ambergris, slaves (at least some originating from Ethiopia), fresh fruit and tortoise shells. It even happened that a live male giraffe was exported from Malindi half way around the world in the early 1400s and the story behind this little-known episode comprises one of the most fascinating tales of the entire history of the Indian Ocean.

China, the Eunuch and the Giraffe, 1417–1419

With the downfall of the huge Mongol Empire in the fourteenth century, trade routes to China were cut off and the Chinese upper class was deprived of many luxurious imports such as spices, fragrant woods and precious stones. It was not until the Ming Dynasty was firmly established that trade once again flourished. The biggest stimulus came from the Emperor Yung Lo (1403–24) who assembled a large fleet of ships under the command of the Muslim eunuch, Cheng Ho. We know very little about this extraordinary eunuch who was born in the Yunnan Province of China around 1371 and in his early years

Aerial view of the old sixteenth-century Swahili town of Gedi, in Kenya.
Source: James Kirkman

studied art and warfare. He was extremely good looking and possessed great height and strength and, on account of his astonishing assets as a courtier, diplomat and warrior, he was appointed Commander of the Emperor's fleet of ships.[21]

His first expedition (1405–7) went to Java, Ceylon and Calicut (which was known to the Portuguese as the 'Pepper Port'); on the second (1407–9) and third (1409–11) he visited more ports in Java and India, while on his fourth expedition (1413–15) he went all the way to Bengal and Hormuz. On the famous fifth voyage (1417–19) Malindi was visited for the first time. But why would a Chinese fleet sail to Malindi, a relatively poor, unsophisticated, small port on the Indian Ocean? The reason the Chinese came to Africa was that a marvellous animal, a reticulated giraffe, had been imported from Malindi to Peking. In 1414, the King of Bengal had sent a giraffe as a present to the Chinese Emperor. The presence of this strange animal caused a terrific stir because the Chinese thought that the giraffe was actually the famed mythical animal, the *K'i-lin*, similar to the European unicorn. The *K'i-lin* was considered a supernatural creature which would only appear in a kingdom which was ruled by an especially virtuous and just emperor, and the eunuchs of the court who were professional flatterers made sure that everyone realized the importance of the appearance of this mystical animal in China. When the Board of Rites went to congratulate the Emperor, he dismissed them modestly saying, 'Let the Ministers but early and late exert themselves in assisting the government for the welfare of the world. If the world is at peace, even without *K'i-lins* there is nothing that hinders good government. Let congratulations be omitted.'[22]

The following year ambassadors from Malindi presented another giraffe plus a 'celestial stag' (oryx) and a 'celestial horse' (zebra) to the Emperor. When the Emperor saw the giraffe and the other animals his officials prostrated themselves and again offered congratulations; he replied:

> This event is due to the abundant virtue of the late Emperor, my father, and also to the assistance rendered me by my Ministers. That is why distant people arrive in uninterrupted succession. From now on it behoves Us even more than in the past to cling to virtue and it behoves you to remonstrate with Us about Our shortcomings.[23]

The archaeologist Dr James Kirkman made some sagacious observations on this lovely quotation: 'The sentiment was admirable. No British Prime Minister has done better. The last phrase of course was not meant to be taken literally; Chinese Emperors had no more time than democratic politicians to heed time-wasting criticisms by out-of-date reactionaries.'[24]

The Malindi ambassadorial entourage had to be returned home, so in the autumn of 1417 a fleet of ships, including the largest junk ever built, which had an estimated displacement of 3,000 tons and a length of approximately 107 metres, commanded by Cheng Ho, sailed for Malindi with eighteen other foreign ambassadors. On the way, Cheng Ho stopped at Java, Malacca, Ceylon, India, Hormuz and Somalia. I find it amazing that Cheng Ho, who later made two more expeditions (making a total of seven), is so little known in the western world. After having read all I could find on this subject, I can only conclude that he was one of the most important explorers of all time. He personally visited so many more places than later explorer-mariners that he should receive recognition for what he did. Imagine what a feat it was between 1405 and 1437 to travel to places as far apart as Sumatra, Cambodia, Malacca and Malindi. Compared to Columbus, Cheng Ho's voyages covered greater distances, and more importantly and unlike Columbus, Cheng Ho knew where he was going. Furthermore, he was an excellent organizer of men and ships which is a trait that Columbus did not possess. For example, on Cheng Ho's first voyage he commanded 317 ships with 27,870 men on board.[25] When new history and geography books are written, Cheng Ho's expeditions should indeed be given prominence instead of rarely even being mentioned, because he was a brilliant admiral and he pre-dates all the great European explorers such as da Gama, Magellan and Drake.

After quoting a Chinese poem in homage to the *K'i-lin* ('with the body of a deer and the tail of an ox, and a fleshy boneless horn, with luminous spots like a red cloud or a purple mist'[26]), Professor Duyvendak sums up this incident in East African history better than I can:

> Thus it happened that the giraffe from the African wilderness, as it strode into the Emperor's Court, became the emblem of Perfect Virtue, Perfect Government, and Perfect Harmony in the Empire and in the Universe. Rarely have such extravagant cosmic claims been made in such refined language for any living animal. Surely, it is the most sophisticated instance of therolatry in history, the apogee of the lore of the unicorn! This is what the discovery of Africa did for Chinese Confucian ideology.[27]

A *boom*, seen through the ruins of Lingeh, Iran

East Africa during
the Portuguese Period

The Arrival of the Portuguese in the Indian Ocean

By 1498, the time the first Portuguese explorers rounded the Cape of Good Hope and sailed into the Indian Ocean, there were many prosperous ports and harbours for coastal trade in East Africa: Kilwa, Zanzibar, Tongoni, Mombasa, Kilifi, Malindi, Lamu, Pate, Siyu and Faza, to name a few. These towns were ruled by Arab Shaikhs as independent city states and there was not even a loose political confederation of the East African coastal towns. This lack of unity made each ruler vulnerable to attack from any outside power or even from any neighbour.

The economies of these towns were based upon agriculture, especially the cultivation of grains such as millet and rice, and the propagation of fruit trees such as oranges, lemons and coconuts. Some of the agricultural commodities were exported by dhow up and down the coast and also to Arabia but most were consumed locally. To pay for the luxury imports which the upper classes required the merchants exported ivory, slaves, ambergris, gum copal (used to caulk ships), coir rope, gold and beeswax. Most of these exports were carried on Arabian, Persian and Indian dhows and there is no reliable evidence that the local sewn craft of the East African port towns ventured much farther than Arabia. The local craft were too small and unseaworthy to cross the western Indian Ocean.

A great variety of luxury items such as gold and silver jewellery, silk clothes, damasks, satin, copper objects, carpets, pearls, perfumes, glass beads, Chinese porcelain and glass vessels came to the ports of East Africa from such rich entrepôt towns as Malacca in Malaya, Calicut on the Malabar coast, Cambay in Gujarat, and Hormuz at the entrance to the Persian Gulf. Food and spices were also brought in by dhows: wheat from Cambay, and cloves, nutmeg, mace and cinnamon from India and Malacca.[1]

The towns of East Africa in 1500 were wealthy as the following description of Kilwa by a Portuguese visitor in 1502 testifies:

> The city is large and is of good buildings of stone and mortar with terraces, and the houses have much wood works. The city comes down to the shore, and is entirely surrounded by a wall and tower, within which there may be 12,000 inhabitants. The country all round is very luxuriant with many lemon trees and gardens of all sorts of vegetables, citrons, lemons and the best sweet oranges that were ever seen, sugar-canes, figs, pomegranates, and a great abundance of flocks, especially sheep . . .[2]

The local rulers impressed the Portuguese with their ornate clothing and their sumptuous taste; and the King of Malindi was particularly admired. The following is a description of him at one of the first meetings the Portuguese had with him:

> The King wore a robe of damask trimmed with green satin and a rich *touca* [cap]. He was seated on two cushioned chairs of bronze, beneath a round sunshade of crimson satin attached to a pole. An old man, who attended him as a page, carried a short sword in a silver sheath. There were many players on the *anafils* [horns], and two trumpets of ivory richly carved and of the size of a man, which were blown from a hole in the side, and made sweet harmony with the *anafils*.[3]

From the ninth century to the coming of the Portuguese in 1498 the pre-colonial towns of East Africa prospered and the Swahili people developed their own culture.[4] Their architecture, with its pleasing and practical qualities, continues to be admired and copied today. House construction was based upon the use of coral rag and lime mortar for the walls and mangrove poles to support the roof. Some houses had elaborate decorative plasterwork inside, and the entrances, with their elaborately carved wooden doors, commanded respect and awe. Craftsmen were employed by the wealthy to construct many different pieces of wooden furniture; jewellers produced outstanding silver and gold ornaments, and it is even reported that silk was woven into cloth on Pate island for the élite.[5] The East African coastal cuisine was original, specialized and tasty.[6] When Ibn Battuta, whom James Kirkman amusingly describes as 'one of the worst scroungers'[7], spent time in Mogadishu, Somalia, in 1331, he was offered a typical coastal meal:

> Their food is rice cooked with ghee, which they put into a large wooden platter, and on top of this they set platters of *kushan*. This is the seasoning, made of chickens, fleshmeat, fish and vegetables. They cook unripe bananas in fresh milk and put this in one dish, and in another dish they put curdled milk, on which they place pickled lemon, bunches of pickled pepper steeped in vinegar and salted, green ginger and mangoes.[8]

Unfortunately, because of political fragmentation, the economies and societies of the East African towns were highly vulnerable to outsiders. When Vasco da Gama arrived in the Indian Ocean in 1498 it was the beginning of the end of these towns. Except for Malindi, which the Portuguese fostered from 1498 until 1593, the major ports such as Kilwa and Mombasa lost their

importance.[9] This was due to the Portuguese attacks and interference with the traditional trade of the Indian Ocean.

In 1505 Francisco de Almeida savagely attacked and plundered Mombasa. Many prisoners were taken and over 1,500 people were killed by the Portuguese.[10] In desperation, the Shaikh of Mombasa sent the following letter to the Shaikh of Malindi:

> May God protect you Sayyid Ali. I have to inform you that we have been visited by a mighty ruler who has brought fire and destruction amongst us. He raged in our town with such might and terror that no one, neither man nor woman, neither the old nor the young, nor even the children, however small, was spared to live. His wrath was to be escaped only by flight. Not only people, but even the birds in the heavens were killed and burnt. The stench from the corpses is so overpowering that I dare not enter the town . . .[11]

This was not the only time that Mombasa was sacked by the Portuguese, who again ravaged it in 1528 and 1589.

By 1512, only fourteen years after having first sailed around the southern tip of Africa, the Portuguese Crown had taken control of the East African coastal towns as well as Hormuz and large parts of the west coast of India and Malacca. Furthermore, the Portuguese commanded the trade of the western Indian Ocean which was an incredible achievement by such a small European country.

The presence of the Portuguese in the western Indian Ocean was not in the least beneficial to trade relations. The Crown wanted to have monopolies over certain products to maximize profit for the home country and this in practice diminished the trade in such commodities as gold and pepper. Dhows in the Indian Ocean were required to carry Portuguese permits, and goods which had not been taxed before were now taxed at six per cent, and after 1596 an additional one per cent was levied at Mombasa for the building and maintenance of Fort Jesus in Mombasa. Most of the towns in the western Indian Ocean were supposed to pay tribute to Portugal but because of interference in their economies and domestic politics, most of them retrogressed during the sixteenth and seventeenth centuries, some, such as Kilwa, almost into oblivion. Some towns, including Pate and especially Mombasa, fought for their independence but on most occasions lost because the Portuguese were amazingly resourceful and aggressive colonialists. They would stoop to any means in order to retain their hold on the East African coast and, in fact, even joined forces with the Zimba cannibals.[12]

The Cannibals, 1587–1589

In 1587 a horde of 15,000 Zimba cannibals, originally from what is now Malawi, encamped on the mainland opposite the island of Kilwa, hoping to overrun the island for human flesh. After many months of waiting, a traitor showed them how to get on to the island at night. Within a few hours, the Zimba had killed 3,000 of the inhabitants of Kilwa, thus ending what remained of one of the richest towns on the east coast of Africa. The Zimba were not satiated with their repast and immediately started to move northwards seeking more people. A year later, after 'killing and eating every living thing, men, women, children, dogs, cats, rats, snakes, lizards, sparing nothing' as an eyewitness reported,[13] they arrived on the mainland next to Mombasa.

At the same time, a Turk named Amir Ali Bey, who was in reality a privateer, had sailed down the East African coast claiming that he had been sent by the Turkish Sultan to free the local inhabitants from the Christian Portuguese. The Portuguese soon heard about the presence of Amir Ali Bey who had been welcomed by the suppressed towns on the northern coast, and a large fleet of twenty vessels and 900 men assembled at Goa and set sail for East Africa on 30 January 1589. The fleet arrived off Mombasa in early March and immediately attacked the Turks. Amir Ali Bey was no match for this huge, well organized punitive expedition. Suffering only a few casualties, the Portuguese rapidly forced the Turks out of the town and into the surrounding bush, but an unexpected ally was to administer the *coup de grâce*; the blood-thirsty Zimba were watching from the mainland with delight as the Portuguese inflicted heavy casualties on the Turks and those Arabs and Swahilis who had allied with them. The leader of the Zimbas sent a message of friendship to the Portuguese and begged to be allowed to come on to Mombasa island to help the Portuguese complete their task. They were granted permission, and on 15 or 16 March they rushed madly across the island, destroying all the vegetation in order to get the Turks out into the open. They then began their terrible massacre. Seeing these cannibals at work, Amir Ali Bey gathered together thirty of his most important men and fled on horseback into the sea to escape slaughter by the savages and gave himself up to the Portuguese, pleading with them to take him aboard one of their ships. The Portuguese agreed, but many of the other Turks drowned when the boats they hurriedly leapt into capsized because they were overloaded. This was the end of the Turkish threat to East Africa, but not the end of the Zimbas.

They continued their mobile feast right up to the town walls of Malindi. Here they were met by an unexpected ally of the Shaikh—a local African tribe called the Segeju. By now the Portuguese were also terrified by the rapacious Zimba and wanted to destroy them, and while the Portuguese were fighting the Zimbas from inside the town walls, the Segeju sneaked up behind the Zimbas and attacked them with their spears, killing hundreds of them unexpectedly. Caught in the middle between two opponents, the Zimbas broke up and ran into the bush followed by the Segeju who killed all but a hundred of them. So ended what the historian Sir John Gray called 'one of the most decisive battles in African history, in all probability comparable in its issue to that which took place over eleven centuries before when Attila and the Huns spent themselves on the plains near Chalons.'[14]

Consequent on the Turkish threat and the opportunity provided by the capture of Mombasa by the Segeju, the Portuguese decided to move their East African capital from Malindi to Mombasa as it was a more desirable base. The harbour at Malindi was poor and defenceless whilst Mombasa, being on an island, had excellent deep water. Entrance into the port could be easily controlled if a fort were to be built. The decision was made, and in 1593 with a labour force from Malindi, artisans from India, and an Italian architect, the great fortification known as Fort Jesus was begun. In the same year, the Portuguese transferred their headquarters from Malindi to Mombasa.

By the middle of the seventeenth century, the Dutch had taken most of the empire that the Portuguese had created in the western Indian Ocean. It was a widespread empire, and one whose people had never accepted Portuguese dominance. In 1650, the Omani Arabs drove the Portuguese out of Muscat, a town in a strategic position at the south-east corner of Arabia, and two years later the Omanis sacked Pate and Zanzibar. The Portuguese were unable to send out more troops from the homeland to support their western Indian Ocean complex, and thus their loss of East Africa became inevitable. The end came when the Portuguese were defeated in the great battle for Fort Jesus, the most spectacular documented siege in the history of East Africa.

The Siege of Fort Jesus, 1696–1698 [15]

In 1696 Mombasa, being the Portuguese capital in East Africa as well as the largest city, was the logical place for the Omani Arabs to attack and in March 1696, they laid siege to Fort Jesus. There were three thousand Omanis, including their supporters, but only fifty Portuguese (some of whom were civilians) inside the Fort. However, the Portuguese had one thousand seven hundred Swahili allies, most of whom were encamped outside the Fort in the surrounding moat. Captain João Leaõ bravely defended Fort Jesus, and the Omanis, instead of immediately pursuing their attack, followed a policy of 'wait-and-see'. After a few months, fifteen more Portuguese slipped inside the Fort, but in October the capable Captain Leaõ died. He was succeeded by a civilian, Mogo de Mello, who made the error of allowing his soldiers to visit the women staying with the Swahilis in the moat outside and the inevitable result was that many of the men caught various types of social diseases. In December, more Omani warriors arrived by dhow and the Portuguese were soon reduced to only twenty men plus their loyal Swahili contingent. Miraculously, a relief mission arrived from Goa on Christmas Day 1696 but, because the captain of this Portuguese fleet was in a hurry to sail down to Mozambique to trade and make himself rich, only a few supplies and a few men were sent inside the Fort.

Unloading mangrove poles in Lamu town

Above, Aerial view of Lamu town

Right, Lamu waterfront

Fort Jesus, Mombasa

By July 1697, in spite of the reinforcements, there were only thirty men left inside Fort Jesus, including Mogo de Mello, an Augustinian prior, and Bwana Daud, the Shaikh of Faza. Warfare, disease and even starvation had claimed the lives of the others. On 20 July the Arabs attacked again and within a few days Mogo de Mello and all the Portuguese soldiers had died. This looked like the end, but Bwana Daud and some fifty women were able to hold out for another six weeks by which time the Portuguese captain, who had preferred to trade in Mozambique, reappeared. He, however, died soon after his arrival, before he could accomplish much. The Fort was supplied with food and guns by the Portuguese for the last time in January 1698 when Bwana Daud and his followers and the women remaining in the Fort were evacuated to Goa. Throughout most of 1698 the Omanis kept up the pressure and, on the night of 12 December, when the garrison was reduced to only ten Portuguese, three Indians and two African women, the new captain sent a boy over the walls to get medical attention. He was captured and told the Omanis of the desperate plight of the survivors inside the Fort.

During the early morning hours of 13 December 1698, the Omanis made their final attack by scaling the walls. The garrison was unable to defend the

21

Fort, and the captain was killed. A brave soldier led the Omanis to the powder store, telling them that gold was kept there, and flung a torch into a powder keg. The powder store blew up, and many Omanis were killed as the consequence of the heroic defender's self-sacrifice at the moment of defeat.

Fort Jesus on that day fell to the Omani Arabs. The siege had gone on for thirty-three months, taking the lives of 400 Portuguese and 3,000 Swahili loyalists. This defeat marked the end of the Portuguese rule in East Africa. In losing Fort Jesus, which had become the headquarters for all their operations on the East African coast, the Portuguese had effectively lost everywhere. The Portuguese had controlled most of the coastal towns from what is now southern Somalia to southern Tanzania for two hundred years. Suddenly, they found themselves without any Indian Ocean empire, and the Omanis, who had hated the Portuguese not only because they were Christians but also because they had interfered disastrously with their profitable trade in the Indian Ocean, were now in the ascendancy.[16]

None the less, the economy of the East African towns remained stagnant and international trade was not, for several reasons, able to recover during the eighteenth century. There is some evidence that an ecological factor such as a significant decrease in rainfall was responsible for a drier environment in which agriculture was more difficult and the water table declined to such an extent that some of the wells in the towns went dry. The Portuguese hindered the possibilities for extensive trade in the Indian Ocean with their innumerable punitive expeditions against the rulers of the major towns which had consequently lost their former wealth but were still customers. After 1700, when the Portuguese had left the coast, overseas trade languished and the petty rulers simply fought one another. The Omanis were never able to exert the powerful control over East Africa which the Portuguese had wielded and, in the early eighteenth century, the Omanis themselves were attacked at home in Muscat by the Persians, which caused further chaos in the western Indian Ocean. Towards the end of the century Pate and Lamu were continually locked in battle against each other and, farther south, the interior in from Kilwa was in confusion because of tribal wars and the French demand for slaves for their plantations in Mauritius. From 1776 to the end of the century, Kilwa was the major exporter of slaves in the entire western Indian Ocean.[17] Also, during the eighteenth century, the Shaikhs of the various Swahili/Arab towns were unable to recover the acknowledged authority which they had possessed before the Portuguese arrived and had no idea how to create a federation which would have given them solidarity to oppose the Omanis or any other outside force. They were even unable to combat effectively the migration of Galla tribesmen who came down from Ethiopia and Somalia. The nomadic Galla wanted more land for their cattle, and in moving south and east they overran the coastal plantations and raided the towns while the local inhabitants seem to have either fled to Mombasa and Lamu or to have simply stood by, aghast at the situation. Except for island communities which had a natural defence, every town from the Somali border to Mtwapa (outside Mombasa) was sacked and abandoned by the end of the eighteenth century and only the towns in the Lamu archipelago and Mombasa survived as trading centres. By 1800 Mombasa and Pate were in fact the only significant towns; the rest of the coast was depressed and the dhow trade suffered accordingly.

The Slave Trade
in East Africa

The very mention of slavery conjures up ill-feeling in East Africa, and historians have seemed loathe to tackle the subject. Even today, there is very little research available on the slave trade that existed for hundreds, perhaps even a thousand years on the eastern coast of Africa. Many historians make sweeping statements about slavery and contradict one another in print, but they do not delve into statistics. Sir Reginald Coupland wrote: 'The Arab Slave Trade was as old as the Arab connection with East Africa.' He added that since A.D. 700, 'a steady supply of slaves was obtained from the interior [of East Africa] for the domestic use of the Arab colonists, and also and in greater volume as time went on, for export overseas to Arabia, Iraq, Turkey, Persia and India.'[1] Dr Freeman-Grenville on the other hand gives the opposite opinion: 'There is, indeed, no evidence to suggest that they [slaves] were exported at all from the coast farther south [than the Horn of Africa] during the sixteenth or earlier seventeenth century, and the contention of Coupland, that the slave trade was continuous from earliest times, rising to a peak in the nineteenth century, cannot be substantiated.'[2] It is a very curious state of academic affairs. One cannot help but get the impression that historians would like to deny the possibility of even studying the subject in so far as East Africa is concerned.

It is true that there is a paucity of information on the East African slave trade, particularly if one wants to tackle the subject on the same basis as has been done in West Africa where calculations are more easily made because of documented sources on the presence of slaves at their New World destinations. One does not have the same kind of information available on slaves arriving from East Africa to their new homes in Arabia, the Persian Gulf and India.

A slave driver and his slave in East Central Africa. *Source: Verney Cameron, Across Africa, 1877*

A witch being dragged away to be burned at the stake. *Source: Victor Giraud, Les Lacs de l'Afrique Equatoriale, 1890*

None the less, one can surmise, using Chinese, Arabic and Portuguese literary sources. Personally, I believe that slaves were exported continuously, probably in small numbers, from East Africa from the ninth to the sixteenth centuries to Arabia, the Persian Gulf and India. There is just too much evidence of the presence of Africans in the Persian Gulf and India in this period not to support this conclusion.[3] For example, it is well documented that the King of the old Muslim Kingdom of Bengal in 1473 had 8,000 African slaves, some of whom held positions in the civil service. Some of the slaves may well have come from Ethiopia and Somalia, but I am confident that the Arabs also sent them out of Manda, Malindi, Mombasa and Kilwa. During the Portuguese period there is no doubt whatever that slaves were exported from East Africa[4] and it is not rare to find quotes such as the following by Gaspar de Santo Bernadino of a Franciscan friar's visit to the Lamu Archipelago in 1606:

> When we reached Pate we were informed that some Moors from Arabia had arrived in a small vessel for the purpose of bartering for African boys whom they carried off to their country. There the boys were made to follow the Moorish religion and treated as slaves for the rest of their lives. Six of them had already been purchased.[5]

I think, however, that gold, ivory and other wild animal products were of greater value than slaves. Throughout the Portuguese period there was a demand for slave labour, including females for domestic use in households, in Arabia and India, and it was from the East African coast that many of these slaves were supplied. All the slaves were sent out on dhows, probably mainly on the sewn boat type known in East Africa in Swahili as the *mtepe*. Such dhows were common in Arabia, the Persian Gulf and India and came to East Africa during the north-east monsoon; it is unlikely that the East African local dhows were used to transport the bulk of the slaves overseas since they were smaller in size. I would estimate that from 1400 to 1600 about 1,000 slaves a year were exported from East African ports to Arabia, the Persian Gulf and India; from 1750 to 1775 perhaps between 2,000 and 3,000 slaves annually were sent across the Indian Ocean, principally to the Mascarenes and to Oman to work on the date plantations and for domestic service.[6]

With the development of coffee plantations on the islands of Réunion and Mauritius, the French began to import large numbers of slaves from eastern Africa. In 1776 a French trader named Morice signed a treaty with the Sultan of Kilwa to purchase 1,000 slaves a year. By 1790, 4,193 slaves had been taken from Kilwa on seven ships to the Mascarenes, and certainly from 1775 to 1800, Kilwa was the most important slave trading port in East Africa.[7] Morice spent several years in the western Indian Ocean and from his records we are able to put together a fairly accurate picture of trading conditions in East Africa for this period.

The French Slave Trading Station at Kilwa, 1776–1800

The Shaikh of Kilwa obtained slaves from the mainland in exchange for coarse cloth, blue calico and beads; money was not used. Most of the slaves were of the Makua, Nyasa and Yao tribes. The Arab and Swahili slave traders were not allowed to penetrate the interior to get slaves; the capturing was carried out by the local Africans. The slaves came from the interior carrying ivory and they were, 'naked with only their genitals and rump covered with a skin . . . [and were] circumcised'.[8]

The slaves were carried on ships from Kilwa to Mauritius, a journey which took from twelve to forty days depending upon the winds. Zanzibar was also a slave port at this time, and Muslim Indians came to collect slaves with their 300 to 400-ton dhows from Surat laden with salt and cloth for exchange. Somalis came to Zanzibar, too, for the purpose of obtaining slaves.[9] In addition, there were Arab dhow captains travelling to various East African ports to pick up slaves whom they transported to Socotra, Yemen and the Persian Gulf.

The Arabs and Indians came to East Africa not only for human cargo; ivory was at least as valuable to them as slaves. Morice tells us that only Africans hunted the elephants, using spears, arrows and firearms to kill them. Some people ate the flesh of elephants but the skin was of no commercial value; however, 'the hair found at the end of the tail is used to make bracelets'.[10] This is the earliest reference I have found to the elephant hair bracelet which is now the 'in thing' for tourists to wear who have visited East Africa, although many of the modern so-called elephant hair bracelets are in fact manufactured in Japan out of plastic. Aside from the slaves and ivory, there were other exports from East Africa in the eighteenth century including rhinoceros hide (for making shields), rhinoceros horn, ambergris, pyrites, wax, ghee, coconuts, millet, rice, maize, whale teeth, cowries, and copal (for making varnish for carriages).[11]

The slaughter of a young elephant. *Source : Giraud*

Morice is quite detailed in his descriptions and observations of the western Indian Ocean sailing craft. The Africans had only dug-out canoes which we

call today in Swahili *mtumbwi* or *hori*. The Arabs on the East African coast, with the assistance of Swahili and African carpenters, made their own boats which were probably very similar to the sewn *mtepe*. They sailed them as far away as Muscat and Mauritius, but most of the overseas trade was done in sailing craft originating in Arabia, the Persian Gulf and India. The Swahilis did not make or purchase their own dhows and had to pay freight charges on Indian and Arab ships whose home ports were mainly Muscat, Surat and Socotra. Morice refers to one dhow which was constructed in Zanzibar and was capable of carrying 300 slaves.[12]

Morice died about 1781 and within a few years French influence in Kilwa had declined. By 1804, Zanzibar had replaced Kilwa as the most important slave port in the western Indian Ocean. Mauritius was captured by the British in 1811, and the slave trade with Kilwa Kisiwani ceased altogether. In this same year James Prior visited the former wealthy town of Kilwa and described it in these words:

> Quiloa, once a place of great importance, and the capital of an extensive kingdom but now a petty village . . . We saw but two or three stone houses . . . Quiloa seems to offer only ivory and tortoise-shell for commerce . . . The number of slaves formerly exported amounted to many thousands, but at present the demand is confined to the Arabs, who do not take many.[13]

The Rise of Zanzibar as the Major Slave Exporting Town on the East African Coast
From 1800 to 1856, the year the famous Sultan Seyyid Said of Zanzibar died, the major towns on the East African coast were Zanzibar, Kilwa Kivinje, Mombasa, Lamu and Pate. Many of the former towns between the Somali border and Mombasa were still abandoned because the Galla had overrun them; only the island communities remained. The towns on the Tanzania mainland such as Tanga, Pangani, Bagamayo and Kilwa were of minor importance during the early years of the century.

From 1812 onwards, Sultan Seyyid Said of Oman was in control of the north coast of Kenya; he was to enlarge his domains to cover the entire East African coast between Mogadishu and Tungi Bay, just south of the Ruvuma River in Mozambique. He took over Mombasa in 1828 and finally, in 1840, he moved the capital of his empire from Muscat to Zanzibar.

With the arrival of Omani troops to man the fort in Lamu in 1813, the north coast of Kenya, except at Siyu, became fairly quiet; the various shaikhs became nominally the vassals of the Sultan of Oman and Zanzibar and they did not fight one another any more. This must have been a huge relief, particularly to the people of Lamu and Pate who had experienced more than a generation of strife. With peace came prosperity, and large areas of land on Manda and Pate islands as well as many acres on the mainland around Lamu were planted with fruit trees and grains to supply the market in Zanzibar. Cattle raising became an important industry; the poor beasts were exported live on dhows to Zanzibar. Prosperity in turn necessitated many slaves to work on the farms and, as the Africans of the hinterland of Lamu were unsuitable for hard work, the labour force had to be imported from southern Tanganyika, Malawi and Mozambique. From 1813 to 1856 thousands of Yaos, Makuas, Makondes, Ngindos and Maravis were brought into Lamu as slaves from ports such as Zanzibar and Kilwa Kivinje and, slavery having therefore become so important to the economy of Lamu, it is unlikely that many slaves were exported from there. However, occasionally some slaves were sent from Lamu to Pate and then on to Somalia as a re-export.[14]

Before about 1890 it is not possible to know how many dhows came into East African ports on a yearly basis because no one kept any records and even information about specific dhow types is often lacking. However, in the first part of the nineteenth century, J. B. Emery reported that in 1826 most exports from Mombasa were carried in *baghlahs*, some over 200 tons in size, and in *bedens*; the crews were composed primarily of Africans and the captains were Arabs. One large dhow in excess of 200 tons which came down to Mombasa from Brava, Somalia, carried 200 Brava merchants who all brought cloth for barter.[15] In Zanzibar, Captain Smee wrote that by March 1818, twenty-one dhows between 80 and 120 tons had come from overseas to trade during the season; however, in the early years of the nineteenth century, Smee was told that upwards of a hundred large dhows came in from Arabia and India to trade with Zanzibar.[16]

The town of Mombasa also expanded during this period, and under the Mazrui family (1735–1837) it became the most powerful town in East Africa. The leading families required quantities of slaves to work on their plantations and in their households, and these slaves came from ports farther south. Towards the end of the eighteenth century, the major exports from Mombasa were ivory, gum copal and ambergris. Slaves were not exported in any significant numbers mainly because the Mazrui Arabs did not want to trade with the French or any other Christians; they could produce at least 6,000 slaves but they refused to sell them to the French for Mauritius, the Seychelles or Réunion.[17] Sir Richard Burton visited Mombasa in 1857 and he does not mention slaves at all as an export commodity; however, he observed that one of the major imports into Mombasa was slaves from Zanzibar, who had originally come from Kilwa. The major exports remained the same as in the late eighteenth century with gum copal being obtained from the Mijikenda tribes, ivory from the Chagga and Kamba peoples, and hippopotamus teeth,[18] rhinoceros horn and cereals making up minor exports. Imports consisted of cotton cloth, glass, beads and hardware.[19] Thus, from the late eighteenth century to 1890 when slaves were finally allowed to purchase their freedom, the Kenya coast was a net importer of slaves. Some slaves, especially women, were of course exported to Arabia and the Persian Gulf, but their numbers were few. Zanzibar, on the other hand, was the major exporter of slaves in the entire western Indian Ocean.

Zanzibar imported large quantities of slaves even before Sultan Seyyid Said began to develop the islands. In 1811 Captain Smee estimated that three-quarters of the entire population of 200,000 were slaves. Smee thought that about 6,000 to 10,000 slaves were annually exported from Zanzibar to Muscat, India and the Mascarene islands.[20] From 1811 to 1821, perhaps an average of 5,000 slaves were sent from the East African coast, Mozambique and Madagascar to Mauritius and Bourbon.[21] In the mid-1840s, the slave trade had expanded enormously. The British Consul, Hamerton, estimated that 20,000 slaves were imported into Zanzibar each year and that from 13,000 to 15,000 were re-exported to the Red Sea, Arabia, the Persian Gulf and India.[22] It is probable, however, that Hamerton's export figures constitute an over-

estimation by about threefold. Many of the 3,500 to 4,500 slaves who were annually exported from 1830 to 1871 to Arabia and Persia were first sent to Oman (where, according to Sir Reginald Coupland, the population was then one-third African[23]), and then on to Arabian and Persian ports; some even went as far as the slave markets at Basra and Baghdad for distribution in the Turkish Empire.[24]

Terry Ryan, an economist at the University of Nairobi, and I have together studied statistics on slavery on the East African coast, and we estimate that from 1770 until 1800 about 3,000 slaves were annually imported to Zanzibar, while about 2,500 were exported from Zanzibar and the East African mainland to Arabia and the Persian Gulf each year.[25] From 1800 to 1830 the numbers tripled, although the exports to Arabia and the Gulf remained roughly the same. There are also references to slaves being exported to India. During the 1830s the importation of slaves to Zanzibar increased to a yearly average of 10,000; the 1840s witnessed 14,000, the 1850s 17,500, and the 1860s 21,000. Surprisingly, during the period from 1830 to 1870, the number of slaves exported out of Zanzibar and the East African mainland remained constant at about 3,500 to 4,000 a year. Most went directly to Muscat, where some were shipped on to other Arabian, Persian, and Indian ports.

The greatest number of slaves imported in the Zanzibar dominions occurred between 1870 and 1876 when 30,000 annually were being brought by dhows mostly from the southern mainland. This was the culmination of the era of massive slave imports, and the Arabs at this time were trying to import both legally and illegally as many as they could before the British stopped the trade altogether. At this time, at least 4,000 slaves per year were being re-exported to Muscat and the Persian Gulf.

Dr Ryan and I conclude that over the hundred year period from 1777 to 1876, roughly 1,200,000 slaves left the East African mainland, mostly for Zanzibar, but also for other markets in East Africa, Arabia, Persia and India.

Slave caravan on the way from the interior to the East African coast. *Source: H. Brode, British and German East Africa, 1911*

29

This figure, of course, excludes the entire export trade from Mozambique. Of the 1,200,000 slaves, we estimate that about 300,000 eventually reached Arabia, the Persian Gulf and India.[26]

Most of the slaves, as was true for the late eighteenth century and early nineteenth century, came from Kilwa. However, by the 1820s, Kilwa Kivinje, on the mainland, had taken over from Kilwa Kisiwani as the major southern port for the export of slaves from East Africa. Fortunately, Richard Burton examined the statistics in the Customs House in Kilwa Kivinje: from 1862 to 1867 an average of slightly over 15,000 slaves were exported annually to Zanzibar, while 4,100 slaves were sent to other ports in the Indian Ocean.[27]

Visiting Kilwa Kivinje in 1859, Burton arrived just at the end of a serious cholera epidemic which had been spread by infected individuals who had arrived here from Zanzibar by dhow:

> There were hideous sights about Kilwa at that time. Corpses lay in the ravines, and a dead negro rested against the walls of the Custom House. The poorer victims were dragged by the leg along the sand, to be thrown into the ebbing water of the bay; those better off were sewn up in matting, and were carried down like hammocks to the same general depot. The smooth oily water was dotted with remnants and fragments of humanity, black and brown when freshly thrown in, patched, mottled, and particoloured when in a state of half pickle, and ghastly white, like scalded pig, when the pigmentation nigrum had become thoroughly macerated . . . The women floated prostrate with puffed and swollen breasts . . . Limbs were scattered in all directions, and heads lay like pebbles upon the beach.[28]

This miserable picture of decaying humanity can almost be equalled by

Preventing slaves from running away in the nineteenth century

descriptions of the slave trade itself. Traders in Kilwa Kivinje wishing to obtain slaves bought them mainly from the Yao who obtained them by trading and raiding around Lake Nyasa. Sometimes an African would sell one of his own relatives to the traders, and David Livingstone relates that a chief in 1868 sold his 'young and good-looking wife' into slavery because he believed that she had been unfaithful to him.[29] After the slaves were captured, they were marched to the coast; some of them were used during this journey as ivory porters, whilst other less fortunate slaves walked for more than a month with a wooden yoke around their necks. If a slave happened to become ill along the way, he was given no help, and was sometimes even killed to discourage others from malingering. Livingstone records such an incident: 'We passed a woman tied by the neck to a tree and dead, the people of the country explained that she had been unable to keep up with the other slaves in a gang, and her master had determined that she should not become the property of anyone else if she recovered after resting for a time.'[30] At night, the slaves were often herded together into a wooden stockade and guarded by the Arab and Swahili traders.

When the slaves arrived at the coast, they were put into pens called *barracoons* or into caves to await the arrival of a dhow to transport them to the auction market in Zanzibar. The horrors of the dhow voyage are graphically described by Captain Moresby, an eyewitness to the misery:

The Arab dhows are large unwieldy open boats without a deck. In these vessels temporary platforms of bamboos are erected, leaving a narrow passage in the centre. The negroes are then stowed, in the literal sense of the word, two adults side by side, with a boy or girl resting between or on them, until the tier is complete. Over them the first platform is laid, supported an inch or two clear of their bodies, above a second tier is stored, and so on till they reach above the gunwale of the vessel. The voyage, they expect, will not exceed 24 to 48 hours; but often it happens that a calm or unexpected land-breeze delays their progress—in this case a few hours are sufficient to decide the fate of the cargo. Those of the lower portion of the cargo that die cannot be removed: they remain until the upper part are dead and thrown over. From a cargo of from 200 to 400 stowed in this way, it has been known that not a dozen at the expiration of ten days have reached Zanzibar. On the arrival of the vessels at Zanzibar the cargo are landed. Those that can walk up the beach are arranged for the inspection of the Imam's officer and the payment of duties. Those that are weak or maimed by the voyage are left for the coming tide to relieve their miseries.[31]

Further humiliation awaited these pathetic people in the slave market of Zanzibar where they were paraded in front of Arab buyers. The females had an especially hard time. The Arabs would take great pleasure in handling the women; they would fondle their breasts and even investigate their private parts for so-called imperfections before they agreed on the price. In 1842, the average price for a slave at Kilwa was $7,[32] but by the time one was landed in Zanzibar the price had substantially increased. In the same year, adult men were sold for $17–$20 and an attractive well-built female was worth $35 or £7.[33] During the 1850s, slaves from Zanzibar fetched between $65 and $100 in Arabia or Muscat, but the risk of being caught by a British cruiser reduced the profits considerably.[34]

Thus, by the end of Said's reign in 1856, Zanzibar had become the most

The remains of the Marahubi Palace built by Sultan Barghash in 1882

important slave trading port in the Indian Ocean. Many of the slaves who had arrived and departed from Zanzibar were transported in dhows, mostly by Zanzibari, Swahili and Arab sailing ships. Zanzibar was also at this time the major entrepôt for East Africa. In 1859 the most important exports from Zanzibar were ivory ($733,330), slaves ($400,000), cloves ($278,330), cowries ($257,220), gum copal ($185,835), hides ($127,765), sesame seed ($104,000), copra ($66,665), and coconut oil ($20,335). Minor exports consisted of: the orchella weed *Rocella fuciformis* and *Rocella rinctoria* which produced a dye of deep purple colour, mangrove poles for house building, hippopotamus teeth used for making sword hilts, knife handles and ornaments, rhinoceros horns which were shipped to Arabia and China for their supposed aphrodisiac qualities (old Chinese men ground the horn into a powder and put it into their favourite drink, hoping that their sex-life would be re-vitalized) and for medicines, beeswax which was eaten for its intoxicating effects, red pepper, ambergris, tortoise-shell, rare woods and arrow-root.

Where did these products go? England and the United States took copra, coconut oil, the orchella weed, copal, ivory, cloves, hippopotamus teeth, hides and tortoise-shell. India and Arabia imported mostly ivory, copal, cloves, coins, hippopotamus teeth, rhinoceros horn, coconuts, beeswax, arrow-root and gums.

As the major import port, Zanzibar received goods from half-way across the world. Silks, cottons, guns, gunpowder, hardware, coins and beads came from the United States and Europe. From India came more cotton goods, beads and hardware plus rice, ghee, spices and sugar candies. Dhows from Muscat brought in ornamental cloths, salt, dried shark and fish oil. Hundreds of small dhows from the Arabian coast brought in slaves, ivory, copal, tobacco, cereals, ghee, cowries, mangrove poles, firewood, rhinoceros horn and hippopotamus teeth. Madagascar exported to Zanzibar only tortoise-shell and rice.[35]

Trade on the East African Coast from 1860 to 1895

The Sultans of Zanzibar—Seyyid Said (died 1856), Majid (1856–70) and Barghash (1870–88)—not only controlled the islands of Zanzibar and Pemba but also most of the mainland from the Ruvuma River on the Mozambique/Tanganyika border to Mogadishu in Somalia. During the early years of Seyyid Said's reign, the Sultan had to use force in several places, including Siyu and Mombasa, to consolidate his power; but by the time of his death the leaders of all the towns of the East African mainland and surrounding islands, except Siyu, had capitulated to the superiority of the Sultan's fighting forces and accepted the new authority.

The expansion of trade on Zanzibar island had a spin-off effect on the mainland towns in Tanganyika and Kenya. During the middle of the nineteenth century, villages such as Mikindani, Bagamoyo, Dar es Salaam, Pangani and Tanga, all in Tanganyika, grew into towns. The slave trade from the coast to Lake Tanganyika and beyond, a distance of over 700 miles, was a major impetus to their development. This was because expeditions to the interior to pick up captives for slavery originated from coastal points such as Kilwa Kivinje, Bagamoyo and Pangani. In these places, the caravan leaders would naturally seek labourers for collecting ivory, gum copal and animal skins along the way. People wanting to join the caravans therefore flocked to

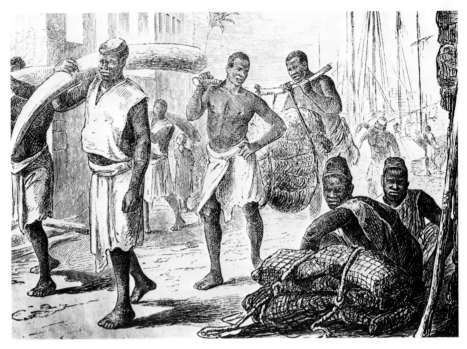

the new towns, adding to the quasi-resident populations. Also, the towns grew
as a result of becoming collecting stations for the agricultural produce being
grown on mainland Tanganyika to meet the demand for supplies required by
Zanzibar. Sorghums, millet, rice and fresh fruit were the main crops. In the
mid-nineteenth century, these towns were far from attractive places, and the
squalor of the inhabitants added to the disgusting atmosphere. Richard Burton
describes one such place, Wasini, near the Kenya/Tanganyika border:

> The climate is infamous for breeding fever and helcoma, the air being
> poisoned by cowries festering under a tropical sun, and by the large
> graveyards—here also, as at Zanzibar, the abodes of the dead are built
> amongst the habitations of the living. The population is a bigoted and low-
> minded race, Hassadin (envious fellows) of evil eye, say the Zanzibarians; a
> mixture of lymphatic Arabs, hideous Waswahili, ignoble half-castes, and
> thievish slaves.[36]

Richard Burton was not known to mince his words. Although he was
favourably disposed towards the Arabs in general, he was one of the severest
critics of the Tanganyika slave trade which flourished at this time:

> It was usual to throw the slaves overboard when the fatal symptoms,
> coprophagism [the eating of dung], appeared amongst them. A single Dau
> (Dhow) belonging to the late Prince Khalid lost when running a course 500
> slaves by sickness . . . A certain Charles L ——, a kiln dried Mauritius man,
> crucified seven negroes in terrorem: two were fastened outside the ship, the
> others were nailed by the feet to the deck . . . Another man, a Spaniard,
> finding his ventures likely to die of dysentery, sewed them up before they
> sent them to the bazar; this slaver made an act of contrition before he died,
> and severely blamed his bowie-knife.[37]

In Kenya, the capture of Africans for slavery was not as common as in

34

Tanganyika in the nineteenth century because it was far easier for a buyer to import slaves from Kilwa Kivinje or Zanzibar by dhow than to attempt to go inland and then face the inhospitable Taru desert and the bellicose Masai, Galla and Somalis. This is not to say that there were not many slaves in Kenya; there were many thousands. In 1885, five years before slaves were allowed to purchase their freedom, I estimate there were between 39,000 and 42,000 slaves on the Kenya coast.[38] Ten years later, when Kenya became a British Protectorate, there were 26,250 slaves remaining.[39]

After 1860, many of the towns which were important during the Portuguese era, such as Malindi and Kilifi, were once again occupied by Arabs and Swahilis. The Galla, who had been terrorizing the Kenya coast since the late seventeenth century, were defeated by the Somali and the Masai. The final showdown took place in the early 1860s when the Somalis invited many influential Galla to a wedding ceremony on the Juba River. There was no wedding, and as soon as the seventy-five Galla leaders had assembled, the Somalis massacred them and sold their children and wives into bondage to the Pokomo and Sanye.[40]

With the revival of many of the Kenyan coastal towns, there was a corresponding demand for slaves to work the enormous plantations of millet, sesame, tobacco, coconuts and fruit trees. There were additional slaves required to do the household chores and female slaves to please the master of the house. Accordingly, the number of slaves on the Kenya coast rose around 1876 when I estimate that there were 50–60,000.[41] Most of these slaves were imported by dhow, but after 1873 most of the new slaves came overland from Tanzania or from the Kilimanjaro area. For example, as late as 1884, several hundred slaves of the Kahe were sold to Bajun coastal traders by Mandera, the King of the Chagga, for $2–$4 per head; they were driven to Kilifi, Malindi and Mambrui where they were sold for $20–$30 each.[42]

Towards the Abolition of Slavery and the Establishment of European Control in East Africa

The British Government led the fight against slavery in the Indian Ocean. In 1822 Seyyid Said signed the Moresby Treaty which outlawed all external traffic in slaves to outside the Sultan's dominions and dependencies, prohibited the sale of slaves by any of his subjects to Christians and allowed the presence of a British agent at Zanzibar or on the mainland, 'for the purpose of collecting intelligence and watching the traffic in slaves with Christian nations'.[43] Slavery in the British colonies was outlawed in 1834.

In 1873, the Sultan of Zanzibar signed another treaty which closed all the slave markets within his territories, and prohibited the movement of all slaves from one part of the Sultan's dominions to another. After 1890, all children born to slaves were legally free, and in Kenya, in this same year, adult slaves could legally buy their freedom. Finally, the status of slavery was abolished in 1897 in Tanganyika, in 1907 in Kenya, and in 1911 in Zanzibar.

Most scholars, including recent ones such as E. A. Alpers, believe that the trade in slaves ended in East Africa around 1880 and that few, if any, slaves were being captured for the local market or sent overseas from Zanzibar by dhow. However, Terry Ryan and I have found a considerable amount of data to the contrary which shows that the slave *trade* (distinct from the *institution* of

An Arab slave dhow off the coast of Africa. *Source: Georg Maercker, Unsere Schutztruppe in Ostafrika, 1893*

An Arab dhow carrying slaves being chased by a British ship of the anti-slavery patrol

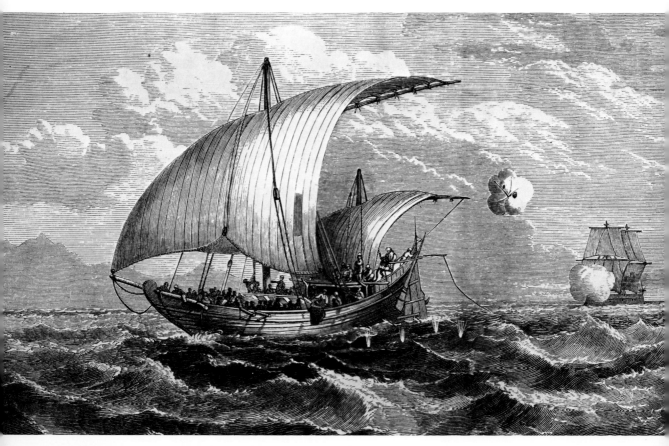

slavery which was still legal in the early 1890s in East Africa) continued at least until 1897. Mention was made above of the Chagga who were trading slaves in the 1880s. It is reliably reported, too, that in 1884, traders in the old slave port of Kilwa were still sending slaves to Bagamoyo.[44] In the same year, new slaves were coming into Lamu district, and these slaves were being supplied and sold by ex-slaves.[45] Some of these were even being exported to Somalia. Other Africans were selling one another into slavery, especially around Takaungu, because of a severe drought and the need for money to purchase grain.[46] In the early 1890s, probably 1,250 slaves were annually being shipped on dhows from the mainland to Zanzibar,[47] while as late as 1896, 350 were still being imported to Zanzibar.[48]

Slave exports from East Africa to Arabia were also common in the 1880s and early 1890s. In the 1880s several hundred slaves a year were arriving in the Gulf from East Africa.[49] In 1890, 400 were sent to Arabia alone.[50] One of the latest references I have of slave exports to Arabia from East Africa is in the year of 1892 when two wealthy Arabs of Malindi sent seven Africans to Muscat in a dhow.[51] Dr Ryan and I estimate that from 1880 to 1889 2,400 new slaves annually were brought to the East African coast and that the figure for 1890 to 1896, also on an annual basis, increased to 2,700. The numbers sent abroad were however much smaller. It is probable that from 1877 to 1896 an average of 400 slaves each year were exported from East Africa.

By the time most of the slaves had become free, Europeans had control of the governments of Zanzibar, Tanganyika and Kenya. The British Government took political interest first in Zanzibar with the appointment of Atkins Hamerton as British Consul from 1841 until 1857. During Consul John Kirk's tenure (first as Acting Political Agent and Consul in 1869) which lasted until 1886, the British consolidated their power and hardly any major decision could be made by the Sultans of Zanzibar without the approval of the Consul. Eventually, in 1890, the British fully legalized their control of the affairs of Zanzibar by declaring it a British Protectorate.

In 1884, Carl Peters went to Tanganyika as a member of the Society for German Colonization for the purpose of setting up a German colony. At first Bismarck refused to become involved in Tanganyika, but he changed his mind within a year and gave the Society a royal charter and sovereign rights within the territory of Tanganyika. In 1890 Tanganyika became officially a German colony with the purchase of the Tanganyikan coastal strip from the Sultan of Zanzibar.

Kenya was the last territory in East Africa to come under a European colonial power in the nineteenth century. In 1887, the British East African Association was able to acquire from the Sultan of Zanzibar a 50-year lease on his territories on the East African coast from Vanga in the south to Kipini in the north. The following year, the Association received a royal charter and became known as the Imperial British East Africa Company. When the I.B.E.A. Company ran out of money in 1895, the British Government incorporated the land nominally under it into the British East African Protectorate, which in 1920 became known as the Colony and Protectorate of Kenya.

The Dhow Trade
at Mombasa

How I became Interested in Dhows

Mombasa is the oldest major city in East Africa and, in my opinion, the most fascinating. I first visited Mombasa in 1964, but I did not spend much time there until 1968 when I began carrying out fieldwork in nearby Malindi for a Ph.D. from the University of Liverpool. Malindi was not quite the booming tourist resort it has now become, and its population of 6,000 could hardly compete with Mombasa's 250,000 so I came down to Mombasa quite often. Besides, James Kirkman was then Curator of Fort Jesus, which he had single-handedly turned into a fine museum.

James Kirkman is a tremendous conversationalist, a master of that cultivated art which sadly seems to be neglected more and more. The talk of an evening with Dr Kirkman and his wife could range from Celtic literature to head hunters in Borneo, but one of his favourite subjects is undoubtedly the expansion of the welfare state and its detrimental effects on mankind. Indeed, James Kirkman broadened our horizons through conversation and no doubt the frequent trips my wife, Chryssee, and I made to Mombasa were arranged mainly in order to spend time with him at Fort Jesus.

There were, of course, Government files for me to check, interviews to carry out and archives that I needed to look into in Mombasa. I enjoyed my work, but it was great to call it to a halt around six o'clock in the evening and make my way back to Fort Jesus. Chryssee and I would arrive there just as the last tourists were leaving and the large wooden gate was swinging on its hinges, ready to be closed and bolted for the night. We would climb the ramparts and stroll along the walls of the Fort. On the eastern side, we overlooked the entrance to Old Port, Mombasa, for centuries the route followed by all sailing vessels entering Mombasa. In the distance and closer by I caught glimpses of the unfurled sails of the dhows on their way into Old Port, and I could sometimes even hear, whistling through the wind, the odd order barked by one crew member to another. There was something magically romantic about watching the dhows from the ramparts of Fort Jesus at sunset. It was almost like becoming part of a world of the past. At first I was content just to watch and absorb the aura of tradition, but after a while I felt compelled to find out about the dhows. I wanted to know how old these sailing craft really were, from whence they came and to where they went, what their cargoes were, and whether there was smuggling going on.

While I continued my research on the historical geography of Malindi from the Portuguese period to the present, I determined that once my thesis was out of the way, I would devote my time to the old sailing craft of the western Indian Ocean. Already notes from my travels, source material from archives and my present work on the Kenyan dhow ports were beginning to yield some answers to my questions on the dhow trade. I was lucky in that my fieldwork in Malindi was so interesting, that it was easy to carry out and that I was not pressed for time. In fact, I was able also to spend five months in Lamu for comparative purposes, and I will admit it now, to look into relevant data on the dhows, which had become my secret passion – secret because a post-graduate student is not supposed to harbour grandiose ideas about future research topics.

My big opportunity came in March 1969 when James Kirkman and Richard Leakey, Administrative Director of the National Museums of Kenya, asked Chryssee and me to take over as acting Curators of Fort Jesus and Gedi (a Swahili ruined town of the fifteenth century which is a major tourist site). James Kirkman was going on long leave to Britain and someone was needed to administer the Fort, pay the seventeen members of the staff and guide V.I.P.s around the historical sites on the coast.

Luckily, the months of March and April are the busiest of the year for the foreign dhow traffic, and I had the wonderful opportunity of being in Mombasa right then. However, first and foremost, I was acting Curator of Fort Jesus and I had to do my work during the day in the Fort or at Gedi. Although I had a large staff, it was not an educated one, and I had to supervise everything, from checking the water meter in the morning (to make certain there was no leakage), to changing light bulbs. While I could let Chryssee handle most of these matters, it was really my duty to pay bills, answer correspondence, handle advances (sometimes I would be asked by a member of the staff for a Sh.1 advance on his monthly salary), and take any visitors who so requested on a tour around the Fort. This was usually interesting, but terribly time consuming; I finally charged Shs. 20 minimum for an hour plus Shs. 5 a head over four people and turned this money over to the museum as donations. Sometimes I would end up with a group of older American women with dyed blue hair. After giving them a full and enlivened explanation of the history of the Kenya coast and of the Fort in particular, and guiding them around the museum and the ruins of the Fort, which might take a full two hours, I would ask them if anyone had any questions. On one occasion, one of these blue-haired Americans raised her hand and asked: 'How did a young, beautiful boy like yourself get the job as Curator of a Portuguese Fort in darkest Africa?' After a question like that, I thought perhaps I should give up my job;

obviously, my lengthy explanations had not made much of an impression.

I also had official work early in the morning and late at night. In early May I was informed by Richard Leakey that he wanted to bring a group of Trustees of the National Museums of Kenya down to the coast to show them Fort Jesus, Gedi, Malindi and Lamu which they had not seen before. I was asked to be the guide and host. At 3.00 a.m. on 16 May 1969, Richard Leakey left Nairobi by car with some of the Trustees and others flew down. By 8.00 a.m. they had all arrived: Makone Ombese, Member of Parliament for Kisii; Ole Kipury, Member of Parliament for Kajiado; John Mbogua, Town Clerk of Nairobi; Peter Kareithi, Inspector of Art for the Ministry of Education; Alfred Vienna, Assistant Secretary in the Ministry of National Resources; and Professor Tom Odhiambo from the University of Nairobi. Also present was John Reader, a photographer for Time-Life Publications who was doing a photographic study on Richard Leakey for *Life* magazine, which was later published. Chryssee and I gave the group breakfast and then I showed them around Fort Jesus. Next on our itinerary was Mnarani, an old ruined town dating from the fourteenth century (abandoned in the seventeenth century). This site had been examined by Dr Kirkman in 1954 but the bush that he had cleared had grown back, and it was very thick indeed. As we approached the large pillar, someone stepped into a bee's nest and all of us were badly stung. A hasty retreat was made without any further approach attempted to the old buildings.

We next visited Gedi where I guided the Trustees around the mysterious old buildings. Gedi is the only main Arab–Swahili town which was not built on the seafront; its location three miles inland has puzzled many people and no one, not even the archaeologists, know definitely why Gedi was abandoned. Upon the completion of the tour of Gedi, everyone was exhausted, and still trying to recuperate from the bee stings. Tom Odhiambo was the only one able still to show enthusiasm, but he laughingly agreed that was because of the tremendous variety of insects that he had been able to collect along the way, and, being an entomologist, he was quite pleased with the morning. After lunch at Malindi, I gave another tour, this time of the Swahili buildings and remaining Portuguese ruins there. After that, we went to see the various local dhows in Malindi harbour: the dug-out canoe known as *mtumbwi* or *hori*, the outrigger *ngalawa*, the larger *mashua*, and the Lamu *jahazi*, the largest craft made in East Africa. We returned late in the afternoon to Mombasa, in time for drinks and dinner at the Curator's house inside Fort Jesus.

The conversation at dinner was stimulating, to say the least. We got into exciting arguments over education and politics and were only interrupted by flash bulbs from John Reader's camera. We talked long into the night, but next morning were up bright and early again in order to fly to Lamu. There were only four of us now: Richard Leakey, John Reader, Tom Odhiambo and myself. Richard had never been to Lamu before, and I was very pleased that we were making this trip together because for some time I had been worried about the fact that many Europeans visiting Lamu were buying up the remarkable wooden chairs, the decorative beds and other pieces of fine furniture made in the nineteenth century, with the result that Lamu was losing its own treasures. A museum was definitely needed in Lamu to preserve some of the items and to display them to the public.

When we arrived at the landing strip on Manda island, we took a small boat

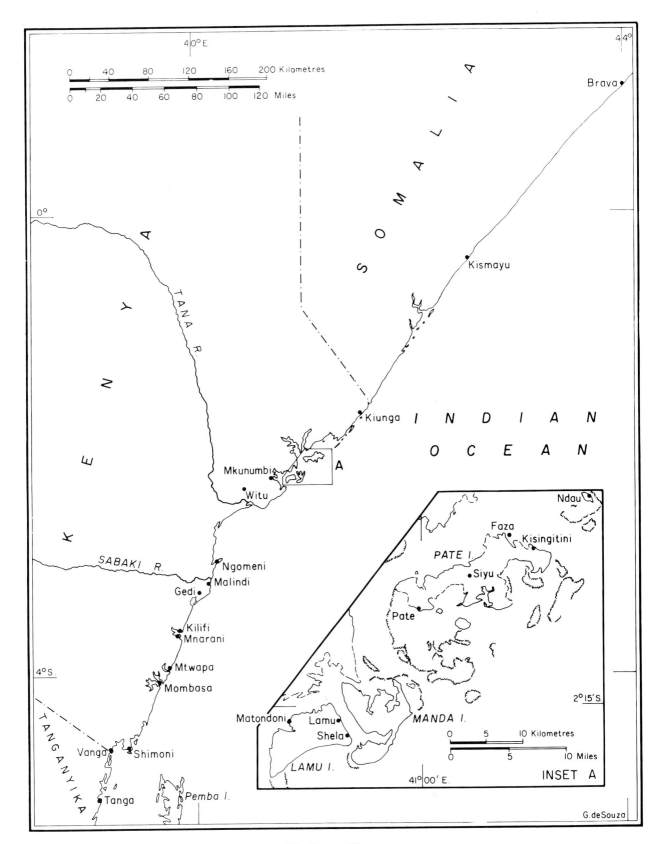

The Coast of Kenya

with an outboard engine across the bay to Lamu town. On the way, we saw several Lamu *jahazis* crowded with passengers making their way to Siyu and Faza. This was a colourful sight, but would have been even better at another time, for in the month of May there are rarely any foreign dhows at Lamu and even the local dhow trade is not active.

In Lamu town we were met by Mr Ngugi, the District Commissioner, who took us to his official residence, a fine nineteenth-century building on the waterfront. I had talked to Mr Ngugi before and he said that he was willing to hand over his residence to the National Museum if the Government would find another house in Lamu for the District Commissioner's residence. He took us all through the building, including the top floor where he had his private apartments. Richard was very interested and thought it would make a very good museum. We continued discussing the possibility of a Lamu Museum at Petley's Inn afterwards, where on view behind the bar was a superb model of a *mtepe*, the old sewn boat which was popular in Lamu until the 1920s.

After a quick lunch, we made a tour of the town so Richard Leakey and Tom Odhiambo could appreciate the architecture and have the chance to examine some more of the fine old buildings and see the beautifully carved wooden doors for which Lamu is well known. Dinner was awaiting us when we returned to Mombasa in the evening, and our excitement about the prospects for a Lamu Museum made us forget entirely how tired we were.

During the two days that the Trustees and Richard Leakey spent in Mombasa, a great deal was accomplished. The Trustees now had a better understanding of the rich history of the coast and the need to preserve the monuments of the past, and Richard was later backed by them in the establishment of the Lamu Museum, which is in the former residence of the District Commissioner. An account of this trip easily demonstrates the tremendous energy of Richard Leakey: he had us up early in the mornings and we worked intensively all day so that by midnight we were all physically and intellectually exhausted. Perhaps that is why we lost some of the group along the way! I have worked for Richard Leakey ever since, mostly in the capacity of a committee member of the Kenya Museum Society, and I can attest to his amazing drive: he is one of the first people to arrive at the Museum in the morning and frequently the last to leave.

Old Town, Mombasa

Chryssee and I continued to work in Mombasa throughout the month of May 1969. Chryssee spent most of her time writing a guide to Lamu entitled, *Quest for the Past: An Historical Guide to Lamu*, which was published at the end of that year. She included a little material on the dhow trade and began dreaming of visiting other ports in the western Indian Ocean. I had completed most of my fieldwork for my thesis and took the opportunity during our last few weeks in Mombasa to write a guide to Malindi, which I have since enlarged and updated. In June the Kirkmans returned to Fort Jesus, and we bid a temporary farewell to Kenya as I had to return to Liverpool in order to write up the material for my thesis. In November 1970, I received my Ph.D. from the University of Liverpool and less than four months later we had moved to Nairobi and made our home there. Once back in Kenya, I began my study of the dhow trade of the western Indian Ocean in earnest. We spent several months in 1971 and 1972 in Mombasa, and for the next three years Mombasa was my research base.

In Kenya, as is the case in most African countries, a scholar must obtain research clearance from the Government to work in the National Archives, see official documents, and to carry out fieldwork. I was fortunate that the Department of Geography at the University of Nairobi was pleased with my doctoral research and granted me permission to remain attached to the Department as a research associate and therefore government clearance was no problem.

Mombasa is really two cities. One part consists of modern buildings dating mostly from 1900, designed by Indian and European architects, and the other, which is locally referred to as 'Old Town', comprises multi-storey Arab/Indian style buildings, tightly lined up together with no apparent overall planning. Most of these were built in the nineteenth century, but in Old Town there are also some of Mombasa's longest standing buildings, including the Mandhry Mosque with its fine minaret which was constructed in 1571.[1] Contiguous to Old Town is Fort Jesus which was built in 1593, and enlarged and heightened in 1636. However, Old Town is not the oldest part of Mombasa: the original settlement was just west of the present toll booth of the Nyali bridge at a place called Mvita, which means island of war. Old Town did not come into being until the Portuguese established their settlement there in an area called Gavana in the sixteenth and seventeenth centuries. They built an Augustinian convent and the Church of the Misericordia as well as many dwelling houses,

Reading the Koran in a mosque in Kenya

but none of these remain today. All that appears to be left is what may be Portuguese masonry still intact in buildings at the north end of Ndia Kuu street.[2] In the eighteenth century the Omanis enlarged Old Town with their own section between the Portuguese quarter and Fort Jesus. Old Town still is the most colourful part of Mombasa, and a considerable amount of business is carried out here in unpretentious buildings. Also, many of Mombasa's residents prefer to do their shopping in Old Town instead of in the more modern part, and tourists enjoy ambling around here and often have jewellery made in the tiny little goldsmith shops. Within this small area, too, most of the activities concerned with the dhow trade take place.

The Foreign Dhow Trade of Mombasa, 1907–1973

For many centuries now, dhows have been coming into Old Port, Mombasa. Unfortunately, we have no accurate statistics until the twentieth century. During the Portuguese period, Mombasa had a population of approximately 10,000 to 15,000, but in the middle of the nineteenth century it had declined to a figure between 8,000 and 10,000,[3] which by 1900 had increased to 27,000. The 1948 census showed that Mombasa had 84,746 inhabitants, but in 1973 there were around 300,000.

From 1907 to 1915, an average of 200 foreign dhows came into Mombasa each year, which is about double the amount for the next largest port, Lamu. The greatest number of dhows arrived during the 1907–8 season, when there were 345, a figure not surpassed until 1945. From the end of World War I to the beginning of World War II, the number of dhows declined to an average of approximately 166 per year.[4]

During the 1912–13 season, among the 341 foreign dhows coming to Kenyan ports, 153 made their way to Mombasa. About half (47%) of the dhows which came into Kenyan ports were Arabian, with the next most important nationalities being Indian (37%), Italian Somaliland (8%), German from Tanganyika (5%), and French. There were no Persian dhows at all, which is odd since they were later to become the most common of all foreign dhows in Kenyan ports. During the 1920s and 1930s, the proportion of Indian dhows coming into Kenyan ports declined sharply. For instance, of the 408 foreign dhows there in 1937, 250 of which went to Mombasa, there were only 28 of Indian nationality. The highest numbers by nationality were Arabian (304) and Zanzibari (37); there were also 17 from Persia.[5]

Why was there a decline in the number of dhows arriving in Mombasa from 1907 to 1940 when the economy and size of Mombasa were expanding enormously during this period? The main reason was that the new port of Mombasa, Kilindini, was developed and modernized to accommodate steamships. Furthermore, in 1921, the Kenya Government changed the currency from the Indian rupee, which had been used as the means of exchange throughout the Indian Ocean for many decades, to the shilling. This created difficulties for the Arab, Persian and Indian dhow captains. There were no banks in the ports of Lamu or Malindi to exchange their currencies. The Government also during this period instituted regulations such as export permits which served to discourage foreign dhows from putting into Kenyan ports. Nor were local dhows spared from multiple fees. The District Commissioner at Kilifi wrote to the District Commissioner at Lamu in 1938

The *dau la mtepe* of Lamu, photographed in 1915; note the matting sail. *Source: James Kirkman*

about the excess number of charges which would have to be paid by an owner of a newly constructed dhow built for him at Lamu: an initial registration fee of Shs.20, a certificate of registration (Shs.5), an annual inspection fee (Shs.20), the purchase of a British flag (Shs.8), a yearly registration fee (Shs.24 for a dhow between 10 and 50 tons), a passenger manifest (Shs.2), a duplicate licence (Shs.10), a sand ballast charge (Shs.2 per ton), port dues (Shs.0.50 per 5 tons), a laying up charge (Shs.0.20 per ton per month), a towing charge, harbour water charges, and if the dhow came into Mombasa for repairs an additional wharfage charge of Shs.0.80 per ton and an unloading charge for cargo of Shs.0.25 per bag would have to be paid. The District Commissioner concluded that, 'It surprises me that dhows can carry on with the various upkeep expenses, ropes, sails and paint etc. added to the various charges mentioned above.'[6]

During World War II, the Germans and Japanese captured or blockaded many of the ports in the British Empire and sank and harassed many British ships on the open seas. Consequently, after 1940, dhows played a larger part again in supplying the imports and exports of Mombasa. In 1945, 371 foreign dhows with a total tonnage of 26,042 came into Old Port, while in the following year a record 433 foreign dhows sailed into Mombasa. The years 1947 and 1948 were also good for dhows with 321 recorded for the latter year. However, from 1948 up to the present, there has been a steady decline in numbers. From 1950 to 1956, the last big year when approximately 225 dhows came into Mombasa, the number of dhows which arrived annually in Mombasa averaged only 180, and from 1956 to 1959 the average dropped to 87.[7]

During the 1960s, the numbers kept declining. The average for the period was a dismal 43 foreign dhows yearly; the best of these poor years was 1963 when 67 foreign dhows came in, and the worst was 1966 when only 30 arrived.

In the 1970s, there was a reversal in the decline of the foreign dhow trade: in 1970, 85 foreign dhows put in at Mombasa; in 1971, 102; in 1972, 65; and in 1973, 54.[8]

From 1963 to 1973, the last year for which I have statistics, the most numerous foreign dhows (excluding those from Tanzania) by nationality which came into Mombasa were Arabian (37%), Iranian (28%), Somali (25%), Indian (6%), Muscat (1.5%), Kuwaiti (1%), British (1%), and Aden (.5%). Comparing these figures with the year 1912–13, the percentage of Arabian dhows remained roughly the same, but the number of Iranian craft increased from zero to an annual average of seventeen.[9]

A few foreign dhows commence their long journey from their home ports in Arabia, Iran or India in November at the beginning of the north-east monsoon, arriving in Mombasa in December, but most of the ocean-going dhows depart later and arrive in Mombasa in March. For example, in a typical year such as 1967, during the month of January 6 foreign dhows arrived; 8 arrived in February, 26 in March, 5 in April, 3 in May, none arrived from June to October, one in November and one in December.[10]

Upon the arrival of a foreign dhow at Old Port, a medical officer rows out to inspect the crew and passengers for any infectious or contagious disease. Kenya has strictly followed this procedure ever since an outbreak of cholera in Zanzibar in the middle of the last century, which was thought to have originated from stricken dhow crew.[11] In 1869 and 1870, 30,000 Zanzibaris

46

died of cholera. Even with inspection, health problems still occur in Kenya as a result of the dhow trade as, for instance, in 1945, when a great influx of Arab dhows, mainly from Sehut in the Hadhramaut, landed in Mombasa bringing a total of 2,654 Arabs. Some twenty-seven men, four children and one woman died during their stay, mainly from relapsing fever.[12]

After the medical officer has carried out his examinations, a customs officer boards the dhow to check cargo and the personal belongings of the crew and passengers. In Kenya, personal belongings and the crews' minor trading items, such as palm frond fans, are allowed in free of tax. After the customs officer signs the papers, the people may come ashore for as long as three months. They leave the dhow at anchor and usually make their way by dinghies which are kept on board ship for such purposes. One more brief inspection is carried out when they land to check that none of the crew is carrying contraband on him personally. At last free to enjoy the comforts and amusements of one of the major cities of eastern Africa, the crew hastily head up the steps of Old Port to their favourite shops and meeting places.

While the dhows are in port, the crews usually work on their craft in the mornings, cleaning and carrying out minor repairs. The *nahoda* (captain) and *sarong* (first mate) may be in town arranging the purchase of goods or attempting to ascertain the best deal in the purchase of mangrove poles and where to go to get them; they sometimes telephone Lamu to ascertain the prices there. The *nahoda* and the *sarong* usually return to their dhow at lunchtime to join the crew for fish, rice and fresh fruit aboard. Afterwards, it is siesta time until about four o'clock in the afternoon when everyone becomes active again, going into town and making plans for the evening. Many dhow crew have friends in Mombasa, and sometimes they spend the night at a resident's house. Except for *nahodas*, they rarely stay at a hotel. After all, there is always their sleeping mat and a blanket aboard the dhow and the crew can make their way freely to the dhow at any time.

The crews from Iran, the Arabian Gulf, Arabia, and Somalia enjoy coming to Mombasa. With Zanzibar essentially closed since the Revolution in January 1964, when an estimated 13,000 people were killed, Mombasa has become the most popular port in eastern Africa for foreign dhows. During the 1971-4 dhow seasons, I spent many weeks in Old Port and interviewed close to a hundred crew members to enquire why they liked Mombasa so well. Some said that they had relatives here; others liked the food, especially the inexpensive fresh fruits; and most agreed that Mombasa was a friendly town with a lot of things to do. The coffee shops they patronize are cheap and it is easy for them also to earn some extra money. Crew members are almost always poor, and the opportunity to sell trinkets from their homeland at a profit is appreciated. Most of the money that they make they spend in Mombasa, and so their presence is good for business. The Arab/Swahili shopkeepers are generally friendly and helpful to members of the crew who often bring news of distant kinsmen and discuss subjects of mutual interest, in particular, politics and Islam. The *nahodas* find Mombasa an excellent place to buy good quality and relatively cheap provisions, to sell their import items, to purchase trade items to sell in ports on the return journey and to make contact with the mangrove sellers from all over the Kenya and Tanzania coast.

An important asset of Mombasa, which many crew members will admit to you privately, is the availability of prostitutes in any price range and ethnic type: African, Arab, Baluchi, Indian and European. Considering that a crew member will be on a dhow for many weeks before putting in at Mombasa, the presence of women of easy virtue is to them a great advantage. One crew member was absolutely blunt and told me that Mombasa had the best prostitutes in the Indian Ocean! There is, though, one area where they are cheaper and that is western India, where, according to Mr Khajamed, an Indian crew member, a prostitute can be bought for only two rupees.[13] On the other hand, ports in Arabia and the Persian Gulf have very few girls available and they are expensive.

For at least 800 years, women in Mombasa have sold their favours to sailors from all over the Indian Ocean, and today female prostitution appears to be common in Mombasa. Although I have not myself carried out any sort of study on the prostitutes, it is obvious that they are highly prized by foreign dhow crewmen and that they are widely accepted. The prostitutes certainly make themselves obvious, hanging out in discothèques, bars, restaurants, movie theatres and coffee houses—in certain parts of Mombasa they are to be seen on literally every street corner after nine o'clock in the evening.

I know of only one scientific study on prostitution in Mombasa and that is to be found in a chapter of the 'Mombasa Social Survey'[14] which was financed by the Kenya Government and carried out by a research team headed by the government sociologist, Dr Gordon M. Wilson. The survey was never completed although thousands of pounds were spent on it. Neither was it printed, but only duplicated in stencil form. Because of the subjects it dealt with, it became an embarrassment to the Government and copies are very difficult to find. Chapter 14, entitled 'A Study of Prostitution in Mombasa', was carried out by Dr Wilson himself, and I present his findings which I agree are controversial and subject to more than one interpretation. Dr Wilson estimated that there were, in 1957, a minimum of 2,000 prostitutes within the municipal boundary: 74% of these women were African, 16% Arab and Bajun, 3% Seychelloise, 2% half-castes, 1.5% Asian and Goan, and .5% European. Over 35% of the total number of prostitutes came from Uganda (32% Buganda and 2% Munyoro) while the Kenya coast tribes made up 15.6% (Giriama 7% and Digo 6%), 12.6% were Tanzanians (mostly Zibasa) and the remaining Africans came from upcountry Kenya. The majority of the Arab and Bajun women congregated in Old Town probably because most of their clients, including dhow crew members, were to be found there.

Dr Wilson found that the average prostitute started her profession at the age of twenty, and had spent ten years in Mombasa and twelve years as a full-time prostitute. Only 5% of the 174 prostitutes in Mombasa who were interviewed were married and 94% of them lived in rooms which they rented in Swahili type houses; only 1% of them owned their own house.

The average prostitute in 1957 earned Shs.350 a month, quite a good salary at that time, considering that a room in a house could be rented for only Shs.20 per month. An African prostitute charged Shs.2 for an occasion and Shs.10 for a whole night. The European charged Shs.30 for one meeting and Shs.60 for the night; the Arab Shs.5 and Shs.20; the Indian Shs.10 and Shs.30. There was a lot of business from the 12,000 port and casual workers who went off work at four o'clock in the afternoon. Many of them had their regular prostitutes whom they visited daily and some even paid them on a monthly basis. Dr Wilson concluded that, 'there was no real need—through poverty or otherwise—to pursue this profession [prostitution], but rather the choice of an easier and more comfortable existence was more important.'

Generally, the results of the 'Mombasa Social Survey' would be the same if carried out today. There are many more prostitutes now, probably in excess of 5,000, and the more attractive girls charge up to Shs.200 for their favours. Dr Wilson found that only eighteen per cent of the prostitutes engaged in 'abnormal practices'.

I have also encountered male prostitution in Old Port, Mombasa. This is for homosexuals. In 1972, during the dhow season, I noticed that every afternoon around four o'clock a Swahili man, more Arab than African in appearance, would climb on to the deck of an Arab dhow and begin preening himself like a male bird. He immediately caught my attention because he was unlike anyone else. He dressed very smartly in tight trousers, had make-up on his face, and always carried a radio. When he was on the deck of the dhow, he would pull out from his pocket a comb and comb his hair for a long time, listening all the while to the music of his transistor radio. Intermittently, he would sip Coca Cola. His presence was extremely obvious, and I presume his antics were exactly what was needed to attract customers. I asked my Swahili and Arab friends about him and they were quick to inform me that he was a notorious homosexual. However, when I attempted to learn more about his profession, people were reluctant to talk about it. After a bit of prodding, I gathered that he came from Lamu and that he was here to obtain clients. That was all the information I could get from people on the spot, but my curiosity was roused and I began wondering how common male homosexual prostitution was in Mombasa during the dhow season.

I learned that there was a chapter on this subject in the 'Mombasa Social Survey', but that it was missing from most copies because such a topic is absolutely taboo. At length, I was able to look at a copy belonging to one of the researchers who worked on other aspects of the survey. In that chapter, Dr Wilson estimated that there were 1,200 practicing male homosexual prostitutes in Mombasa, 75% of whom were Arabs, the remainder being mostly Baluchi, Buganda and Swahili. I was startled that there could be so many. I have no idea how many there are now, some twenty years after this study was carried out, but I occasionally see them, much less obvious than the man described above, milling around Old Town, and I have also seen transvestites skipping along the winding, narrow streets of the oldest sections of Mombasa.

Dr Wilson discovered an unusual arrangement: 12% of the male prostitutes lived in Swahili-type houses in which they rented out rooms to female prostitutes for additional income. Of the male prostitutes, 40% remained in their homes and depended upon procurers to get their business, while 30% worked out of their houses with clients who knew where they lived. The average male prostitute earned Shs.500 a month and had considerable material wealth, usually in jewellery and gold work worth Shs.3,000. Almost all of this wealth came from their clients who were Arabs, Swahilis, Asians and Europeans. Dr Wilson was told that male prostitutes refused to co-habit with Africans. Homosexuality is illegal in Kenya and homosexuals, including Europeans, have been jailed by the Government. However, I have never heard of a lesbian being jailed or deported though there are some, particularly in Lamu district.

Male prostitutes are introduced to their profession at an early age. Dr Wilson found that 75% of the boys first became prostitutes between the ages of twelve and fifteen. Of the male prostitutes practicing in Mombasa, 40% were born there; 35% in Lamu and 12% in other areas on the Kenya coast. Many of the boys were introduced to homosexuality by older men, especially in Lamu:

> When he was twelve years old he was taken from school one day to a 'club' where several adults were watching a performance by young dancers; he recognized the dancers—all of whom were wearing female apparel—as being boys of his own age. As the dancing progressed he was asked to participate, which he did, and he was given something strong to drink. During the dance he gradually removed parts of his clothing until, finally, he—like the rest—was naked; eventually, the dancers joined and consorted with the men in the audience.

The above is a description by Dr Wilson of how one boy learned about homosexuality and came to take part in its activities. Some of the boys who do find out about sex this way do not remain homosexuals all their lives and instead turn away from it in their late teens or early twenties and marry and lead ordinary family lives.

Dr Wilson concluded that the main reason male and female prostitution exists is because of economics. In 1957, many of the Arabs and Swahili did not have the education or technical skills that many Africans were beginning to possess, mainly through Christian missionary schools, and therefore they could not compete in the job market and were finding that their living standards were falling far behind those of some Africans. Because the Swahili and Arabs believed that they had a higher culture than the Africans and should consequently live at a higher economic standard, many of them turned to prostitution as the only means by which they thought they could excel so as to earn sufficient money. Whatever the reasons men and women become prostitutes on the coast, prostitution remains a problem in Mombasa today and the dhow crews support both the males and females there.

Foreign Dhow Cargoes

Within a short period of their arrival in Mombasa, the crew members begin to unload their import commodities. Surprisingly perhaps, the products have hardly changed over the past hundred years. One reason is, of course, that few modern manufactured goods are produced in the Yemen, Arabia and Iran and those that are would come to East Africa in modern ships docking at Kilindini Harbour because of the difficulty in obtaining insurance among other things. There is still ample demand for traditional commodities from the Gulf. It is not so easy, though, to find out exactly what all the imports and their values are, because no statistics are compiled. There are neither monthly nor annual reports on imports and exports for dhows in Old Port. What I had to do was to look at each and every transire note for every import item from every dhow, and total them. Fortunately, these notes are written in English, Swahili or Italian (for the Somali dhows), and so at least there was no translation problem from Arabic or Persian. None the less, it is a tiring job, particularly if you are perched on a high stool in a clerk's office on a sultry day. It took me several weeks to compile the following table but from an interest point of view I think it was well worth while.

TABLE I
IMPORTS INTO OLD PORT MOMBASA CARRIED ON FOREIGN DHOWS FOR 1970

Commodity	Value in Kenya Pounds
Dried salted fish	£32,748
Salt	14,960
Dried shark	10,240
Antique and new wooden chests	8,000
Carpets	7,490
Seashells	780
Kikois	740
Fresh dates	255
Henna	162
Copper wire	153
Earthenware pots	75
Tobacco	55
Braziers	35
Miscellaneous items	273
Totals	£75,966

Source: Transire Notes, East African Customs and Excise Department, Old Port, Mombasa.

The dried salted fish comes mostly from Arabian ports such as Sehut, Ghidha, Jazir and Shihr.[15] The next most important place was Aden. Socotra and Kismayu (especially during the months of October, November and December when other foreign dhows do not come into Mombasa) also supplied large quantities of dried and salted fish for the Mombasa market and Tanzania. Dried fish were even sent as far away as Zaïre. Most of the dhows which brought dried salted fish were of Iranian, Arabian and Somali nationalities. In 1970, twenty-two Arabian dhows brought dried fish worth on average £1,042 per dhow; nine Somali dhows brought an average load valued at £245; and six Iranian dhows discharged an average cargo of £817, a relatively small amount considering that the Iranian dhows are the largest of all. The reason for this is that the Persian dhows carry many other products to Mombasa such as chests, salt, carpets, tobacco, dates, henna and clothes. Although dried fish is in great demand in East Africa, less of this commodity has recently come into Mombasa because the East African Customs and Excise Department keeps increasing the duty. Before 1970 there was no duty at all, in 1970 a tax of twenty-five per cent was introduced, the following year it rose to thirty-seven per cent, and in 1975 to fifty per cent. No wonder that fewer foreign dhows are coming into Mombasa.

Salt is mostly imported into Old Port in Iranian *booms* since these are the largest and therefore most profitable dhows for transporting this heavy, inexpensive product. In 1970, fourteen Iranian and three Arabian dhows picked up salt at Aden, worth an average £907 per ship. The salt is packed in

Dried fish and shark meat being transported to auction in Old Port, Mombasa

bags and has to be unloaded with the help of *hamalis* (porters) at Old Port. In 1970, salt had a tax of Shs.4.40 per 100 kilos.

Dried shark comes next in value and it is in great demand by the coastal people as well as by up-country Africans who have once lived on the coast and become used to it in their diet because it is half the price of beef. In 1972, a kilo of shark meat sold for Shs.2.50. The fins of the shark are considered to be a delicacy by the overseas Chinese and during the dhow season there are agents who buy the fins and ship them as far away as San Francisco; apparently, the white fin is more valuable than the black fin. Most of the dried shark originates in Arabia, Aden and Somalia. The auction of dried shark and fish in the Old Port of Mombasa is a fascinating scene which I will describe later in this chapter.

If you ask the average long-term European resident of the Kenya coast what he thought was the most valuable commodity carried by overseas dhows, he would probably reply without hesitation that carpets or wooden chests fell into this category. This is of course not true: in 1970 dried salted fish was worth four times as much as the imported chests. In 1970, all 459 wooden chests which came into Mombasa were imported in Iranian dhows.[16] This, however, does not mean that they were all made in Iran. Only the more valuable old Shirazi chests were made in Iran, while the majority of the ones which now come into Kenya were made recently in Pakistan or India. Cynics tell me that even the so-called antique ones are new and that they are thrown into the sea to make them old looking. I admit that when I was in Iran I never saw any antique wooden chests for sale in shops in Khorramshahr, Abadan, Bushire, Kung, or Bandar Abbas, the main ports of the country. However, I understand that

52

Above, A man in a traditional dhow toilet, in Old Port, Mombasa

Left, Sailing a *mashua* between Mafia and Chole, in Tanzania

Left, A boy sleeping in a dug-out canoe in Lamu

Inside a Koranic school in Lamu

some of the really old chests can be purchased from poor Iranians in the Gulf ports; usually they have been treasured family possessions for generations and are only sold when these people are in great financial need. Chests are often found on dhows because crew members use them to store their personal belongings.[17] I have not seen antique wooden chests for sale either in Kuwait, Bahrain or Abu Dhabi, and the only shops in the Gulf where I discovered them for sale were those in Dubai. My guess is that in so far as the real antique chests are concerned, the crew members bring them in for sale on the request of friends of theirs living in some of the less sophisticated and poorer areas of the Gulf. As for the new ones made in India and Pakistan, they lack the beauty of older ones. Antique chests now sell for £700 to £1,000. On the East African coast some chests are being made now in Zanzibar, but the metal work on them is not up to the quality produced by Arabian craftsmen.

Most of the chests which are brought into Mombasa by dhow, even when relatively new, are in poor condition and a lot of work is required to make them look presentable. As soon as they are landed in the main Customs House, buyers such as Hatim and Shariff Mohamed Abdulla Shatry purchase them directly from the dhow captains. The declared sale value of the average wooden chest in 1970 was £18, with a range in value from £5 to £25; obviously, in that year there were no antique Shirazi or Malabar chests in the consignment! The import duty was 33% (now raised to 50%) which was usually paid by the buyer to the customs officer since the dhow crews have little money or do not wish to go to banks. Exactly what the buyers paid, I do not know, but a lot of bargaining went on that year and no chests went back on the dhows for lack of buyers. If the declared value of a chest was £18, then the duty was an additional £6, costing the buyer £24; some repairs, cleaning the brass and polishing of the wood would be required before the chests could be offered for sale to the public. Shariff Shatry told me that in 1971 he sold carved Malabar chests for an average price of £60 and so-called Arab chests for £70. This seems to provide an attractive profit. The major sellers of wooden chests on the Kenya coast in the early 1970s were Shariff Shatry and Noel Gateja in Mombasa, Hatim and Tom Allfree in Malindi and Fakrudin Gulamhusein in Lamu.

Of the 629 carpets which came into Old Port in 1970, all but one came on Iranian dhows. The exception was one which came in on an Indian dhow which had put into Muscat before coming to Mombasa; the total value of the dhow's cargo was a pathetic £37. The average carpet in 1970 had a declared value of £12 which gives some idea of their relative poor quality. The duty charged on carpets was thirty per cent; their values ranged from £6 to £125. Almost all these carpets were new and woven in Iran and Pakistan. Very few valuable Persian carpets are now imported by dhow; these come into Kenya instead by air. Carpets are sold in Mombasa in the same manner as chests, with the buyer (usually a shopkeeper) paying the duty. In the Customs House they are unrolled and spread on the floor for inspection. Anyone can go to look at them there, and as the Customs House is a rather charming old building and business transactions are often carried on by very traditionally dressed older men, some with long white beards, it gives one the impression of stepping back into a former era.

In 1971, Shariff Shatry sold carpets priced from £10 to £700, with an average price of £90. The most valuable carpet he had in his shop in July 1971, was a modern Persian blue carpet. Shatry is the main carpet retailer in Mombasa. His family has been in the business of selling carpets and chests longer than any other family in Kenya. His great grandfather was born in Shihr in the Hadhramaut, and so was his great grandmother who claimed a pedigree all the way back to the days of Mohammed in the seventh century. Shatry calls himself a shariff, that is he claims that he is a blood descendant of the prophet Mohammed. He is very proud of this distinction, and one often sees men come up and kiss his hand in respect. About a hundred years ago, Shariff Shatry's grandfather set up a shop near the Bohora mosque since at that time the dhows landed their cargoes in that area because steamships putting into Old Port before Kilindini was built had priority. Around 1930, Shatry's family moved the shop to the area immediately in front of Old Port from where he still carries on his carpet business. He also purchased dates, salt and dried fruits which he handed over to brokers in Mombasa. Business boomed during World War II when many European soldiers came into Mombasa and bought Arab and Persian chests and carpets. Today, Shatry sells carpets, wooden chests, brass Arab coffee pots, furniture and metal trays, and his most important customers are British, American and German.[18]

Although the remaining imports are of little value and significance, they show what the people on the coast want to buy from abroad. Some of these products are used mainly in Swahili households. Eight dhows, all of Somali nationality, brought in seashells valued at £780. The dealers who purchased them in turn sold them to collectors. *Kikois*, rectangular pieces of cotton cloth which are wrapped around the body and tied at the waist and commonly worn by Arab, Swahili and African men on the coast, came in on one Arab and two Iranian dhows. Some *kikois* were manufactured in Indonesia and others in Arabia. Dates used to be a very important import to East Africa, but they are not any more, perhaps because of the fifty per cent import duty; only five dhows carried dates into Mombasa in 1970; all of these were Iranian. Henna is a powdered dye made from a shrub found in Arabia; it is used to make the hair and palms of women's hands a rich auburn colour. The henna imported here was from Mukalla in the Hadhramaut. Copper wire and braziers are unusual imports; all I can say about the braziers is that two dhows brought them in, one lot having been made in China and the other in Britain. The earthenware pots came from the Kutch-Mandvi area of India and are used for holding drinking water. Nowadays, about the only commodities brought from India on Indian dhows are these earthenware pots and clay tiles for roofing buildings. The dhow trade between East Africa and India and Pakistan is almost dead.

The twenty-three Iranian dhows which came to Mombasa in 1970 carried the most valuable products, averaging £1,364 per dhow, and the range was from £50 to £6,550. Rationally, it would be expected that the Persian dhows carried the largest amount of cargo since they are the largest craft in the western Indian Ocean and, except for the Indian craft, are coming the farthest distances. Their commodities were also the most profitable. The twenty-five Arab dhows carried slightly less than their Persian counterparts, £1,277. The twelve Somali dhows only carried £356 per ship and eight of them came into Old Port during the months of October, November and December when no Iranian or Arab dhows put in. In 1970, only two Indian *kotias* arrived, one carrying Shs.1,000 worth of earthenware pots and the other Shs.750 of them. Five Kenyan *jahazis* came in from Somalia with £1,150 of dried fish, £475 of shark meat, and £275 of marine shells. A sixth Kenyan dhow came in from Southern Arabia with £575 of salted fish and one Tanzanian dhow came into Old Port with £800 of dried fish which had been loaded at Jazir in Arabia. It is rare for either Tanzanian or Kenyan dhows to go as far as Arabia, and the fact that there were two dhows which did so in 1970 is highly exceptional.

The foreign dhows which come into East Africa do not usually sail directly from their home base non-stop to Mombasa but trade on the way and often back-track. Let me give some specific examples. On 1 January 1972, the 300-ton Iranian dhow *Jamil* which had been constructed only a year previously at Kung, left her home port for Abadan near the Iran/Iraq border with wooden chests and carpets which were mostly Turkish and Iranian. No products were sold in Abadan but fresh dates were purchased by the *nahoda*, Ahmed Abeid. The *boom* next stopped at Aden and then at Berbera, Somalia, where all the dates were sold to an agent. It then returned empty (except for the chests and carpets) to Aden where the *nahoda* bought salt and fish for the East African market. On 16 March the *boom*, having a crew of seventeen, arrived in Mombasa.[19] Such an itinerary is quite typical for Iranian dhows. A slight variation is the following. The 200-ton *boom*, *Nasiri*, which is twenty-five years old, left Lingeh in Iran in October 1971 for Basra with no cargo. At Basra, the *nahoda*, Ahmed Abdul Rahman, picked up £5,000 of fresh dates for Berbera, stopping on the way only briefly at Muscat. At Berbera the captain purchased 600 goats and sheep which he brought back to Qatar and Dubai for sale. From Dubai, he sailed empty back to Lingeh, his home port. There Ahmed Rahman loaded carpets and chests and departed for Mombasa on 1 March 1972. On the way, the dhow stopped at Dubai and Oman to pick up shark and fish before proceeding non-stop to Mombasa.[20]

The Arabian dhow is usually smaller than the Iranian *boom*. For instance, in 1971, the average Iranian dhow had a tonnage of 156 and a crew of seventeen, whilst the average Arabian dhow was 120 tons with a crew of fourteen.[21] The Arabian dhows follow a slightly different route from the Iranians. On 20 March 1972, the *beden, Al-Husseini*, which is twenty-two years old and might, I was told, sell for £8,500, departed from its home port of Sur with a crew of twelve carrying no cargo and made its way to Muscat where the *nahoda*, Swaleh Ali, purchased rice, sugar and cooking oil. The *beden* carried this cargo to Salala where it was sold and dried fish for the East African market was purchased. The dhow arrived in Mombasa on 1 April.[22] The Arabian dhows which come to East Africa generally do not trade with Iranian ports.

Dhows from the Yemen usually originate at Hodeidah and sail directly to Mombasa with salt and fish, or, if they think they can obtain a better price, the captains buy these products at Aden on the way. The voyage from Hodeidah to Mombasa non-stop takes twenty days. The Yemeni dhows tend not to go very far afield and spend most of the year trading from one Yemeni port to another. They are smaller craft than either the Iranian or Arab dhows.[23]

The Indian dhows, mostly *kotias*, travel the longest distances of any craft in the Indian Ocean. Most of them originate from around Bombay or Kutch-Mandvi. Some of the Indian dhows sail directly without making a stop between the west coast of India and Mombasa. In 1973, two Indian dhows, the

60-ton *Alimadat* and the 80-ton *Lakshmin* sailed from Kutch-Mandvi non-stop to Mombasa, and neither had an engine. The journeys took twenty-one and sixteen days respectively. These dhows brought with them 2,500 cream-coloured clay water jugs which they had purchased for a rupee (Shs.0.70) each. The duty on them was Shs.1.50 and the Indians sold them for about Shs.4 each. Thus the dhow captains grossed only £225, a pathetic sum for such a long voyage with nine crew members aboard who had to be paid.[24]

I find the Indian dhow trade with East Africa an enigma. Most of these dhows have no engines although they travel the longest distances. Almost all Arabian and Iranian dhows, on the other hand, do have engines. Engines were probably first installed in dhows in Sharjah by the British during World War II;[25] however, foreign dhows with engines did not come in any numbers to East Africa until after 1957. I asked the Indian captains why they did not get engines and they replied that they could not possibly afford the £5,000 needed to purchase and install them. After all, the captain of the *Alimadat* pointed out to me, his ship might have sold for only £1,400 in India because it was forty-five years old, in poor condition and only sixty tons. Where was the dhow owner going to find £5,000 for such an expense? Accepting that, why don't these dhows bring in more cargo and make money? In the recent past they obtained more income when they brought in large quantities of Mangalore tiles for roofing, but since a factory has opened in Mombasa to produce the same article and the demand for foreign, imported ones has dropped, one would think that the Indian dhow captains would find alternative goods to bring in, particularly since India is much more industrialized than most underdeveloped countries, manufacturing many products from refrigerators to medicines which would probably be competitive on the East African market. The dhows do take clothes, cotton cloth and other items to the Arabian Gulf shaikhdoms[26] and even these would seemingly be more profitable for them than clay pots.

The Somali dhows generally bring goods to Mombasa from Somali ports such as Berbera, Hafun, Mogadishu, Brava and Kismayu. They seldom go to Arabia to purchase commodities for the East African market but they do trade fairly extensively between Somalia and the Arab shaikhdoms carrying primarily goats and camels. The Somali dhows are not large and have usually been constructed in Arabia. For example, Said Farah, the first Somali dhow captain to grant me an interview, purchased his *sambuk* with an engine in Aden in 1968 for £5,000.

The Somali dhows tend to be the most unkempt and filthy in the western Indian Ocean; the Indians take second prize for dirty ships. One reason why the Somali crews themselves are so shabby is that they are paid very low wages. On the *Saad-el-Rizek*, the ordinary crew members, in 1973, received only Shs.100 per month and the *nahoda* Shs.200, plus food. For comparison, in the same year, the average Indian got Shs.110 per month as crew (with no profit-sharing), while the average Arab sailor earned Shs.400 a month and the Iranian Shs.330 for long-distance voyages to East Africa.[27]

A curious aspect of the Somali dhows arriving in Mombasa is their extraordinarily large crews. For example, in 1969, four Somali craft came to Mombasa with tonnages of 80, 49, 45 and 79; the numbers of crew were 47, 30, 31 and 53, respectively. This contrasts with an average crew of 17 for a 200-ton Iranian *boom*. I do not believe that all of these so-called crew received a salary,

56

but think that most of them were passengers in disguise who called themselves crew for convenience. Being a member of a ship's crew allows one to land and to move around a town without a visa or restriction, and a large number of the Somalis on board dhows were actually no more than tourists who wanted to come to Mombasa for a visit. For the past ten years, conditions have not been very good in Somalia due to droughts and political instability and the fact that there is little money; Mombasa allows a change of scene and it appears to be relatively easy for a Somali to sign himself aboard a dhow as crew and have the chance of a holiday in a Kenya port, where life is much freer. Some of the more adventurous Somali have left Somalia for long periods; there used to be many of them in Aden and now you can find many in the Arabian states, driving taxis, running shops and managing smaller hotels.

Mombasa Auctions

Some of the first commodities to be unloaded at the beginning of the dhow season in Mombasa are the dried fish and shark. It is quite a sight to watch. Dhows carrying these goods lay at anchor off Pwakuu, a few hundred yards away from the jetties near the original settlement of Mombasa. Porters wade into the water to take the fish from the small boats ferrying it; they stack it upon their heads and walk up the steps to the place where it is to be auctioned. During the dhow season, there is at least one auction a day so the *nahodas* quickly receive Kenya shillings.

There are three main auctioneers of dried fish in Mombasa: Hadi Ahmed Bashughewan, Swaleh Sherman and Rajab Garwan. Hadi is the best known and the most successful.[28] Every day during the dhow season, one can see Hadi auctioning dried fish and shark. He sits on the ground near a pair of scales surrounded by his assistants and heaps of smelly dried fish, calling out prices of

Hadi Bashughewan presiding over a fish auction in Mombasa

various bidders. He starts his auction at noon during the heat of the day and may not finish until four p.m. He likes to work during the middle of the day so that he can spend the morning in his office in Old Town or go to the Mwembe Tayari market to collect his commissions from the fish buyers.

From 1971 to 1974, shark meat sold at auction for about Shs.3.40 per kilo; and in the Mwembe Tayari market the retail price was Shs.5. Fish, on the other hand, is sold by piece rather than by weight. The price of one salted fish about three feet long was Shs.14 in 1974, or about Shs.5 a kilo. The auctioneers such as Hadi and Swaleh make their money from commissions ranging between two and four per cent of the price that the fish fetch at auction. From January to the middle of April Swaleh and Hadi earn £750 to £1,000, after expenses, and their expenses are little and consist primarily of the wages that they pay to their assistants who help them with the auctioneering. During the rest of the year, Hadi, Swaleh and Rajab hold auctions for dried fish which comes either from Somalia to Mombasa or from Lamu, via lorries and dhows. These auctions, however, are infrequent and not as profitable as those held during the dhow season.

Most of the wholesalers who buy the fish and shark meat are Arabs and Bajuns. The largest single purchaser is a Mombasa-based company, Al-Ikbal. Much of the dried fish and shark is sent down to Tanzania where there are occasional severe shortages of fish. Usually, several days are required before the auctioneers get paid by the fish merchants, and Hadi sometimes gives advances to the dhow captains whom he cannot pay fully until he gets the money. Swaleh, however, does not do this and perhaps that is the reason why Hadi has more business. Hadi and the other auctioneers maintain good relations with the *nahodas* of the foreign dhows and help them in all their business affairs. Being fluent in Arabic, which is not commonly spoken by Mombasa residents, they have a welcome asset as far as the dhow captains from Somalia, the Yemen, Arabia, the shaikhdoms and Iran are concerned.[29]

The dried fish and shark are eaten in a variety of ways by coastal people. Some of them simply fry it or make a sort of fish soup, but the better cooks turn out a delicious curry made from the dried fish which is called in Swahili *mchuzi ya nguru*. Shark curry is called *mchuzi ya papa*. Another popular dish is dried fish simmered in coconut milk or ghee.

Some of the dried fish is not sold immediately to consumers as food but is first used for another purpose. All around Pwakuu are warehouses where fish, mostly kingfish, is stored. Inside these godowns are wells seventeen feet deep and seven feet across, into which the fish are lowered. Salt is added at various levels, and at the very top, when the well is filled, two tons of stones are placed, putting tremendous pressure in order to extract the fish oil. The smell from these warehouses is strong, to say the least, and very obvious to all around the area. After two to three months, the oil has oozed out. This oil is called *sifa* and is used by the *nahodas* to coat their ships for protection from insects. In 1972, a gallon of *sifa* sold for Shs.4. After the oil is extracted, the remains of the fish are then sold for about Shs.17 per kilo (in 1972).[30]

Life in Old Town during the Dhow Season

At any time of year, Mombasa is a fascinating city, as I said at the beginning of this chapter. And during the dhow season Old Town truly exudes charm and hums with activity due to the presence of some thousand foreign dhow crew members from Somalia, the Yemen, Arabia, Dubai, Kuwait, Iran and India. These people are very colourful with their elegantly wound turbans, their flowing robes which are often rich in embroidery, their daggers at their side, and their black, glistening eyes darting here, there and everywhere. Suddenly, in the dhow season, the old buildings seem to re-awaken and their architecture takes on added value when you notice the foreigners congregating in little, but vociferous, groups on the door steps. Old Town becomes a cosmopolis, possibly more eclectic in its variety than any other place in the western Indian Ocean. Walking through just one small, narrow street in Old Town during the dhow season in a matter of two or three minutes one may bump into a Punjabi from Pakistan, a Chinese contemplating the cost of shark fins, a Somali buying sugar, an Arab from the Yemen hawking trinkets, a Persian counting up his Kenyan coins, an Englishwoman doing her shopping, a German tourist with a camera, and an upcountry, heavy-set African working as a porter. Because so many of Mombasa's own residents form a great variety of cultures—Eastern, Western and African groups are all mingled here—the appearance of foreigners from some of the most exotic corners of the world does not seem out of place at all; instead, they enhance this city which not only has some of the oldest inhabited buildings in East Africa but also has witnessed the comings and goings of traders from distant ports for nearly a thousand years. Zanzibar used to be like this, but since the Revolution in January 1964 much has changed. Walking through the streets of Zanzibar in the evening hours, one has the impression of being in a ghost town: there is no activity at all. Yet, in Mombasa, coffee shops are crowded, Swahili and Indian type restaurants exude spicy aromas, and all around are peregrine sights and sounds. Zanzibar officials, when asked why it is now so quiet there at night, reply that it is because they now have television. So does Mombasa, but this modern amusement cannot compete with the excitement engendered by diverse groups of people gathering together to discuss their lives, their politics, their religious beliefs and to enjoy the company of one another while partaking of the pleasures offered by night life in a vibrant city.

Most of the inhabitants of Old Town, Mombasa today are coastal people. Some anthropologists, historians and geographers call them all Swahilis as most of them have Swahili as their first language. The Swahili people are really a very mixed cultural group whose main components are coastal African, Baluchi, Arab and Indian. If you asked the coastal people of Kenya what tribe they were, as I have done in Malindi and in the Lamu archipelago, few would use the general term Swahili but would be more specific and call themselves, for example, Bajun, Giriama, or perhaps Arab. None the less, Swahili is a convenient term and generally accepted for the Muslim people who live, mainly in towns, on the East African coast and whose language is Swahili.

During the dhow season, there is a lot of social intercourse between the Swahili and the foreign crew members. Some of the Arab crews spend the night with relatives or friends who have connections with their countries. The Yemenites are often seen supporting the local Arab restaurants and the Iranians like to purchase coffee from street vendors who go around with a large brass coffee pot, clapping two porcelain cups together to attract customers. The coffee sold in this manner in Mombasa is not quite as strong as the Turkish

The making of lime juice in Old Port, Mombasa, for the voyage across the Indian Ocean

variety nor is it as thick, but it has a delicious aroma and is very tasty. Almost all the crew are devout Muslims and they go to Mombasa's many mosques to say their prayers; on Fridays, especially, the mosques are brimming with these foreigners. Of course, the crews also support the local night life, going to Indian films, spending entire evenings in coffee houses, playing card games and enjoying the girls.

How does a typical Swahili spend his day in Old Town? I can say from experience that the day begins at 5.00 a.m. When I lived in Fort Jesus from March to May 1969, the first thing I heard every morning was the call to prayer from the mosques. Unfortunately, *muezzins* have been phased out and replaced by recordings, and the loudspeakers are particularly piercing to the ears at dawn. Both the men and women get up, but only the men go to the mosques for *assubh* (morning prayers). By 5.30 a.m., they have finished and return home, and some go back to bed for a while. Before breakfast, they will usually take a cup of black coffee. The first meal of the day ordinarily comprises *mbaazi* (peas) prepared with coconut milk, peppers and salt. *Mbaazi* is accompanied by fried sweet cakes such as *kitumbua*. The breakfaster might also help himself to pieces of bread and will have tea with lots of milk and sugar. Afterwards, the boys and girls go off to school, the women begin their household tasks and the men go to work.

Swahili men are involved in a variety of occupations in Old Town. Some are porters, called *hamalis*, who load and unload cargo from the dhows. During the dhow season there are about a hundred in Old Port and they are not paid for the hours they work but for the particular jobs that they do. They start at eight o'clock in the morning and carry on until four o'clock in the afternoon, with a two-hour lunch break at noon. The maximum they can earn is about Shs.50 a day without doing overtime.[31] I found the *hamalis* were not very pleasant while at work, but that is certainly understandable: their work is very tiresome and requires a great deal of strength so there are no old *hamalis*. Few Swahilis want to take on such a back-breaking job with no long-term prospects, and, in fact, many *hamalis* were not born on the coast but are men from other parts of Kenya who come to the coast in the desperate search for jobs.

Quite a few of the Swahili people own and/or run *dukas*, small shops which sell a variety of common necessities such as salt and sugar, rice and maize meal. Cigarettes, matches and soft drinks are also always found in the *dukas*. There are a number of fresh fish mongers, like Mohamed Antar. He also supplies fishing equipment to two fishermen who catch fish in traps off Mombasa, and when the fish are caught and brought back to Mombasa, half the catch goes to Antar who sells it in his stall at the fish market near the Customs House in Old Port. The fishermen keep the other half and what they don't eat themselves, they sell privately. Antar's fishermen make about Shs.500 a month and Antar himself does only a little better, making roughly Shs.600 on a gross of Shs.3,000 a month. Antar is lucky to have a stall in the market: he only has to pay Shs.35 monthly rent to the Municipality for it and business is good there. He also supplies some fresh fish to the Nairobi market.[32]

There are many Swahili fishermen who fish from the 109 registered sailing craft in Old Port.[33] They are some of the poorest regular workers, and the majority of them do not own a house or have a farm. Fishing is a hard job, too. It means going out in the morning, depending upon the tides, at around six o'clock before the sea gets too rough, and hauling fishing lines and nets in and out of the water, under the glare of intense sun, for they do not get back to shore until noon or one o'clock.[34] Even then the day's work is still not done; late afternoons are spent mending and repairing nets in front of Fort Jesus or in other open places in Old Town. In 1974 the average daily catch per fisherman was about Shs.25 worth of kingfish, sea bass, rock cod, mullet, red snapper and other fish.

Naturally, the local dhows provide considerable employment for the Swahili people. Some are crew members on *mashuas* and *jahazis*, and many of them originally came from the Lamu archipelago, especially from Kisingitini, Lamu town and Shela. Most started as fishermen with little formal education. Depending upon the particular *mashua* or *jahazi* they work on, they are either paid a straight salary plus food or, more commonly, obtain a portion of the ship's profit for carrying cargo.[35] A very good portion is allotted to crew members of the *Zaliha*, a *jahazi* registered in Lamu which carries cargo between Mombasa, Malindi and Lamu; her crew obtain two-thirds of the profit with the other third going to the dhow owner.[36] More usually, in East Africa, the crew and owner split the profits on a fifty-fifty basis. The crew of the *Zaliha* also spend a considerable part of their time in Mombasa cutting mangrove poles around Port Reitz, Tudor Creek and Jomvu and selling them in Mombasa to people who wish to construct houses and use the poles as beams. Ali Kuppi, the *nahoda* of the *Zaliha*, told me that if he makes the trip between Mombasa and Lamu four times in a month, the owner will receive Shs.700 and the crew will split Shs.1,400 among them which means Shs.360 for each man. On other, more typical, ships such as the *Ikbal-Alkheir* a crew member will receive only Shs.250 per month plus food.[37]

There are several tramp steamers which regularly ply between Mombasa Old Port and Lamu. On the *Kole Kole*, for example, the regular crew are paid only Shs.170 to Shs.200 a month; however, as the steamers can work all the year round, as opposed to the dhows for which the season is sometimes only eight months long, due to the monsoons, the owners of the steamers, who are usually Indian, seem to think that the lower salary is fair enough. Of course, the more senior members of the crew on the *Kole Kole* are better paid; in 1974, the assistant captain received Shs.280 a month and the engineer Shs.350.[38] It appears, too, that crew members on steamers often have to dig into their own pockets to purchase more food than regular dhow crews; they supplement their rations with extra rice, maize flour, tea, sugar, salt and green peas when in port. Most local steamship crews come from the Lamu district and some own small farms there.[39]

A few people from Old Town make their living as agents providing the cargo for the dhows and steamers going to and fro between the various ports in Kenya, Tanganyika and Zanzibar. The best known agent in Old Port is Mohammed Abdulla, affectionately known by many as Badi. Chryssee and I got to know him when he was in Lamu as the Customs Officer in Charge. We would meet him almost daily in Petley's Inn at noontime. It was a sort of custom then for the government officers to gather there, and we found that Badi was a particularly good conversationalist. He was born in Mombasa in 1914 and was educated for seven years in a government school. In 1934, he joined the East African Customs Department and worked all over East Africa until his retirement in 1968. In 1970, Badi became the agent for Paul Stimert's *jahazi, Ikbal*. Stimert, a German, was the only European at the time who owned a dhow for the purpose of carrying cargo up and down the East African coast. He installed an engine on his *jahazi* as soon as he bought it, thereby greatly increasing its efficiency. From 1970 to 1973, when Stimert sold the craft for £1,500, Badi was his sole agent in Mombasa and organized the cargo (rice, maize meal, onions, bananas, etc.) for his shipping which was almost always taken to Lamu. For his work, Stimert paid Badi Shs.300 monthly during the season but nothing at all when the monsoons were so strong that the *jahazi* could not get down to Mombasa. The new owner of *Ikbal* also retained Badi but only paid him Shs.250 for the same job, which is little indeed when one considers that each morning during the dhow season Badi is in Old Port to solicit business for his ship. Badi also receives a pension from the Government for his past service.[40]

These are typical occupations of Old Town inhabitants. Most of a day's work is carried out in the morning when it is cooler. By noon, all the shops and government offices are shut. Unlike many tropical countries, though, the government offices re-open in the afternoon for two hours beginning at two o'clock. The shops usually stay closed until about four o'clock in the afternoon and carry on their business until fairly late in the evening.

Almost all the Swahili men return to their homes for lunch, which is generally the big meal of the day. A typical one would consist of a fish curry and a vegetable dish, *mchicha*, which is prepared with coconut cream.[41] Fresh orange or mango juice is sipped with it, and it is usually followed by black coffee with ginger. Around 1.30 the entire family will retreat to bed for an afternoon rest. Upon rising again, they usually have some tea with lots of sugar and milk to fortify them for the rest of the day until supper time. Between 4.00 and 4.30 p.m., there is the afternoon call to prayers; some return to their businesses afterwards, while others hang around their local mosque, talking to their friends. Again at 6.30 p.m. they are summoned to the sunset prayers; these only last ten minutes.

It is just after these prayers that Old Town becomes very active socially. Little boys will be seen running around the narrow streets, sometimes pretending to shoot the pigeons who come in to roost. Coffee vendors begin crying out for business as they kindle the charcoal burners under their big brass coffee pots. Competing with them are the tea stalls that sell tea heavily laden with sugar and milk for only Shs.0.25 a glass and sweet cakes such as *mahamri* for just Shs.0.10 a piece. Many of the men sitting around tables in tea stalls and in little restaurants play cards, draughts, *bao* or dominoes. During the early evening hours, the women also emerge into the open, covered from head to toe in black *buibuis*. These were worn in the past mainly for protection from men's eyes, but now are looked upon by the women as a great convenience for secret sorties and there are few coastal women who would wish to give up this customary garment. The women in little groups dart from one shop to another to look at, and occasionally purchase, jewellery and clothes. They move in and out of neighbouring households to chat with one another or to borrow something. The flutter of black *buibuis* renders the women totally indistinguishable from one another.

One of the bizarre sights in Mombasa is the madman telling the news. There is a half mad Swahili who can be heard in the morning around the market making 'music' by scraping a piece of metal. This grating sound attracts the attention of the throngs of people in the area, and when they have gathered around him, he begins to recite the news in a very loud voice in Swahili, having earlier heard it on the radio and possibly also having read the newspaper. When finished, he plays his raucous instrument again in the hope that the people will throw him ten cent pieces.

Children's street games, the men's cards and dominoes and the women's excursions are interrupted a little before eight o'clock in the evening when most return home for supper. This is a light meal and may only be a vegetable curry with *chipatis* or a cassava dish cooked in coconut milk. Some of the men do not go out again after dinner but instead talk with their wives and children, read a newspaper or listen to music on their radios. Most families go to bed in Old Town around 11.00 p.m.

The weekends are much freer; most of the men have to work only a half day on Saturday, as is common throughout East Africa. In the afternoon, there is almost always a football match to watch and after that Indian musical films and American westerns attract large crowds at the cinema houses. On Sunday mornings the young boys dress in a clean white *kanzu* (a long robe, usually made of cotton) and put on a *kofia* (embroidered cap) and, with their little sisters tagging behind, go to a Koranic school where they are taught to recite the Koran in classical Arabic. Some of the *madrassas*, as the schools are called, also teach a little about the history and geography of the Islamic world, but the major emphasis is always put on the holy book of Islam and, from the age of five until about thirteen, children attend Koranic lessons. After lunch on Sunday the entire family may go to the beach at nearby Bamburi or the men may go pleasure fishing. In the evening they might go to the cinema again, and it is interesting that, although the Swahili do not know Hindustani, Indian love films are popular with them. The Swahili also enjoy playing tombola, a type of bingo, and this is another favourite entertainment on Sunday evenings.

Maintenance of Foreign Dhows

After the foreign dhows unload their cargoes and the crew members have spent a few days relaxing from their long voyage, the *nahoda* moves his ship towards Pwakuu to await his turn to beach his craft to make the necessary repairs and carry out proper maintenance, especially careening. At high tide, the mast is removed and any remaining cargo is taken off to lighten the craft which is then slowly moved inland. Long poles, usually mangroves, are driven into the mud on both sides of the ship and rope is attached to the poles to support it when the sea recedes. Eventually, at low tide, the dhow is high and dry settling on the sand.

Now the hard work begins. The entire crew and occasionally some local Swahilis as well carefully take off the barnacles and vegetation from the wooden planks which make up the hull. To caulk the hull, cotton will be jammed between the planks. After this, the entire lower hull of the ship will be covered with *shahamu*, a greasy substance made out of fat and lime. *Shahamu* is made on the beach and stored in tin cans. It is a white paste which is coated by hand all over the dhow's underwater timbers. The process takes many hours but when the *shahamu* is finally added to all the crevices, the ship is protected relatively well from rot and attack by insects for that season.

On the upper part of the hull fish oil is applied to protect the wood from insects. This also brings out the colour of the wood, and after the oil application the patina of the wood becomes most attractive—a shining deep reddish-brown in colour. At this time, also, the blocks and tackle will be examined for any deficiencies and the sails will be taken to an open area in Old Town, sometimes in front of Fort Jesus, to be mended.

Commodities Exported from Mombasa Overseas by Dhow

During this maintenance period, the *nahodas* will be going around Mombasa purchasing cargo for the homeward journey. Some will even make arrangements to take their dhows down to the Rufiji Delta in March to pick up mangrove poles and then return to Mombasa for other commodities. Mombasa is by far the most popular port in all of eastern Africa for dhow captains to purchase goods. There is a greater variety here and the prices,

Preparing *shahamu* for protecting the hull of dhows, in Old Port, Mombasa

except for mangrove poles, are cheaper than elsewhere in Kenya, Ethiopia, Somalia or Tanzania. Furthermore, communications are far superior in Mombasa to other ports and there are more agents in Mombasa who supervise the captains' exchange of foreign currency, purchase their goods for them and assist them in transporting the commodities to their dhows.

Almost every *nahoda* uses an agent because he can save the captain hours of time and also interpret for him in Arabic or Kutchi. Already mentioned are the three best known agents: Hadi, Sherman and Rajab. But there are also wholesalers who sell directly to the dhow captains, most of them specializing in specific commodities. The main suppliers of ghee are Khamis Rashid, Mohammed Salim Bakhit, B. Faiel, Khamis Mohamed, Juma Abdulla, Nassor Ahmed, Rashid Ali, Mbarak Mdelwi and S. S. Alhajri. The largest suppliers of cotton seed oil are Roshanali, Shantilal Pethraj and Ali Kassim; the biggest wholesaler of ghee and coconut oil is Parshottam Bhimji; and Devchand Keshavji supplies most of the sorghum. Coffee is mostly supplied by Rashid Moledina and tea by Abdulla Ali and Shariff Abdurehman; and the captains purchase their coffee husks from Suju Sufi Suja and their sisal rope from Anjarwalla. Thus, most of the wholesalers supplying goods to dhow captains are Arabs and Indians.[42]

TABLE II
EXPORTS FROM MOMBASA BY FOREIGN DHOWS IN 1970

Commodity	Value
Ghee	£31,550
Cotton seed oil	22,875
Sorghum	22,400
Wheat flour	20,850
Tea	17,075
Coffee	14,609
Coconut oil	11,295
Coffee husks	10,075
Rice	7,775
Simsim (sesame)	6,750
Old newspapers	5,375
Charcoal	4,025
Aluminium kettles	3,515
Tamarind	3,350
Metal cooking pots (*sufuria*)	3,175
Misc.	35,415
Totals	£220,109

Source: Transire Notes and Mombasa Dhow Registers, Old Port, Mombasa.

Some of the more unusual minor exports in 1970 were: sisal rope (£1,765), locally made iron beds (£1,200), betel nuts (£143), and mangrove poles from Mombasa (£130).[43]

If you asked educated people in Mombasa, I do not think that one out of a hundred would know that the most valuable single export from Mombasa carried on foreign dhows was ghee. This is clarified butter and used throughout the Muslim world as a cooking oil. Of the ghee, eighty-three per cent is produced in Kenya, with the remaining amount coming from Tanzania. There is a tremendous shortage of animals and animal products in the high income shaikhdoms in the Gulf so there is consequently a great demand for East Africa's ghee.

Cotton seed oil is also used for cooking in the same way butter is used; over sixty per cent came from Uganda where cotton is one of the major cash crops. The oil is sent down to Mombasa on the railroad.

Grains—sorghum, wheat flour, rice and sesame—made up just over one quarter in value of the total exports carried by foreign dhows from Mombasa to overseas ports. This is very understandable since Arabia and the Arabian Gulf produce hardly any grain at all because their rainfall is too low. Kenya produced all the wheat flour, rice and sesame, while Tanzania produced 100 per cent of the sorghum for export.

Next in importance are the various commodities to make beverages: tea, coffee and coffee husks. Most of the tea came from Uganda, but there was a considerable quantity (£6,675) from Kenya, and some (£500) came all the way from Zaïre. Of the coffee, eighty-six per cent came from Tanzania with the remainder from Kenya. In Somalia and Arabia coffee husks are pounded and then roasted to make a drink which is mainly consumed by the poor people because of its cheapness. According to consumers of this beverage it has two advantages over coffee: the drink does not cause insomnia and gives a cooling effect unlike the warmth generated by bean coffee.[44] Of the coffee husks, eighty-eight per cent originated in Uganda with Kenya supplying the remainder.

Coconut oil is the most common type of cooking oil used on the coast of East Africa. It is cheaper than ghee and butter but is coarser in texture and therefore not generally used by the wealthier Indian and European communities. Over ninety-five per cent of the coconut oil is produced in Kenya.

Old newspapers are a curious export but, unlike all the other major exports carried on foreign dhows, the newspapers are not local. Over ninety per cent (£5,225) come from Denmark. These old newspapers, which are imported in great quantities to Kenya are used for wrapping foods such as rice and sugar when purchased at small *dukas*. Old Scandinavian newspapers are to be found in most of the countries in the western Indian Ocean.

Charcoal is not usually an important dhow export from Mombasa because of its bulk and low value. However, charcoal is in tremendous demand in places such as Kuwait and Qatar where there is no wood at all. When I was in the city of Kuwait during Ramadhan, I could detect the strong smell of shish-kebabs and shash-lish cooking over charcoal in the late afternoon while the people waited for their fasting period to end at sunset. Although the shaikhdoms have the highest per capita incomes in the world, many Arabs prefer to cook with charcoal instead of gas or electricity. Kenya until 1975 exported large quantities of charcoal mostly made from acacia trees which are common on the coast and in the surrounding drier hinterland called the *Nyika*. But almost all this charcoal was sent out on steamers from Lamu and Kilindini.

All the products already discussed which originate in East Africa and are exported by dhow are primary products, not semi-manufactured or manufactured goods. This state of affairs of course is typical of most underdeveloped countries. However, Kenya does export two manufactured goods on dhows: aluminium kettles and metal cooking pots which are called *sufurias* in Swahili. These cooking utensils are popular throughout the Indian Ocean countries.

Where are all these food products and oils going which are shipped out of Mombasa on dhows to foreign countries? It is impossible to give exact figures because the dhow captains themselves, before they leave Mombasa, do not know, for example, precisely how much coffee they will unload at Mukalla instead of at Muscat. If the price is low for a specific commodity in one port, the *nahodas* may move on to the next port to try to get a better one. In some countries, accurate statistics on imports and exports by dhow are not kept, and it is impossible to get the figures for Kenyan imports from many Arabian Gulf ports, but we can make some generalizations.

Almost all the dhows which depart from Old Port, Mombasa, to foreign ports between January and March are Somali and go to Kismayu and Mogadishu. In 1970, during the months of January, February and March, eighteen dhows left from Mombasa and all but one first stopped at Kismayu.[45] The most valuable export for them was sesame, worth £6,580. This was followed by wheat flour (£3,500), tea (£2,350), coffee husks (£2,000), kettles (£1,800), and metal cooking pots (£1,800). Since all but one of these eighteen dhows were of Kenyan and Somali nationality, it is likely that most of these goods would remain on the Somali market.

In early April of each year, the larger Arabian and Persian dhows depart from Mombasa. Most of the *booms* avoid trading with Somalia because the Somali merchants are mostly taken care of by Somali dhows. They, therefore, sail directly for Arabia and the Gulf. During the month of April 1970, fifty-five dhows left Mombasa for foreign ports. The dhow captains gave as their first foreign port of call the following places, but it is probable that in those instances where great distances are involved, some of them may have pulled into other foreign ports along the way: Dubai (26), Sehut in Arabia (5), Basra in Iraq (3), Kismayu (3), Qatar (3), Kung in Iran (3), Bandar Abbas (3), Merca in Somalia (1), Khor Fakhan in Arabia (1), Abu Dhabi (1), Aden (1), Muscat (1), Hafun in Somalia (1), Kuwait (1), Socotra (1), and Beila in Somalia (1). Forty-six per cent of all the dhows chose Dubai as their first foreign port of call and this is easy to comprehend: Dubai is the major entrepôt port for the entire Arabian peninsula, the Gulf and Iran. More dhows come into Dubai in a year than any other port in the entire western Indian Ocean with the possible exception of Bombay.

Of the fifty-five foreign dhows which departed at the beginning of the south-west monsoon during the month of April 1975, twenty-eight of them had Iranian nationality, eighteen Arabian including Oman, five Somali, three Kenyan and one Indian (a *kotia*). But nationality did not have that much influence on their choice of first destinations. Both Iranian and Arabian dhows went to Basra in Iraq, the sole Indian dhow went to Dubai and many of the Arab and Iranian dhows went to Dubai. Eventually, by June, however, most dhows would be in their home ports.

Examining the various commodities, there is not a great difference between those which go to Dubai and the Iranian ports. However, tamarind, which is

made into a beverage and also used as a spice, seems to be more popular in Iran than elsewhere; only once in 1970 did a dhow come in to Bandar Abbas or Kung without tamarind to sell, although the total sales in Iran were only £830. The Iraqi port of Basra, which used to be one of the major ports of East African goods, especially mangrove poles, has not recently been so important. In 1970 the most important imports for Basra from Mombasa were cotton seed oil (£1,150), coffee (£775), ghee (£450), and coconut oil (£315).

In May 1970 there were six Arabian dhows which departed late from Mombasa, and it was not until the 15th of the month that they had all left. From 15 May to 31 December twenty-six Kenyan dhows and five Somali dhows sailed to Somalia with cargoes of coffee husks, wheat flour, tea, coffee, tamarind, spices and miscellaneous goods. For this six-and-a-half-month period, there were only two other dhows which went to foreign ports. One was an Indian *kotia* which first went to Mukalla with £450 of coffee husks and the other was an Arabian dhow which departed from Mombasa on 12 October (a most unusual time of year) for Sehut with £3,100 worth of sorghum, ghee, tea and straw mats. It is rare to find foreign dhows (except Somali ones) on the east coast of Africa between May and the end of the year since the monsoon winds make travel difficult. For instance, if an Arabian dhow wanted to come to Mombasa in June it would sail against the wind the whole way. Even though most Arabian and Persian dhows now have engines they still rely on their sails. Furthermore, the trip would be much slower and consequently more expensive. To get the monsoon to return to the Gulf, the dhow would have to wait until April, a long period, or use the engine against the wind all the way to Arabia, thereby using up a lot of fuel and still going slower than if the dhow travelled by the winds of the monsoon. Consequently, it is not surprising that from 15 May to 31 December 1970, only £48,435 of cargo moved out of Old

Port to foreign ports by dhow, which was twenty-one per cent of the total exports for the whole year.[46]

Dhow Passengers

Along with the overall decline in the number of foreign dhows which put into Mombasa,[47] there has been a corresponding drop in the number of passengers carried by dhow. For example, in 1945, 2,654 foreign Arabs (of whom only 28 were women) came into Mombasa;[48] in 1970, the figure was only 115.[49] The reasons for this decline are obvious: since Independence in Kenya, immigration has been tightened, and work permits and trade licences are required which naturally discourage job hunters from the Gulf. Also, and more importantly, since World War II the great quantities of oil found in many of the Shaikhdoms lessened the need for Arabs there to emigrate. Life has indeed become easier for these people.

Most of the passengers who arrive in Mombasa are now from Lamu in Kenya. In 1970, 545 passengers, both locals and foreigners, disembarked at Mombasa from dhows, 69% from Lamu, 21% from Arabia and 3% from the Persian Gulf. In 1964, a higher percentage came from Arabia (28% of the total), and from Kismayu came 7%, followed by Zanzibar with 6%.

In 1970, only 216 passengers left Mombasa by dhow. Three-quarters went to Lamu and 10% to Kismayu, while in 1964, 61% had gone to Lamu, and 14% to Mukulla in Arabia, and 11% to Kismayu. Today, the foreign passenger traffic by dhow to and from Mombasa is almost dead and is unlikely to revive in the foreseeable future.

Only rarely do Europeans travel by dhow between the Gulf and Mombasa. I remember being amazed one day when I glanced up from taking notes in Old Port to see a dark haired European girl disembarking from a foreign dhow. It was 11 April 1973 and I took my camera and started photographing her talking to the Persian crew. She looked tired and quite wind-blown. I went up to her, suddenly realizing that she might well be Marion Kaplan, whom I had heard about several months previously, a single girl who had proposed to travel from Dubai all the way to Mombasa by herself. I asked her if she were, and she replied that she was indeed. She knew of my work on the dhow trade, but we had never met before, though we are both Nairobi residents. She said the one thing she really wanted at that point was a shower and a clean hotel room. I lent her my Land Rover and when I saw her again that evening heard first-hand all about her exciting journey.

It had taken her five months to complete the trip on an Iranian *boom* from Dubai all the way down to the mosquito-infested swamps of the Rufiji and up to Mombasa. She is the only European woman known to have made such a trip on her own. In fact, I can think of only one other person who has made a similar trip and written it up in detail and that is Alan Villiers who travelled on a Kuwaiti dhow in 1938–9 and wrote subsequently the excellent book called *Sons of Sinbad*.[50] Marion was financed by the National Geographic Society to make this epic voyage. She decided to become a passenger on an Iranian dhow because she was told that the Iranians would probably take better care of her than Arabs. In December 1972, she embarked on a dhow from Kuwait to Dubai to pick up an Iranian dhow sailing to East Africa. She met the *nahoda*, Issa Abdullah, who eventually allowed her to board his 170-ton *Mihandust*.

A *boom* in the Gulf in 1938.
Source: Alan Villiers

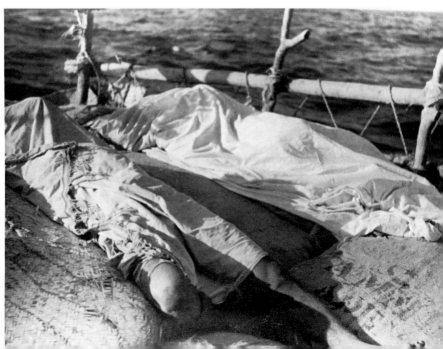

Passengers' sleeping
accommodation on a *boom*,
photographed in 1939. *Source:
Alan Villiers*

Marion had to pay $500 as a passenger, ten times the normal rate. The reason for having to pay so much, according to Marion, was that the *nahoda* was not certain he wanted to go to East Africa, since carrying cargo between the ports of the Shaikhdoms and Iran is often more profitable than the hazardous trip to East Africa. If he was going to make this trip, he wanted to make it worth his while. Furthermore, he was worried that the presence on board of a European girl might well be a distraction and nuisance to his all-male crew.

Finally, Marion departed on the *Mihandust* from Dubai. Her biggest difficulty at first was communication; although, of course, she knew some Swahili and brought along a book on colloquial Arabic, the crew's first language was Persian. For the first week or so she just stared at the crew, but after a while talking in Swahili became easier and questions began flowing from both sides. The crew and the *nahoda* were primarily interested in Marion's private life. Marion does not particularly care to discuss intimate subjects with anyone, but she said that she had to cope with one very personal question after another—they wanted to know exactly her age, whom she slept with, etc. She became exhausted with all the prying and it seemed very strange to the crew and captain that she was not interested in discussing these matters.

Marion endured the hardships of travel with good cheer, which was appreciated by the crew members. There was rain sometimes and choppy seas which made all work difficult. Insects were a real nuisance, too. Marion worried about not having any privacy aboard, but the crew seemed to sense her need to be alone at times, and they would move away from her. The crew members all behaved as gentlemen towards her and at the end of the journey in April, Marion had made good friends with most of them and she told me afterwards that she did indeed miss their company for a long time. Her good-byes to them in Old Port were fond and sad on both their part and hers.

One aspect of this unusual trip specially interested me. Marion comes from a Jewish family and she was travelling with a very conservative and devout Muslim group of people. She never mentioned her Jewish background when in Kuwait, Dubai or anywhere else in the Gulf, and she thinks that her crew never stopped to consider whether or not she might be Jewish.

I am not going to relate Marion Kaplan's fascinating journey as she herself has written it up for the September 1974 issue of the *National Geographic*.[51] However, there is one related incident in which I became involved which has not been written up. One night while the *Mihandust* was off the Somalia coast, the second engineer got his *kanzu* caught in the flyshaft of the 250-horsepower engine. He was immediately dragged down into the engine and received a very severe neck injury before he could be rescued. He lost a tremendous amount of blood and the other members of the crew thought he was going to die. However, he made a rapid recovery and within only a couple of days he was able to walk a few steps by which time the *boom* pulled into Lamu where the local surgeon patched him up until he could be operated on in a modern hospital in Mombasa. The operation was successfully carried out but the engineer was too weak to return home on the dhow. How was he possibly going to get back? There was no passenger ship going to Iran and the airfare to Tehran was almost $1,000. His salary was a total of only $42 (Shs.300 in 1973) monthly and he could not even afford to stay in Mombasa for very long.

Marion suggested that the *nahoda* should go to Nairobi and see someone in the newly opened Iranian Embassy. Since the *nahoda* spoke no English and only halting Swahili, she asked me to take Issa Abdullah to Kenya's capital. I agreed and I personally dropped him off outside the Imperial Iranian Embassy. I later heard from Marion that the Ambassador, when he heard of the poor man's predicament, decided that the best thing to do was to get him home as soon as possible and that he should go by plane. The Ambassador put up the money for the airfare himself. I found this gesture so outstanding and kind that I wished personally to tell the Ambassador. But, to my horror, I ran up against a bureaucratic stone wall when I went to the Ambassador's secretary to make an appointment. I thought it was not appropriate for me to tell the secretary about the Ambassador's fantastic generosity, but was refused an appointment because I would not state my reason for wishing to see him. I could not understand why I could not get an appointment so I tried to find another way of seeing him through a mutual friend. I called the secretary a second time and she refused again to allow me to make any appointment but said I could see the Ambassador's assistant. By this time I was embarrassed about the whole matter since all I had wanted to do in the first place was to express my appreciation. Finally, however, I agreed to have a talk with the assistant and explained my predicament of not being able to see the Ambassador and my embarrassment at having used the name of a close friend in an attempt to get through to him. The assistant, who was the First Secretary, started laughing uproariously and found the whole incident most amusing. He said that he had heard about my unsuccessful efforts and thought that I was trying to get a job in Iran! All was well in the end; soon after this meeting I was invited over to the Iranian Ambassador's Residence and at last had a chance to convey my thanks to the Ambassador for his considerable generosity to a crew member of an Indian Ocean dhow.

Lamu

The Mangrove Trade

The mangrove swamps around Mombasa are not very extensive and also lack the longer and larger poles known as *boriti*, which are the favoured ones abroad. What poles are available there find a ready market among the local population who use them both for fencing and house building. Therefore, the foreign dhow captains who wish to purchase mangrove poles to sell in the Gulf have to go up the north coast or down to the Rufiji in Tanzania where the supply is more abundant. While still in Mombasa, they ascertain from dealers in various areas the year's prices and make arrangements for picking them up, rather than depending on the local *jahazis* and *mashuas* to transport the poles down to Mombasa. It is, of course, cheaper for the foreign dhow captains to pick up the poles themselves, and by going up to the source of supply, they can also check their order before any loading is undertaken.

For many years Ngomeni, with its natural deep-water harbour, was a particularly popular pick-up point. For example, statistics show that from 1969 to 1971 a yearly average of twelve foreign dhows (mostly Iranian) came in for mangrove poles. The cutters would bring them in from the Mto Kilifi swamps about twenty miles farther north and the Forest Department would grade them right on the beach at Ngomeni. However, there was so much overcutting from the 1950s onwards that the Forest Department had to close the swamps in 1973 to allow the Mto Kilifi trees to rejuvenate. With poles no longer available at Ngomeni, not a single dhow put in there that year;[1] instead, they all sailed past and on up to Lamu which then became the most important mangrove centre in Kenya.

The Lamu mangrove swamps cover a huge area which extends from the

Tana River delta up to the Somalia border. In 1971 the gazetted portion of the forest totalled 114,121 acres,[2] the main commercial areas being around Mkunumbi, Kimbo Creek, Mongoni, Chunguni and Dodori Creek;[3] close to Lamu and Manda islands the mangroves are stunted and almost useless. *Rhizophora mucronata* is the species which produces the finest *boriti* poles.

For centuries, the mangrove swamps in the Lamu archipelago have been exploited. The demand for poles has come from traders in Iraq, Arabia and the Persian Gulf where there has always been a shortage of wood.[4] Traditionally, mangrove poles have been used to hold up the roofs of houses built with stone, mortar and cement. In the old sections of Arabian and Persian towns, houses with mangrove pole ceiling beams can still be seen today. Now, however, since oil has been discovered in many of the shaikhdoms and there is much more wealth generated, iron and steel are beginning to replace mangroves; hardly any mangrove poles have been imported into Qatar or Abu Dhabi in recent years. Elsewhere in the Gulf, mangrove poles are now used mainly for scaffolding. Additionally, a lot of cheap, Indian wood is now being imported into the Gulf by dhow, but it is not as sturdy nor as long-lasting. The demand for mangrove poles, while considerably less than in the 1950s, still exists, particularly in Iran and Iraq and, ironically, is very high in Somalia which used to be a great exporter. Somalia is a perfect example of a country which did not adequately control the cutting of mangrove poles and allowed its swamps to become so devastated that now the people have to import poles for their own use. It is a very poor country with hardly any forests remaining and the Somalis now have to buy more mangrove poles from Kenya than does any other country.

TABLE III

MANGROVE POLE EXPORTS FROM LAMU BY DHOW (in scores)

	Somalia	Iran	Iraq	Kuwait	Dubai	Saudi Arabia	Bahrain
1966	0	200	770	0	0	100	0
1967	0	3,505	3,263	200	440	100	0
1968	5,107	4,203	3,893	0	200	0	300
1969	14,604	978	548	300	0	109	0
1970	3,197	1,060	0	2,600	0	0	0
	22,908	9,946	8,474	3,100	640	309	300

Source: Forest Department Annual Reports, Lamu, 1966–70.

The largest number of mangrove poles ever cut and exported from Lamu was in 1916–17 when 75,000 score or 1,500,000 poles were sent to Basra in Iraq for the war effort. During the 1920s this trade decreased partly as the result of fewer Arabian dhows coming to Lamu on account of the Kenya Government's changing its currency from the widely used Indian rupee to sterling and also because of the low price for mangrove poles in the Arabian Gulf. During the 1930s in an attempt to improve the mangrove pole export trade, the grading of poles for quality was introduced, and this certainly helped to boost the exports from 1936 to 1940, which averaged 19,000 score annually.[5]

During World War II there was a great demand for poles within East Africa. Local dhows transported about seventy-five per cent of them to Mombasa and the remainder to Tanga. Immediately after the War, very large quantities of poles were cut. The forest officers, who were in charge of setting quotas, believed that because of the tremendous oil wealth in the Persian Gulf, the demand for poles would decline severely as more and more people would begin to build modern houses. Therefore, between 1947 and 1956, they allowed a very high average of 30,918 score to be cut each year, and in 1955, a record year, 83,650 score were removed from the swamps of the Lamu archipelago. From 1957 to the present, strict cutting quotas were revived to counter the overcutting allowed in the War years and afterwards; thus from 1957 to 1970 the average number of poles exported was only 17,072 score on an annual basis. However, because the demand was still great in Somalia, Arabia and the Gulf, prices were high. From 1962 to 1970 the Lamu people earned £186,000 or an average of £20,666 a year from the sale of mangrove poles.[6]

Although from 1969 to 1973 an annual average of only six foreign dhows came into Lamu to pick up mangrove poles,[7] this trade directly employed hundreds of local people in the district. The cutting of the poles in the surrounding swamps is one of the major occupations in the Lamu archipelago. The Bajun people do most of the cutting and transportation of the poles. They are a hard-working people who make up about two-thirds of the population of the district. The job of cutting mangrove poles is arduous. The season begins in January, and in April, when it ends, all are exhausted. Owners of *mashuas* and *jahazis* hire the Bajuns at the beginning of the year to take their dhows into the swamps to cut the poles and to bring them back. The Bajuns receive in advance as much as half the season's wages which they use to purchase goods they need or to pay their bills. Sometimes little money changes hands between the prospective employee and the dhow owner who instead agrees to assume responsibility for the cutter's previous debts, which may even be owed to another dhow owner. The system of advances is an old one and is also common in Lamu's fishing industry, although the Bajuns lose money in the long run due to the interest charges deducted by the dhow owners which I have heard are as high as twenty-five per cent.[8]

Just as soon as wages and advances are settled, the cutters form crews and sail out to the swamps. They search the area for the longest and strongest poles which will bring in the most money to their employer. When they decide upon a good cutting place, they get out of the dhow and wade through the muddy water which comes up to about knee height and begin hacking away at the mangroves with *pangas* (large knives). Paddling a *ngalawa* through the mangrove swamps as a sightseer is entirely different from slogging barefoot through cloying mud and having to spend time in one spot cutting the poles while mosquitoes swarm viciously around. The tourist keeps moving, creating a breeze which deflects the insects, and he can admire the vivid green leaves of the mangroves and appreciate the white flowers which cover the branches at a certain time of the year. He will also find an abundance of birdlife in the swamps; of special interest to him will be the osprey, the sooty gulls, and the carmine, Madagascar and European bee-eaters.

The cutting season is the time of year that Lamu is at its best. During January, February and March the north-east monsoon is blowing, the sky is

clear, and there is little chance of rain. It is also the busiest time of year for
Lamu residents and dhow owners. Besides the activities of the mangrove
cutters, other dhow crews are unloading goods such as coconuts and coconut
fibre which come from the islands in the area. Coconuts are processed at Lamu
into copra. Since the weather is particularly favourable now for sailing, trade
with Mombasa flourishes. Somali cattle traders who have come down from
Somalia with large herds of cattle to sell to local traders are actively bartering
for tea, sugar, rice and coffee to bring back home. More fishermen go out in
their boats during the north-east monsoon because the sea is not very rough
and there is a greater demand for fish due to the many visitors who flock to
Lamu at this time.

Life in Lamu

Lamu has a unique charm among the towns of East Africa. However, the
average visitor has a strong tendency either to love or hate it. I am, of course, in
the former camp and am amazed at how many people say that Lamu is just a
crowded, disorganized and dirty place, complaining also that there is no beach
in the town and nothing much to do. To some extent, there is truth in these
criticisms. Lamu is crowded and the mud-and-thatch houses in the southern
part of the town have been built in a haphazard fashion, but the stone
buildings in the northern part of town are often most attractive and possess
magnificent carved wooden doors. Inside some of the older stone houses of the
eighteenth and nineteenth centuries are walls carved with plaster work and
niches where family treasures are displayed; often these are fine pieces of good
old Chinese porcelain. There is no doubt that some of the back streets of Lamu
are dirty, but people often mistake the open drains for open sewers. As a matter

of fact, the sewage system was one of the most advanced in Africa when it was constructed in the eighteenth and nineteenth centuries. It has its problems in some houses today where insufficient maintenance has been carried out and when new chemicals and detergents have been used which tend to clog up the pipes. The household drains, on the other hand, work very well indeed, but there is a favourite trick that little boys sometimes pull. At high tide, when the seawater level is almost as high as that of the drains, rats are forced up through the drains. Little boys enjoy catching them and showing them to little old ladies from Chicago. After such a display of doubtful goodwill, it is highly unlikely that the ladies will want to make another visit to Lamu. Attempts have been made to eliminate the rats, many of which are much larger than the Lamu cats. The last really major effort was made in the late 1950s. In 1959 the District Commissioner proudly reported that 949 rats were caught, but a little later he lamented, 'Again the courage and stamina of the Lamu cats failed them and it is believed that the rats actually eat the cats here.'[9]

These imperfections must be overlooked as all urban centres, even including London, have their problems and certain unattractive aspects. Lamu is really a jewel. There is no town in East Africa which has the overall architectural style that Lamu possesses. One would have to go to a Sahelian town such as Djenné or Agadès or to one of the North African towns like Rabat, Medenine or Temacine to get a similar feeling. Zanzibar used to have an architectural 'presence', but since the Revolution there the Government has allowed many of the old buildings to collapse, and on the outskirts of the stone town the revolutionary government has constructed modern, ugly, high-rise blocks of flats whose concrete shells dominate the skyline. Lamu, unlike so many towns in Africa, has not been spoiled by modernization. Houses which have recently been constructed conform to the old Swahili-type of architecture. New stone houses are still made of coral limestone with roofs supported by mangrove poles. Since mangrove poles are rarely longer than ten feet, the rooms are generally long and narrow. Most rooms face an inner courtyard which may be exquisitely landscaped. The houses are built close together and sometimes project over the street. Pedestrians are thus sheltered from the sun in narrower streets. This type of Swahili architecture which once was predominant on the coast from Somalia down to southern Tanzania, is unique and an admirable achievement, both on aesthetic and practical grounds.

My favourite time of day in Lamu is the late afternoon. Around 4.00 p.m. the town slowly begins to reawaken. Almost everyone has retired after the midday meal for a siesta, and upon re-emerging from their houses, the shopkeepers unlock the bolts on their doors and begin the best part of the day's business. This is the time when the fishermen and dhow crews come to buy their goods, having been too busy in the morning to do so. The shops are friendly places and news flickers from one to another. A crier goes past all the shops through the main streets, bellowing out advertisements for the film that will be shown in the evening which will very probably be an Indian musical. Many of the men make their way to the mosques to say their prayers and to chat with friends, for mosques in Lamu serve as social meeting places. Here the talk may well centre on religious topics interspersed with titbits of news from the Hadhramaut or elsewhere in the Indian Ocean where Lamu people may have friends or relatives. Strangers to Lamu usually gather at the mosques in

the afternoon and, upon telling their news, they receive a hospitable welcome from the residents. The strangers have been led to the mosques by the sound of the *muezzin* calling the faithful to prayer.

By sunset, the town is a hub of activity. It is a traditional and particularly enjoyable pastime to walk along the seafront just as the sun begins to go down. There is a tendency for the various groups of people to walk together. The Swahili and Arab ladies, covered from top to toe in their black *buibuis*, but with their eyes carefully made-up with khol, dart back and forth, visiting friends' houses and gossiping about who is with whom. The Ithnaashariya women gather in little groups together, their *buibuis* usually being a dark royal blue. The Arab men look the most aristocratic of Lamu's populace, and though they now lack the money to buy the colourful silks that they wore way back in Vasco da Gama's time, their waistcoats are still beautifully embroidered in front, sometimes in matching white thread, sometimes in pale beige. Often whole families gather together on the benches looking out to the sea towards Manda and the mangrove swamps.

In the early part of the evening, the aroma of charcoal-roasted meat pervades the streets throughout the southern part of town. Tiny kiosks sell roasted beef on skewers to the passers-by, and there are also small restaurants which offer Swahili cakes and other sticky sweets along with tea. Inside these places are long benches and trestle tables where mainly the Bajuns gather to spend the evening together. They take their tea in the old-fashioned manner, pouring it from their cup into the saucer and sucking it up.

Later on, the coffee vendors appear on the streets. They have lovely old brass pots which they set up on charcoal braziers on any street corner. They also have with them little buckets (sometimes old paint tins), filled with water in which they rinse the china cup that is used by everyone who buys a cup of coffee. Lamu coffee is not as thick as the Turkish variety, but it is heavily sugared and has a superb aroma. After supper, you find many men sitting on the benches outside their houses or outside the restaurants playing dominoes, the favourite game in Lamu. There are also games of *bao* and draughts. The boards vary considerably; at one time an enterprising soap company in Kenya printed the checkered squares on the back of their boxes of soap powder which must have boosted their sales in Lamu tremendously! Lots of these are seen around Lamu, but there are also many home-made boards. Quite a few of the Arab, Swahili, Bajun and African residents play rummy with dog-eared cards that have been cherished for years. It is said that the Portuguese introduced playing cards to East Africa.

Meanwhile, the ladies are up to other activities. Women's Lib takes a peculiar turn in Lamu. When a little girl reaches puberty she is usually strictly guarded inside the women's quarters of her home until a suitable husband is agreed upon by the family members. Before she is married, the older aunts explain to her the art of love, and both the Swahili and Arab women of Lamu are notorious for their skills in making love. The prospective bride is almost always a virgin, but she already knows how to give pleasure to a man. Quite often she is still under sixteen when married. Once she has a husband, she is

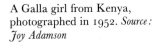

A Galla girl from Kenya, photographed in 1952. *Source: Joy Adamson*

freer than she has been since reaching puberty. She may not remain faithful to her husband, but keeps up appearances. If her husband loses his temper with her he may divorce her; indeed divorce is common in Lamu.

The wife's girl friends are very helpful in arranging rendezvous with lovers. Since men are not allowed at the parties women give for one another, it is very easy for a woman to borrow a friend's pair of shoes at such a time and if she wraps herself modestly up in her *buibui*, no one will recognize her when she goes out on the street. With the borrowed shoes (she usually borrows them from someone with an entirely different shape, so that woman won't be thought to be the one 'out on the loose' either), she slips out of a back entrance of the house where the party is being held to go to wherever it is that she has agreed to meet her lover. If her husband happens to come to the house to pick her up from the party and take her home, the one who opens the door will of course not allow him entry to the women's quarters and will instead offer to go and fetch his wife for him. She finds out who knows where the wife has gone and sends a friend to get her while the husband waits. Back to the house via another entrance, the wife changes into her own shoes and demurely meets her husband. He accepts having had to wait for her, for everyone knows how difficult it is for a woman to break off a gossipy conversation with another woman! Besides, he may have come just at the time when tea and cakes were served and it would have been rude for the wife to leave without sampling the delicacies provided for guests.

Undoubtedly, the Lamu women twist to their own advantage the etiquette that is centuries old. Lamu men may not be so naïve as to be unsuspecting of their wives, but they would never risk causing the virtue of a friend's wife to be called into question by barging into the private quarters of the women in any house. A man would never even walk inside the house where a woman was on her own. In fact, whenever anyone wishes to enter someone's house, there are strict rules of etiquette to be followed. One knocks on the outside door and calls 'hodi!' Since no one usually lives on the ground floor of a stone house, the visitor must wait until enough time has passed for someone to descend the stairs to let him in. He will be told immediately whether entry is possible or not, depending on who is inside. If a woman's husband is not present, she will not allow a man to come inside, even to the public rooms of her home, unless he is a very close relative or possibly a foreigner. For some reason best known to the residents themselves, a foreigner who is not a Muslim does not count as a potential threat to a woman's virtue! He may come inside and carry on a conversation in the parlour with a lady without subjecting her to any slanderous gossip afterwards. He may have wanted solely to talk to her husband but may well end up spending hours discussing trivialities with the lady.

Despite Lamu's rather notorious sexual life the people are sincerely religious. Lamu's particular brand of Islam is recognized by Muslims throughout the Indian Ocean as strictly conservative. The local shariffs, who claim descent from the Prophet Mohammed, are believed to have 'karama', special blessedness, and the ordinary mortals of Lamu, when meeting a shariff, will kiss his hand as a token of respect. One particular Lamu shariff, Habib Salih, became a highly revered Muslim teacher at the end of the nineteenth century.

Like many Muslim communities, Lamu commemorates each year the birthday of the Prophet Mohammed at what are called *Maulidi* celebrations.

At Lamu, however, they take on special significance because of the renowned holiness of Habib Salih who introduced there the *Habshi Maulidi*, in which praises of Mohammed are chanted to the accompaniment of tambourines. Some people even believe that a visit to Habib Salih's tomb after the *Maulidi* confers special favour in the eyes of God. Lamu's *Maulidi* celebrations therefore attract many more visitors than such festivals held elsewhere in Africa. They are far more exciting and certainly more colourful than those I have witnessed in Mombasa, Zanzibar or even in Kairouan, in Tunisia. Preparations for the *Maulidi* in Lamu are begun months in advance and Muslims from all over East Africa and even as far away as the Sudan and Zaïre come to Lamu to participate in the activities.

The celebrations always commence on a Tuesday afternoon when a parade forms of men dressed in long white *kanzus* who carry large banners; they make their way through the streets of the town to the square in front of the Riyadah Mosque, followed by children and various onlookers who are all in a holiday mood. A crowd is already waiting in the square for the parade and when it arrives it forms a column and leads the singing of joyful songs in praise of Allah and his Prophet Mohammed. After a while, the people divide up into different groups to take part in, or to watch, special dances and games. In one corner of the square there is a stylized stick fight which generally attracts the greatest number of spectators, including women in their black *buibuis*, which are not as tightly drawn as usual since the women have practically all splurged on new dresses and they like to show them off—even though they have to do so discreetly! The stick fight ritual is practised as follows: each of the two participants holds a three-foot long stick near his chest. The men move around a circle in a manner similar to that of boxers, and one of them will take a sudden swing with his stick in an attempt to hit the stick of his opponent and make him flinch without actually hitting his body. Throughout the performance, a group of drummers gradually increases the tension by drumming faster. When one of the participants gives way or becomes too tired, someone else immediately takes his place. Sometimes the fighters get so worked up into a trance that they have to be removed from the ring by force. Somewhere else in the square, at the same time, a less violent and more subtle dance takes place. This is one variation of the Cane Dance, and it is also performed only by men. A group of about forty stand in a row, each one holding a cane or an umbrella in front of him. While the drums roll softly, the dancers follow the cadence by swaying from side to side. When dusk falls, the performers stop and make their way home for their evening meal.

On Wednesday, the crowds around the Riyadah Mosque in the afternoon are even greater, and recitations and similar dances take place, but with greater intensity. Thursday is the most important day. The dances start a little earlier in the afternoon and at sunset they stop, and the people break away to rush home for a quick supper. At eight o'clock they all return again. The square has now been partitioned into several sections by means of string attached to little stakes in the ground. On one side of the square next to the Mosque hundreds of women with their small children gather to sit in the sand quietly together. The men and boys settle in different sections depending to some extent on their rank in Lamu's society or their importance as visitors. When everyone is in place, noted religious personalities inside the Mosque pray aloud with the male audience outside periodically joining in the refrain. The *Maulidi*, the praise of Mohammed in verse, is softly chanted and punctuated by sounds of tambourines. I had been invited to sit on the steps of the Riyadah Mosque when I attended my first *Maulidi* celebration there, and I found myself fascinated by the communal spirit of devotion. For a long time I was so awed I didn't budge. Finally I decided I wanted to see what was happening behind me, inside the Mosque. I slipped away as unobtrusively as I could and walked around to the side where I could peer into the latticed windows and watch the holy men kneeling on mats and swaying from side to side as they led the chanting. Together with the musicians they glanced from time to time at small books in which the prescribed *Habshi Maulidi* is handwritten in ornamental Arabic script. I later walked up to the top of the hill behind the Mosque from where I could look down at the vast crowds so subdued and intent on their devotions, so in contrast to their earlier frenzied exhilaration. I will always remember standing there in the fresh night air observing below me the brilliantly lit Riyadah Mosque surrounded by what seemed to be acres of people solemnly attesting to their faith in Islam. It was an emotional experience, the most beautiful and thrilling of its kind that I have ever seen.[10]

The majority of visitors who come to Lamu for *Maulidi* are fellow Muslims who accept without ado the peculiarities of its customs and reciprocate their hosts' generous hospitality with little gifts and mementos. The Lamu people are proud and their generosity towards guests often belies their real financial means, thus the simple pieces of clothing or staple foods brought to them by

Boats decorated for the 1952 *Maulidi* festival, Lamu. *Source: Joy Adamson*

friends or relatives at *Maulidi* mean more to them than perhaps they care to admit. As for foreigners who come to Lamu, a certain pretence of well-being is made towards them: rare indeed would be the Lamu man who admitted to poverty. In colonial times, the British civil servants and a handful of eccentrics who came to Lamu understood and in a few cases shared similar desires to keep up appearances despite monetary setbacks. Consequently, when the hippie invasion happened, the Lamu people were genuinely shocked by what they saw.

It all began in 1970 when the hippies, or overlanders as they prefer to call themselves now (as distinct from tourists who jet from one part of the world to another to stay in identical international class hotels), were kicked out of Nepal. They began looking for new sanctuaries, and quite a few of them came by boat to Kenya where they soon discovered that there was an island just off the coast of the northern part of the country where life was relatively cheap and the authorities few in number. One after another, they began to move into Lamu with packs on their backs and little cash in their pockets. In 1971 rumours began floating around Nairobi that there were hippies bathing in the nude at Lamu and even love scenes on the beaches. The national Government became concerned while the Lamu locals decried their indecency in other matters, too. Cleanliness of person is strictly observed there, and the hippies' disdain of a good bath or shower caused more than wrinkled noses. Perhaps the most shocking of all which happened was that a few of the overlanders actually stole from the Swahili. One evening, I went around to some of the rest houses where the overlanders were putting up. It was certainly true that they had a shaggy appearance and that the taking of marijuana, called *bangi* here, was common. On another occasion, when I was in Lamu again, while I was walking down the beach in daylight at Shela, a German girl was making love in the sand to a Bajun with elephantiasis. A secret love affair would not perturb Lamu people, but the brazenness of public display and the probability of the girl having paid the man would disgust even the most 'progressive' Lamu resident. One of the Kenyan newspapers, the *Daily Nation*, sent a reporter to Lamu who interviewed an old man at Lamu called Bakari Abedi. He said:

> I am surprised to see these youths in this condition. They stink and are dirty with horrible shaggy hair. There must be something wrong with their country, either drought or famine which forces them to come to Lamu island. They are almost like beggars and when buying the cheap food on the street they bargain for hours.[11]

The government administrators in Lamu began clamping down on the overlanders, forbidding them to camp on the beach and carrying out searches in the places where they hung about. Several of the overlanders objected and felt that they were being discriminated against because they did not spend much money. A debate about the overlanders ensued, with the national press having a field day airing divergent opinions. A Nairobi resident wrote to the Editor of the *Daily Nation*:

> Travelling by the time honoured methods and sleeping in bad hotels, a traveller comes into intimate contact with the local inhabitants, something that ordinary tourists never do . . . So what if they have long hair? The Samburu and the Masai warriors do not even notice the hippies' long hair,

Maulidi festivities in Lamu

Dhow crewmen repairing a
sail in front of Fort Jesus,
Mombasa

The collecting of eggs from
marine turtles off Chole
Island, in Tanzania

whereas they are puzzled by the short hair of other young men. It was said that they sleep together unsegregated by sex but sex is natural and, like their hair, they prefer to let it grow.[12]

The argument still rages today and hippies continue to come into Lamu but generally in reduced numbers as compared with 1970 and 1971. The hippies in Lamu have not had much of a long term effect on the place except for a few local people who have converted old houses into boarding houses to lodge them. On the other hand, the tourists in Malindi, who are not hippies, have had a far greater negative effect on the morals of the local population. In Malindi there are many more prostitutes, people taking hard drugs and indulging in anti-social behaviour than in Lamu. Fortunately, Lamu cannot accommodate many tourists and the town itself has changed little in overall appearance for a long time. Lamu continues to be basically a nineteenth-century Swahili town with tremendous ambience and interest.

Lamu's uniqueness remains primarily because of its remoteness. It is not easy to travel to Lamu by road, and for this reason too, it is more dependent upon the local dhow traffic than any other town in Kenya. Still today the main road from Malindi to Mkowe, the village opposite Lamu island, is a rough dirt road. As recently as the late 1960s, the road would be closed for up to eight months of the year because of the flooding of the Tana River. While I was studying the economic history of Lamu, I often got bogged down on the tracks of Lamu district, especially between April and July. One of the worst episodes occurred in 1968 while I was driving back from Witu. I was in a Land Rover with Chryssee, Terry Maginn (the Forest Officer for Lamu), and another government officer who was going to take over from Terry during his leave. We had a driver, who was one of the fattest men I've ever seen in the Lamu archipelago, and most of his conversation centred on his preferred foods. All day long it had been raining heavily, and by the time we headed back towards Lamu, the road had about three feet of water on it. It was still pouring, and the whole area had begun to look like a lake. At one point we caught a three-foot fish on the radiator of the Land Rover, much to the driver's delight, I might add. He proudly placed it on the windscreen ledge and rapturously eyed it, paying less and less attention to the splashing of the wheels through the water. Finally, as the water flowed on to the bonnet of the vehicle, the engine stopped. By this time it was late afternoon, so we decided that the wisest thing to do would be to abandon the Land Rover and walk to the nearest village to spend the night. The only catch was that the village, Mkunumbi, was seven miles away, and it takes more than twice as long to slog through knee-deep mud puddles than walking on dry land. The rain had mostly stopped and there were now only little intermittent showers, but there was no breeze at all and the mosquitoes were out in full force. Our small group decided, nevertheless, to move on by foot, and we waded for hours through the swampy land. We could hear lions roaring around us and we were fully aware that many cattle in the district had been killed by lions, and we also knew for fact the incredible story of a lioness who had swum from the mainland to Manda. We had no idea what we would do if we came upon a lion—we didn't even have a long stick for protection, let alone firearms! However, our biggest problem that evening was not our imaginings of lion encounters but the reality of the awful mosquitoes which delighted in drinking our blood. Around 10.00 p.m. we more or less stumbled into Mkunumbi and a dear old Swahili elder, who was a friend of Terry's, put a house at our disposal. It was a very simple hut with a coconut-frond roof and mud floor. About an hour after we had installed ourselves, the elder brought us a magnificent dish of chicken, bananas, coconut milk and a mound of fluffy rice. When we had finished and I was beseeching Terry and Chryssee to stop their chitter-chatter so that I could get at least forty winks, our host re-appeared with a red silk pillow with gold fringe, 'for Chryssee to rest her head upon'. It was rather amusing to see Chryssee there, on the mud floor, curled up with that pillow! However, neither she, nor Terry, nor the government officer nor myself got any sleep at all—it turned out that our gigantic driver snored like a rhinoceros and dawn came as a blessed relief to the tremors he caused in that tiny one-roomed hut! By mid-morning we were able to get word to Lamu and another Land Rover came to pick us up. Fortunately, the rain had completely stopped during the night and the return journey that day was very easy.

The Coastal Dhow Trade of Lamu

Lamu is the second most active dhow port on the Kenya coast, but the town of Lamu and the surrounding district is far more dependent on goods transported by dhow than Mombasa or any major town on the Kenya coast, as Table IV shows. The local dhow traffic from 1962 to 1973 has declined for most parts of Kenya but not for Lamu. The reason for the decline elsewhere in Kenya is easily explained by the remarkable improvement in roads. The town of Malindi serves as a perfect example of the change: from 1935 to 1940 an average of.554 dhows came into that town each year[13] and the road connecting Malindi to Mombasa was in an appalling state.[14] In 1964, when I first went to Malindi, the road was still not tarmacked and it was in fact very sandy in spots; in that year 123 dhows came into Malindi.[15] When the road was finally given a tarmac surface, the dhow trade to Malindi and to the town halfway between the two major ports, Kilifi, practically collapsed. While in 1954, 289 local dhows came into Kilifi (262 from Mombasa), by 1970 only ten put in, all from Lamu.[16] Another example is Shimoni where during the decade of the 1950s an annual average of 154 local and foreign dhows came in; this figure dropped to only 53 during the 1960s.[17] Here again road transport was made easier.

Of all the goods imported at Lamu by dhow and small steamships, ninety-five per cent came from Mombasa. In 1970, the only year for which I have detailed statistics, the major imports consisted of alcoholic beverages, flour and grains, sugar, rice and cement (see Table V). Alcoholic beverages being the most valuable important raises some eyebrows since the population of Lamu is over ninety per cent Muslim. There are of course up-country Africans in the administration and government departments, and about a dozen full-time European residents, plus the tourists who come in for the day or even to spend a holiday on the carefree island—still these people can hardly account for such a figure and there must be quite a few local people imbibing! I checked the figure for 1969 to ascertain whether 1970 was a freak year but it wasn't: in 1969 £17,650 worth of alcoholic beverages was imported to Lamu by dhow.[18] Most of the other imports for 1970 were exactly what one would expect; the only

TABLE IV
KENYA DHOW TRAFFIC: LOCAL AND FOREIGN DHOWS
COMING INTO THE MAJOR PORTS OF KENYA FROM
1962 TO 1973

Year	Mombasa*	Lamu*	Malindi	Shimoni	Kilifi
1962	600	312	131	55	60
1963	584	261	58	40	66
1964	454	228	123	48	31
1965	363	227	70	45	9
1966	331	203	74	58	19
1967	428	290	84	42	15
1968	553	364	89	18	6
1969	615	N/A	72	56	4
1970	550	370	60	35	13
1971	688	310	30	N/A	N/A
1972	507	324	50	N/A	N/A
1973	514	294	40	N/A	N/A

*Includes small steamships as well. There are fewer steamships coming into Mombasa but a higher proportion to Lamu.

N.B. These figures refer to dhows travelling to major ports; they do not include dhows making short trips such as from Lamu to Faza or from Mtwapa to Mombasa.

Source: Dhow Registers for Mombasa, Lamu, Malindi, Shimoni, and Kilifi, 1962–73.

TABLE V
MAJOR IMPORTS TO LAMU FROM MOMBASA FOR 1970 BY SEA

Commodity	Value
Alcoholic beverages	£21,785
Flour and grains	20,210
Sugar	17,900
Rice	15,875
Cement	15,240
Cigarettes	9,900
Fuel (diesel, paraffin)	9,250
Tea	8,945
Vegetables	4,250
Soft drinks	2,950
Building materials (mostly wood)	2,705
Cotton piece goods and clothes	2,175
Misc.	37,895
Totals	£169,080

Source: Lamu Pass Notes, East African Customs and Excise Department, Lamu.

three which might be called unusual were ice (£1,420), betel leaves (£790) and Arab chests (£650). The ice is used for food storage and there always has been a shortage of ice-making facilities in Lamu. The importation of betel leaves is frankly a puzzle since Lamu is generally a main exporter but perhaps there was a shortage that particular year in Lamu. It is also surprising that quite so much in value of chests was imported. The Arab chests brought up from Mombasa are put on sale in retail shops in Lamu, the best known being that of Fakrudin Gulamhusein, the major tourist shop in Lamu which sells antiques.

Besides the imports from Mombasa a few dhows from Malindi also brought goods to Lamu. In 1973, 225 tons of produce came in from Malindi by dhow. By far the bulkiest item was the 126 tons of maize husks, called in Swahili *wishwa*. These maize husks or chaffs are obtained after the maize seed is cleaned at home by the women, who save them to supplement their incomes. However, the price is low in Malindi for *wishwa*, being only about Shs. 10 for a thirty-five kilo bag. The maize husks are used in Lamu as feed for the cattle and they are in considerable demand as Lamu island is mostly sand and there are both milk and beef cattle on the island. The other main imports from Malindi, in order of tonnage, in 1973 were salt, diesel fuel, broken rice and cement.[19]

The number of dhows registered at Lamu has been steadily decreasing since the 1950s. In 1957 there were 237 sailing ships registered in use;[20] in 1963 there were 204,[21] and by 1973 only 118 remained.[22] The main reasons for this sharp decline is that it is no longer very profitable compared to other businesses to own a dhow since returns are low and the owner must spend a considerable amount of time supervising the entire business of trading. In the 1950s some of the wealthier Arabs such as Said Bujra and Indians such as Sadakali Nurbhai owned several dhows each, but now Said Bujra does not have even one and the Nurbhai family have also sold theirs. During World War II when Said Bujra owned four *jahazis*, he made a lot of money transporting food from Kenya to Somalia. After the War, he continued to make a good profit with these *jahazis* by supplying goods to Mombasa and transporting mangrove poles within the Lamu area. However, by 1973 Said Bujra and his family had sold all their *jahazis*; I asked Ahmed Bujra, his son, why and he told me that the crews were becoming very difficult to control and that dhows now made very little profit for their owners. He strongly hinted that a major problem was that some crew members steal the cargo for their own use.[23] It is true that theft occurs much more now than in the past and several people in Lamu have admitted this. Maintenance on dhows now is also costly; each year a *jahazi* requires a major overhaul, caulking and re-painting, and one *jahazi* owner told me that these expenses alone amount to Shs. 700 a year plus the purchase of new equipment such as ropes, a new palm-frond roof and stern gallows. Another reason for the decline in the profitability of dhows is that within the last ten years schooners such as the *Seifee, Salaama*, and *Marigo* have begun regular service between Mombasa and Lamu and back, taking a lot of business away from the traditional local dhow trade. Motor boats have advantages over the dhows because the latter here usually do not have engines. Not only do the motor boats get to Lamu much quicker, they can also go at any time of the year, even against the monsoon.[24] Furthermore they can get insurance for all cargo, including diesel fuel, which dhows cannot. Between 1970 and 1973 there were in fact more arrivals of small, modern steamships in Lamu than traditional dhows. Finally, although the road to Lamu is still fairly poor, road transport service has been improved and that, too, competes with the dhows.

Today, most of the remaining dhows in Lamu are owned by poorer members of the community; those who sold their craft with a certain profit, particularly the Asian families, including Ithnaashariyas and Ismailis, put their money in shops which were a better investment. No longer will one find in Lamu a man owning a fleet of dhows; sadly, that age has ended.

The average Lamu *jahazi* now in service is 27 tons and has a crew of seven. The largest *jahazi* continuing in use in Lamu is the 42-ton *Nash-kuru* (registration L. 481), owned by Bakar bin Mohamed Haji. Only recently has the *Zuljanah* (L. 84) of 93 tons been removed from service.[25] Many of the crew members who worked on the cargo dhows come originally from Pate island, but they usually have a temporary house in Lamu or Mombasa. Of the nine crew members and captains I interviewed in 1974 who travelled between Lamu and Mombasa, six had not been to school at all and the average number of years of schooling for the others was less than four.[26] The average crew member earns about Shs.250 per month, plus all food, but this is not a regular salary which can be depended upon; instead it is a portion of the profits. The usual division is that after expenses the dhow owner gets one-third of the profits, the captain and the crew splitting the remaining two-thirds; on some dhows the captain or *nahoda* might receive as much as one-third of the total profits.[27]

Although Shs.250 (roughly $35 in 1974) is not a lot of money, it is higher than the average wage in the private sector of Lamu. One must also remember that food is included and that the job is not particularly exhausting in that there is considerable travel involved and that these people almost always have friends and relatives in Mombasa whom they enjoy visiting. Most crew members seem pleased with their job and several have told me that they can make more money in the dhow trade than they could dream of making in agriculture in the Lamu area. Alternative full-time employment for the uneducated is practically nil. Since most dhow crewmen have small family plots, they return home during the south-west monsoon, when the winds are too strong to sail by dhow, and help with subsistence cultivation.

In studying the local dhow trade, I have had more difficulties in trying to ascertain how much money a *jahazi* owner actually does earn a year than anything else. Both *nahodas* and owners were very reluctant to supply me with the figures I needed and in most cases I do not suppose they even keep track of the amounts themselves. Of course, because the dhow trade is so seasonal, there are some months when there are nothing but expenses and others when the trade flourishes. For instance, during the months of January, February, March and April 1973, an average of eleven dhows came into Lamu each month, compared to fifteen steamships, but not one came in from May to August.[28] This is a typical situation because, during the south-west monsoon, the sea is too rough and the dhow owners are limited to trips within the Lamu archipelago. Besides general cargo, dhow owners can also make money by transporting passengers. Taking all the various factors into consideration, I can tentatively make the following estimates. On a 27-ton *jahazi* during the months of January, February and March, the owner may make Shs.1,000 a month after paying expenses, including Shs.500 to the *nahoda*, Shs.250 to each of the crew members and buying all the food. During the months of June, July and August the dhow will be undergoing repairs and maintenance work and some of the crew will take about two months' holiday; only if the owner is lucky will he make as much as Shs.500 a month on average by carrying cargo and passengers around Lamu, Pate, Siyu, Faza, Kisingitini and Kiunga because there will be fewer goods to carry and greater competition for them. This is the time, however, when passenger traffic is highest.[29] From September to December a dhow can again safely sail for Mombasa and can earn Shs.1,000 a month. Thus, in a year an owner of a *jahazi* perhaps earns Shs.8,500. Yet out of that amount, towards the end of the season, he will have to make repairs to his craft and purchase new equipment, expenses which probably total close to Shs.1,500. Consequently, at the end of a year a dhow owner who has managed his affairs well can make Shs.7,000 profit. However, one must remember that the Lamu dhow owner has to spend a considerable amount of time and energy making sure that he can get cargo business in Mombasa, prevent the crew from stealing the cargo and supervise the maintenance work. If the dhow owner's time were to be calculated to be worth only Shs.20 an hour, one hour a day of supervising his single dhow would eliminate his total profits!

Lamu's exports by sea-going dhows constitute a curious assortment of mostly primary commodities which have been sent out of Lamu for decades, and in some instances, for centuries.

TABLE VI
LAMU'S EXPORTS BY SEA IN 1968

Cotton and cotton seed oil	£52,000
Charcoal	30,000
Coconut oil	22,000
Fish	17,000
Mangrove poles	16,000
Mats and mat bags	13,000
Cashew nuts	12,000
Simsim (sesame)	6,000
Copra	3,200
Tobacco	2,500
Mangoes	2,400
Betel leaves	1,800
Antiques (chests, old wooden doors, etc.)	1,800
Cowries and other shells	1,700
Coir	1,700
Beche-de-mer	1,400
Tamarind	1,100
Ivory	300
Totals	£185,900

Source: Lamu Pass Notes.

Most of the cotton sent out of Lamu town is not grown in the Lamu archipelago but on the Tana River around Galole. The cotton is sent to Lamu by lorry where it is ginned into 400-pound bales at the Lamu Ginners. Afterwards, the cotton is usually sent out by road or schooner, dhow transport being only third choice.

Charcoal production in Kenya is a controversial subject. In the entire country only three per cent of the land is covered by forests. Within the last decade hundreds of thousands of trees, especially acacias, have been felled to make charcoal. In the late 1960s at Makinnon Road, fifty miles inland from Mombasa, a pile of charcoal a couple of hundred feet long and thirty feet high could be seen awaiting train transport to Mombasa; this charcoal was sent out by steamship to the Arabian Gulf. The reason that so many trees have been cut down in the Coast Province to make charcoal is that the price for charcoal is very high in the Shaikhdoms and Arabia. For example, in early 1975 the price for a bag of charcoal in Nairobi was about Shs.10, but in the Middle East the same bag was worth Shs.300. No wonder that exports of charcoal from Kenya rose from 2,500 tons in 1967 to 80,000 tons in 1975, and huge areas around Tsavo National Park and along the Tana River came to be completely denuded of trees.

The charcoal sent out of Lamu by small steamers and dhows in the late 1960s was not made from acacias but from mangrove wood. Some of the charcoal was made by Fakrudin Gulamhusein in primitive kilns at Shela. In 1967 Fakrudin exported 1,000 tons of charcoal and 2,000 in 1968; he had his share of problems both in producing the charcoal and getting it exported. I remember when I was in Lamu in May 1968 that a Greek ship called the *Kallianus* arrived and no sooner had it dropped anchor than a Swiss bank had it 'attached' with the result that the ship stayed in Lamu for over a year while the lawyers haggled with one another. On most mornings, as I was making my way into Lamu town from Shela, I would pass exhausted crew making their way back to the ship after having spent the whole night carousing about the town. The *Kallianus* had one disastrous effect on Lamu: while stranded off Shela oil leaked from the hull and polluted one of the most beautiful beaches in all East Africa.

The coconut oil is produced at the Lamu Ginners and in two primitive presses in the town. Many of the coconuts come from Lamu island where in 1968 the farmers were paid Shs.120 for every 1,000 coconuts that they brought to Lamu Ginners.[30]

The continental shelf is wider off Lamu than elsewhere on the Kenya coast, which is the main reason why fishing is good here. Large quantities of fish are caught and put on ice to be sent down to Mombasa on small schooners. Very little fresh fish is sent by dhow due to lack of cold storage facilities aboard and the additional time required by dhows to make the trip. On the other hand, quite a lot of dried fish and shark meat is transported to Mombasa by dhow.

Mat bags have been made for centuries in the Lamu archipelago from the Doum palm (*Hyphenae thebaria*) and mats are made from the *Phoenix reclinata* tree. The bags are made from the leaves of a young tree which are cut and taken home to be dried in the sun for two or three days. They are then plaited into strips four inches wide and woven by hand into bags. From the 1920s onwards, most of the mat bags and mats have been made by children in the Koran schools and by women at home. The bags used to be a major export from Lamu to Zanzibar where, until fairly recently they were used for packing cloves. Palm fibre is also made into flat mats to cover floors in houses and

The mid-nineteenth century fort at Siyu, Kenya. *Source: Mohamed Amin*

mosques, and it is woven into bulwarks for the *jahazis* as well.

There are many additional agricultural commodities which are exported by dhow from Lamu including sesame, coconuts and mangoes. There are also three unusual ones, tobacco, betel leaves and tamarind, which are worth a brief description. The tobacco is mostly grown around the old town of Pate where about twenty-five acres were under cultivation in 1968.[31] How long it has been regularly grown there I do not know, but it certainly was there in the nineteenth century. During the past decades many of the older and once important buildings of Pate have been pulled down to make more agricultural land available for tobacco, and this really is a tragedy. In the eighteenth century, Pate was the centre of the arts in Kenya. Its architecture, fine arts and poetry were the finest in Kenya, and to see so many of Pate's splendid old buildings not simply in a crumbled state, but even being recklessly razed for the sake of a few more tobacco plants, is indeed very sad. The betel leaves, on the other hand, enhance the tiny gardens and courtyards in the town of Lamu. The betel leaf is a beautiful glossy dark green and even if it had no economic value it would be worth cultivating for the delightful aesthetic contrast it gives to the white buildings. It is so appreciated by chewers of the leaf all along the coast that when planes began coming into Lamu with supplies in the mid 1960s and there were few passengers on the return trips, seats were pulled out to make room for enormous baskets full of betel leaves going to Mombasa for sale. In

almost all of the East African coastal towns are found little kiosks selling the betel leaf with a pinch of tobacco on top mixed with lime. During the late 1960s about £4,000 worth were sent out each year from Lamu and remembering that only the leaf itself is exported, that is a lot of leaves![32]

One might be rather taken aback by the darkish-brown gooey lumps for sale in the little kiosks in Lamu. They are tamarind (*Tamarindus indica*), obtained by squeezing the moist and pulpy seed pods from the tree. During the season when the mango is not available, Swahili cooks add considerable amounts of tamarind to their dishes to supplement Vitamin C to their diet. One might expect the Lamu people to make use, instead, of the delightful limes which are plentiful throughout the year, but there is a superstition that limes cause elephantiasis of the testicles and many people avoid eating them.[33] Food flavoured with tamarind takes on an acid taste, which many visitors to Lamu find unpalatable. However in India and Zanzibar tamarind is often mixed with curries and made into a chutney. Before the advent of Coca Cola and other bottled soft drinks to Lamu, tamarind juice, which I find to be a tasty and refreshing drink, was quite popular. The tamarind drink is made by simply squeezing the pulp into fresh water. I have frequently seen people using tamarind in Lamu as a brine for curing fish and as an excellent cleaner for brass and copper. Also, many of the walking sticks that the shariffs carry have been made from the root of the tamarind tree.

For many centuries the Lamu archipelago has been the centre of dhow building in Kenya. The famous sewn boat, the *mtepe*, which dates from the time of Christ was made in the Lamu archipelago and undoubtedly in other places in East Africa as well, but the last *mtepe* may very probably have been the one made in Lamu in 1933. There are two types of *mtepes*: the 'original', older *mtepe* with the bird-like prow which is supposed to represent the head and neck of the favourite camel of the Prophet Mohammed, and the *dau la mtepe* which is similar but without the bird-like prow. The *mtepe* probably originated on the East African coast and, if so, is one of the most interesting creations of the people here.

The older type of *mtepe* disappeared from the East African coast by the 1920s, but the *dau la mtepe* continued to be used for transportation into the 1930s. We have a full description in 1933 of the construction of a *dau la mtepe* by the District Commissioner of Lamu at the time, J. Clive:

> As I write one *mtepi* is being constructed at Faza. Roughly sawn timbers, usually *mkoko* or *mlilana* (mangrove timbers) are used and are sewn together with coconut rope . . . Holes are bored in the timbers and the rope is passed through the holes, rather as if one were lacing a shoe. The rope is tauted and then a wooden mangrove plug is driven into the hole to fix the rope. Not one nail is used in the *mtepi*'s construction, and even the rudder is fastened to the vessel with rope. The masts are mangrove poles (the writer has seen one mast 60 feet high), and the sail is square made of matting and swivels around the mast . . .
>
> These *mtepi* are used almost entirely in the boriti trade, and the average capacity is 1,000 korjas of boriti (about 20,000 mangrove poles usually 18 feet in length with a base diameter of 4 inches).
>
> They are usually decorated with numerous flags and streamers. The big white streamer at the mast-head is an indication that the vessel comes in peace, a survival of the Nabahan Portuguese period when, as often as not, the ships sailed intent on war. The small white flags on the bowsprit, and the ornament under the bowsprit are supposed to indicate the importance of the passengers, the ornaments being referred to as the 'beard' of the *mtepi*— presumably to indicate that it is no longer young and irresponsible . . .
>
> The crew are invariably Bajun and on the bigger *mtepi* as many as fifteen are employed, as they are required to pondo (punt) the *mtepi* along in shallow water when heavily laden, and also the boards being sewn together only, it is necessary to bale half-hourly both day and night. Two children are also taken aboard, one as a cook and one to man the *hori* (a small dug-out canoe) which is used to communicate with the shore when the *mtepi* is at anchor.
>
> At the end of a trip any profit that may have been made is equally divided among the crew, the *nahoda* getting twice as much as any individual . . .   *Mtepis*, when on a voyage of any length, travel in threes or more, and on dark nights drums are beaten hourly so that the craft may keep in touch.[34]

I have quoted in length Mr Clive's remarks because they are the most complete on the *dau la mtepe* that I have found, and his description of the *mtepe* may well be the last given by someone who actually saw a *mtepe* sail. By the late 1930s, all the *mtepes* had disappeared, being replaced for the most part by Lamu *jahazis*.

During this century, no one has kept records on the number of dhows built in Lamu district, and my information is limited to only a few years in particular.

The true *mtepe* (sewn boat) in Old Port, Mombasa, in 1890; note the bird-like prow. *Source: Kenya National Archives*

I know that between 1938 and 1942, between five and twelve dhows were constructed on Lamu island in each of those years.[35] During the 1940s and 1950s, Pate island appears to have been the centre for dhow building, but the numbers were already decreasing then. In 1959 six dhows were built, two at Kisingitini, two at Faza, and one each in Ndau and Siyu. One of the largest dhows built between 1950 and 1960 was the *Queen Mother*, launched in 1959, with a tonnage of seventy-eight.[36] Since the late 1960s, *jahazis* have only been built in Matondoni, on Lamu island. They are used for carrying cargo and passengers, and many of them operate in Tanzania, especially between Dar es Salaam and Zanzibar. *Jahazi* crew members are mainly Bajuns, from Kisingitini, Faza, Ndau and Matondoni.[37] *Mashuas*, on the other hand, because they are smaller and more easily constructed, continue to be built more widely in the Lamu district, but construction of them is also severely declining.

The most famous Lamu *jahazi* is the *Hodi Hodi* which was commissioned for refitting by a European in 1967 and was to sail through the Suez Canal and then across the Atlantic ocean, up the Saint Lawrence Seaway to Montreal for the World Fair. However, the Middle East June 1967 War broke out and the *Hodi Hodi* never made it through the canal. This was most disappointing because if the *Hodi Hodi* had sailed across to Canada it would have been the first time that a Lamu dhow would have crossed or even got into the Atlantic Ocean.

It has been an era of both decline and change for dhows in Lamu since the 1920s. The *mtepe* and the *dau la mtepe* ceased to exist first; then the double-masted *jahazi* with its two sails disappeared in 1944 (the last one was the

95

Detail of the stern of a *dau la mtepe*, the famous sewn boat found on the coast of East Africa; the photograph was taken around 1915. *Source: James Kirkman*

Nidhamu). The latter type of dhow had been used to sail all the way to India. Until the late 1960s, Lamu families owned whole fleets of dhows. For example, Abdulla Kadara had four *jahazis* in his fleet up to 1964; Kadara had sent these *jahazis* to trade in India but stopped in November 1957 because it was no longer economical to do so. Since the late 1950s, the *jahazi* itself has become a much smaller vessel and its sailing grounds have been confined from Arabia and the Gulf to simply the East African waters in the 1970s.[38]

In the future, foreign dhows will continue to come into Lamu in small numbers to pick up mangrove poles to take back to the Arabian Gulf. The local dhow trade will play an important part in transporting goods between Lamu town and Pate island where some 7,000 people live. Since petrol prices have increased sharply over the past few years and also because the harbours of Pate, Siyu, Faza and Kisingitini are shallow, and the distances between these ports short, Pate will continue to rely on local *mashuas* and *jahazis* for supplies in the foreseeable future. However, with the continued improvement of the road between Lamu and Malindi and more air traffic, the dhow trade between Lamu and Mombasa will surely decline rapidly, as is the case with most of the other Kenyan ports. I doubt whether many *jahazi* owners will put engines in their craft to modernize them since they are not presently making much of a profit on their business, and, inevitably, the *jahazis* will be replaced by motor boats. When that happens, a long tradition, covering some two thousand years from the time of the *Periplus* to the latter part of the twentieth century, will come to an end. I suppose the day when the *mtepe* no longer sailed in the waters of East Africa presaged the finale of the dhow trade in this part of the Indian Ocean.

The Tanzanian Mainland

Since 1962, when Tanzania received independence from Britain, the political economy of the country has changed considerably which has greatly affected both the domestic and foreign dhow trade. The sequence of events, leading down a socialist path of development chosen by the leaders of Tanzania, is complex, and I will therefore only summarize those highlights that illustrate the situation in respect to the dhow trade.

Until the mid-1960s, most of the land was held either communally, by a tribe or a family. Although the majority of the Tanzanian farmers did not individually have a government title to their land, they tilled it privately and sold the produce either to traders or to co-operatives. However, after the Arusha Declaration of 1967 and other government pronouncements, farmers were encouraged to form *Ujamaa* villages and farm communally. The *Ujamaa* village is a concept expounded by President Nyerere whereby people work together and do not compete against one another. President Nyerere believed that capitalism exploited the peasants and that only through collective efforts, co-operatives and state-owned enterprises could Tanzania develop uniformly. By the late 1960s, he could rightly claim that Tanzania was moving towards becoming a socialist state. By then, the entire wholesale trade of the country, which had previously been mostly in the hands of Asians, was nationalized, along with all the banks and certain other businesses.

The formation of *Ujamaa* villages was to be voluntary; farmers were expected to join willingly these new socialist villages which were expected to offer more amenities and greater efficiency. However, this was not the case. The more productive and enterprising farmers, including the Chagga coffee and banana farmers around Mount Kilimanjaro, the Haya farmers to the west of Lake Victoria, and the people in the southern highlands, for the most part refused point blank to leave their homelands voluntarily and re-establish themselves in new villages.

By 1972, the Government realized that the peasants on the whole were not taking the initiative to form *Ujamaa* villages on their own as only thirteen per cent of the population of the country had joined, and also that the few who had moved were tilling their land individually. Even then, most of the fourteen million people in Tanzania were living in highly scattered homesteads throughout a country almost as large as western Europe, and the Government could not possibly provide the necessary amenities to the majority of them. On paper, the *Ujamaa* concept sounded plausible—people in strategically located villages could be catered for so much more easily and economically. Roads, schools, clinics, piped water and communal halls would make life better for all concerned. Furthermore, the Government felt that the farmers' individualism contravened the principles of socialism. The administrative officers were asked to give more encouragement to the people to move away from their traditional areas and into new villages. Unfortunately, some of the officers became over zealous in implementing the government policy. One method that they employed was to appear suddenly at a small farm and ask the head of the household whether he was ready to move; if he said no, the officer would say that he would return the following morning with a lorry to load his personal effects. When the lorry came, the man might plead that he and his family had lived in the area for generations and possibly add that he needed his land for grazing his stock. If he continued to resist the proposal, the officer would attach a rope from his lorry around a corner of the house to pull down a wall. He would then ask again if he were ready to move. To prevent the family from returning to the homestead, he might even burn down some of the buildings. I actually saw burnt out houses when I flew over Tanzania in a small plane in 1975.[1] While such practices were definitely not condoned by the Government, they certainly had the desired effect of moving people quickly. Stories of the use of force in a few cases made others concede to government wishes more readily.

Valiantly, the Government made an enormous effort to help the people once they were resettled, but there were too many unforeseen problems and it was not realized in time that hydrologists and soil scientists were needed to plan where new villages should be located, so some were consequently established in areas where the soil was poor and the water insufficient. In certain instances there was not enough roofing material, cement or pipes for construction, and some of the villages were not improvements on the older scattered settlements. By moving too quickly economic chaos was inevitable.

Agricultural production fell drastically and Tanzania, which had hitherto been self-sufficient in food grains, became an importer. Between March 1974 and September 1975, the country imported £60,000,000 worth of grain from America, Canada and even Kenya. This unexpected expenditure practically drained Tanzania's foreign currency reserves which could have been more wisely used to purchase machinery, spare parts and for making technological improvements.[2] The official explanation for the severe shortage of food in 1974 and 1975 was drought. But Kenya also experienced drought during this period and was still able to produce food for its own consumers and for export. Incidentally, Kenya is the only country in tropical Africa which does produce

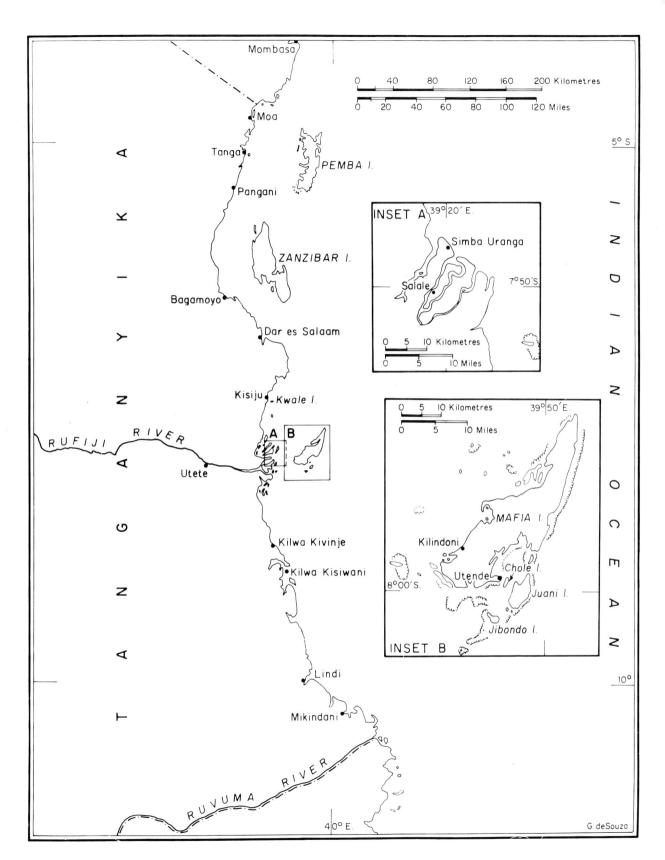

Tanzania

ample fresh milk, cream, butter and cheese and, in fact, it usually exports these products. The drought was of course partially responsible for the decrease in agricultural production in Tanzania at this time, but its effect was compounded by mismanagement of some of the *Ujamaa* villages, by poor transport facilities, by low prices paid to the farmers for their agricultural output, and, perhaps most serious of all, by the loss of incentive. It was because of the problems experienced at this time that the Government decided to allow the farmers to work the plots allocated to them on their own, rather than carrying through their original programme of collective agriculture, whereby all the farmers share the profits equally, irrespective of how much work each farmer does himself.[3]

The translocation of the rural majority of the population to villages was quite a feat in Tanzania, since the country is only five per cent urbanized. It was certainly unique in Africa. In the long run the project may prove successful, if the Government does not resume its original policy of collectivization of agriculture, a concept they probably adopted from China. In all the major grain exporting countries of the world—U.S.A., Canada, Australia and France—the land is farmed individually and is mostly private land. In order to boost agricultural production in Tanzania the Government should continue to aid the farmers by making available to them subsidized fertilizer, by expanding the road network, by improving transport and by making life in the *Ujamaa* villages more worthwhile to the peasants. It was extremely interesting to me to be in Tanzania in 1974 and 1975 when millions of people were being moved. Intellectually, the *Ujamaa* concepts are exciting, but from a practical viewpoint I am glad I was not one of the peasants.

For a socialist country, Tanzania allowed an amazing amount of criticism and debate in its government-owned press during the period when people were being translocated. The University openly entered into discussions of the problems involved and there were no reprisals against those who pointed out failures in enacting the policy. The Government even answered through the press some of the criticisms raised.

Concurrent with the radical experiments in rural areas was the continued process of nationalization of large companies and some other sectors of the retail trade. This resulted in some curious shortages, which affected me to a small extent, and certainly were annoying to the dhow merchants. For instance, between January and March 1975, there was no colour film available (this was especially frustrating to the thousands of tourists that were still coming to Tanzania particularly to visit the magnificent game parks), nor even such a common item as black ink. I could not find a nail of any size in Dar es Salaam, the capital city, and the lack of toilet paper became a national issue! There was petrol rationing in a sense: from 9.00 p.m. on Friday until 6.00 a.m. on Monday no petrol was sold to public consumers, and from 2.00 p.m. on Sunday until 6.00 a.m. on Monday no cars except diplomatic and a few public vehicles were allowed to move. Cities such as Dar es Salaam and Tanga became like ghost towns on Sunday afternoons and evenings. The price of petrol was also raised. One side effect of this was that the dhow trade became a more competitive means of transporting goods from one place to another.

'Nationalization of the means of production', a common definition of socialism, brings along, almost inevitably, a left-wing foreign policy. Tanzania became a leader of the so-called Third World countries and began attacking many western countries as capitalist exploiters. It also made some new 'friends'. At least 15,000 Chinese were imported to help build the Tan-Zam railway from Dar to Zambia, and anti-colonial forces such as FRELIMO were welcomed in Tanzania. An obvious anti-west sentiment was officially encouraged, especially in the government-owned and controlled newspapers. Therefore, permission to do research like mine, which entailed living in the countryside and interviewing people, was not easy to obtain. I had applied for research clearance in September 1973 only because I had two close friends in Tanzania who said that I would receive approval from the Government. I was rather doubtful none the less, knowing so many American and British scholars who had been turned down. I wrote many letters and was given several recommendations. I was actually in Tahiti, some nine months after I had sent in my application when the permission came through. I immediately made arrangements to spend from December 1974 to October 1975 in Tanzania to carry out fieldwork and archival research.

I was pleasantly surprised that the government officials I came across during my stay in Tanzania were so extremely helpful. Once I had obtained official clearance, and that was the major difficulty, the many government officers with whom I held various discussions were most generous with their time and they allowed me to see any statistics germane to the dhow trade. None of the officials were arrogant, as I have found on occasion elsewhere in Africa, and many of them were genuinely interested in my research. There could be two reasons which might partially explain why. I was surely the first person ever to have made a study of the dhow trade there and I was also one of the very few people doing any type of research in the field, other than those concerned with wildlife preservation. Therefore the officials were not inundated by students asking questions as so often happens elsewhere today, and some of the officers obviously enjoyed the novel opportunity to talk about the lists of statistics in their files.

My permission entitled me to study the dhow trade from the Kenya border down to the Rufiji Delta. I had not asked to be allowed to work farther south because the southern coastal areas were essentially closed to outsiders due to the war then being fought in Mozambique. Following a north to south itinerary, I did fieldwork in Moa, Tanga, Pangani, Bagamoyo, Dar es Salaam, Kisiju, on Kwale island, the Rufiji Delta and the Mafia archipelago. I became very security conscious since I was so conspicuous. With me at all times was a Tanzanian assistant and a folder full of official documents permitting me to do research. When I went into a new region, I would go to the Regional Development Director to introduce myself and obtain a letter of introduction from him for me to present to the District Development Director. The latter would in turn write another letter to the local TANU (Tanganika African National Union—the sole political party) Chairman. Finally, for the major ports of Tanzania I had to have written permits from the East African Customs and Excise Department and from the various officers in charge of customs statistics. In all, I had over twenty-five official letters and documents and I needed all of them as occasionally I would be stopped by a TANU official who would ask me what I was doing and check on each letter of authorization. There was, however, one letter I could never get: written

The building of a *mashua* on the beach in the middle of Dar es Salaam

permission to take photographs in the Dar es Salaam dhow wharf. I was concerned about this since earlier a European had come up from South Africa and taken photographs and made sketches of the Dar es Salaam harbour. The police caught him and he was convicted and jailed as a South African spy. Naturally, I didn't want a similar incident to occur and I consequently made many trips (eleven in all) to the appropriate authorities to request written permission. Every time I was told that there was no problem whatsoever and that I could just go ahead and take what pictures I needed of the dhow wharf. I really wanted more than oral consent but I finally gave up after having spent weeks getting nowhere. I wanted photographs of the largest dhow port on the Tanzanian mainland so I talked a customs officer into coming with me. I went out with my cameras and began snapping away and as the customs officer saw no one around he returned to his office. I continued photographing and when I had finished and was making my way back out of the port, a policeman stopped me and tried to confiscate my cameras. I argued and argued and was beginning to wonder what the outcome was going to be when to my relief the customs officer re-appeared and settled the matter amicably, insisting to the policeman that everything was in order. This was not the only time while in Tanzania that I had trouble with a policeman but I decided at that point not to attempt again anything for which I did not have explicit written permission.

The Foreign Dhow Trade of Tanganyika prior to 1963

The foreign dhow trade of Tanganyika from World War I up to Independence was less significant than that of Kenya (see Table VII). The simple explanation for this is that Mombasa and Zanzibar were more attractive. The former had more to offer to foreign dhow crews in trading commodities and amenities, and

Zanzibar, only twenty-five miles off the Tanganyika coast, was, from 1840 until the Revolution in 1964, the main entrepôt for foreign dhows for the entire East African coast. Most of the commodities traded by dhow from Tanganyika, such as ivory and gum copal, were shipped to Zanzibar so there was no need for foreign dhows to come to mainland Tanganyikan ports except to pick up mangrove poles. On account of Zanzibar's paramount importance as the centre for foreign dhows (and still today as the major coastal dhow port), I will devote a separate chapter to the dhow trade there.

For at least a hundred years and likely for many centuries, Arabian dhows have been coming to Tanganyika, mostly to the Rufiji, to pick up mangrove poles. Regrettably, not until about 1900 do we have statistics on the numbers of poles that were cut in the Rufiji swamps so we can only guess at previous quantities. Since there are many historical descriptions about the mangrove pole trade in Tanganyika for the earlier part of this century,[4] I will confine my comments to contemporary conditions in the midge- and mosquito-infested swamps.

TABLE VII
NATIONALITIES AND NUMBERS OF DHOWS COMING INTO TANGANYIKA PORTS FOR SELECTED YEARS FROM 1895 TO 1948

Year	British*	Indian	Arabian	Zanzibari	Italian	Mozambique	French	Belgium
1895	699							
1921	2,522		98	439	4	4	9	31
1925	2,091	49	24	75		16	9	5
1930	1,895	29	53	48		14	12	17
1935	2,488	18	146	7	10	7	7	
1939	2,068	15	175	12	10			
1945	2,940	31	151	376		3		
1948	2,334	32	31	478				

*Mostly Tanganyikan (after 1917) and Kenyan dhows Source: 'Annual Report of German East Africa for 1896', Residency F2, Zanzibar Archives; and *Blue Books 1921–1948*.

The main port for foreign dhows since the beginning of this century has been Dar es Salaam, the largest city and the capital of Tanganyika. Most of the foreign dhows come from Arabia but there has also been a considerable number from India: from 1921 to 1939, an annual average of 60 foreign dhows departed from Dar, but during the War years and up to 1948, the dhow traffic boomed with an annual average of 300 dhows.[5] Salted fish was the major dhow import. I do not have the figures for fish imports into Dar es Salaam *per se*, but for all the ports of Tanganyika grouped together, and these show that, for instance, in 1932, £3,960 of fish came from Arabia and this figure gradually increased, and by 1944, £29,884 of fish were imported from Arabia. The peak year was 1948 when Tanganyika imported £38,880 from the Hadhramaut, £4,090 from Kuwait, £1,296 from Aden and £963 from Oman.[6] Dates were also imported in the various ports of Tanganyika by dhow. During the 1930s, most of the dates came from Arabia, but some also came from Iraq and India; their import value was roughly £1,200 annually. During the war years, there was a tremendous upsurge in date imports, averaging £9,400 yearly, and the dhows continued to be their major means of transport.[7]

During the first half of the twentieth century, the second most important port of the country was Tanga (see Table VIII). From 1921 to 1939, an average of 41 foreign dhows came into port there each year, and from 1941 to 1948 the traffic increased to an average of 105 dhows a year. Tanzania's minor foreign dhow ports include Kwale island, which is mainly a stop-over point for dhows travelling on to the Rufiji (averaging yearly 73 foreign dhows from 1932 to 1948), Bagamoyo (averaging yearly 18·5 dhows between 1921 and 1948), Lindi (exactly the same during this period), Mikindani (16), Pangani (15.5), Mafia (5), and Kilwa (less than 1.5).[8] These ports are of little significance and do not warrant individual discussion so far as the recent foreign dhow trade is concerned.

TABLE VIII
NUMBERS OF EAST AFRICAN AND FOREIGN DHOWS WHICH DEPARTED FROM TANGA FOR SELECTED YEARS FROM 1921 TO 1974

Year	East African Dhows	Foreign Dhows (including Zanzibar)	Total
1921	206	73	279
1925	892	18	910
1930	372	34	406
1935	331	35	366
1939	391	42	433
1945	280	49	329
1948	154	130	284
1970	220	17*	237
1971	200	17*	217
1972	85	14*	99
1973	183	3*	186
1974	281	1*	282

*excluding Zanzibar

Source: *Blue Books 1921–1948* and Tanga Dhow Registers, East African Customs and Excise Department, Tanga

The Foreign Dhow Traffic of Dar es Salaam since Independence

In 1948, 364 foreign dhows came into Dar es Salaam directly from overseas. In 1974 only one arrived. What has happened? Unfortunately, I was unable to obtain statistics for the 1950s as they seem to be missing. After weeks of searching the Tanzania National Archives, the East African Community and the Dar es Salaam Customs Office, I gave up. Even without the statistics, however, we may assume that there was a decline in dhow traffic, and this decline has continued, becoming more severe since 1967. Table IX shows that from 1961 to 1967 an average of seventeen dhows came into Dar yearly, while from 1968 to 1974 the average dropped to less than four. We must remember that these figures refer to dhows which came directly to Dar from abroad, not for instance those which first stopped in Tanga. They are counted at their point of arrival and their point of departure from the country, which explains why, for example, it looks as though there is a discrepancy in the number of dhows in Dar in 1970: nine arrived but eleven departed (see Tables IX and X).

TABLE IX
NATIONALITIES OF FOREIGN DHOWS COMING DIRECT TO DAR ES SALAAM FROM 1961 TO 1974

Year	Indian	Somali	Arabian	Total
1961	18	1		19
1962	13	1		14
1963	20	1		21
1964	16		1	17
1965	8			8
1966	22			22
1967	15	4		19
1968	1		1	2
1969	2		2	4
1970	6		3	9
1971	8			8
1972	2			2
1973				0
1974	1			1

Source: Dar es Salaam Dhow Registers, East African Customs and Excise Department, Dhow Wharf, Dar es Salaam.

The Kenyan foreign dhow trade has also declined over this period of time, but not to the same extent. The main reason for Tanzania's decline is directly linked to the political and economic policies discussed earlier in this chapter which have resulted in shortages of goods available in Dar es Salaam. Furthermore, in comparison with Kenya, what goods there are are more expensive. Even aesthetically, the city of Dar es Salaam has deteriorated. I first went to Dar in 1964 and it was then a beautiful clean city overlooking the Indian Ocean. On the waterfront were many attractive large German or coastal Arab buildings dating from the late nineteenth century. The suburbs around the Museum and the State House were attractively landscaped with colourful tropical bushes and plants. Over the past few years the physical appearance of Dar has so changed as to make this description almost unbelievable. The entire city needs a coat of paint. There are refuse dumps near the Lutheran Cathedral and on the waterfront. The public gardens are poorly maintained and even in the Kilimanjaro Hotel garden the weeds are more numerous than flowers. The streets have far too many potholes. Most of the small independent restaurants and cafés which gave Dar its friendly atmosphere are now closed.

The explanation is that the upkeep of Dar es Salaam is very low indeed on the list of government priorities. Since ninety-five per cent of the people are rural inhabitants, money is planned to be used to improve the standard of life in the countryside. Under colonialism, a far higher percentage of the Government's revenue was going into the cities than the present Government believes appropriate. Furthermore, it is argued that if city life becomes too pleasant, people will be attracted from the rural areas to towns where there are no jobs for them. Even today, government officers periodically go around Dar and collect unemployed people and prostitutes and send them back out to their home areas.[9] Although I can understand the point of the Government's policy to build up amenities in the countryside, the infrastructure in the cities must also be maintained. However, the basic problem in Tanzania is lack of incentive. Since the Government owns and controls almost everything, it is not really worth anyone's effort to try to do something as an individual. It has even come to the stage where an innovation designed by an individual cannot be implemented by him. A state where one is forbidden to own a second house or buy a new car, as in the case of Tanzania, may well diminish incentive.

The nationalization of the wholesale trade and the taking over of privately-owned business enterprises in Dar es Salaam has been the major cause for the decline of the foreign dhow trade. The following incident is just one of many which is typical of the present state of affairs. On 13 February 1975 the Somali dhow *Iqbaal* with a crew of seven arrived at the Dar es Salaam dhow wharf from Mogadishu with 2,500 kilos of dried shark and salted fish for sale. When the *nahoda* attempted to sell his fish, his agent told him that the Government had refused to renew the licences of the fish agents because the Government wished to take over the wholesale purchase of fish. But the catch was that the Government in February 1975 had not yet set up its own business to purchase the fish and thus there was no way whatsoever that the dhow captain could sell his cargo. Since regulations prohibit the importation from abroad of Tanzanian shillings and the dhow captain could not sell his fish, he had no

The dhow harbour of
Dar es Salaam

money to purchase food in Dar. For fifteen days the captain's agent went around town trying to get permission for the fish to be sold while the crew got hungrier and hungrier. On 28 February I talked to the captain and asked him why he did not sail to Zanzibar and sell his fish there; he said that he thought that the price would not be profitable (a correct assumption). He told me that his family had been coming to Dar for the past fifteen years to sell fish but that this was the last trip he was going to make to Tanzania. The next day he left for Mombasa to sell his fish there. The irony of the story is that Tanzania is a net importer of fish and everyone lost out in this affair: the poor Tanzanians who eat dried shark and fish were deprived of purchasing this cheap food supply, and the dhow captain and his crew who sailed a long way to learn without prior warning that the market was in effect closed. Although this was a temporary situation the tragedy of it is that this sort of news is carried back to Somalia and Arabia and discourages further ventures.

TABLE X

NUMBERS OF EAST AFRICAN AND FOREIGN DHOWS WHICH DEPARTED FROM DAR ES SALAAM FOR SELECTED YEARS FROM 1921 TO 1974

Year	East African Dhows	Foreign Dhows (including Zanzibar)	Total
1921	374	153	527
1925	723	50	773
1930	665	33	698
1935	1,030	76	1,106
1939	666	41	707
1945	999	277	1,276
1948	692	364	1,056
1968	911	13*	924*
1970	869	11*	880*
1971	815	18*	833*
1972	735	9*	744*
1973	1,403	11*	1,414*
1974	1,486	1*	1,487*

*excluding Zanzibar dhows

Source: *Blue Books 1921–1948* and Dar es Salaam Dhow Registers.

Of the twenty-six foreign dhows that have come into Dar es Salaam from 1970 to 1974, seventeen brought in roofing tiles from Mangalore in India, and the average dhow brought in 20,000 of these clay roofing tiles. From 1972 to 1974, only three foreign dhows (all Indian) have come into Dar directly from abroad and their cargo was limited to 1,867 clay water pots. I am unable to understand how it could be economic to sail all the way from the west coast of India to Dar es Salaam with less than 2,000 pots to sell for a few shillings each. I spoke to one Indian crew member about it. He told me that the captain had picked up the clay pots in Kutch-Mandvi and sailed (his *kotia* had no engine) down to Calicut with a small amount of cargo. From Calicut he sailed directly to Zanzibar which took twenty-four days. A few days later he came into Dar to sell some of the pots. The captain did not plan to buy anything in Dar because of bureaucratic difficulties.[10] The dhow then went to

Kenya where the captain planned to purchase mangrove poles and cement to sell in the Arabian Gulf.[11] One wonders why the captain sailed into Tanzanian waters at all when he perhaps could have brought cargo to sell in Mombasa.

From 1970 to 1974 about one third of the foreign dhows that have departed from Dar es Salaam have gone to Somali ports, one third to Aden and one third to Arabian Gulf ports. Their cargoes have consisted of mangrove poles (mostly from the Rufiji), tea, rice and sorghum.[12]

The Mangrove Trade

Some of the foreign dhows which come to the Tanzanian mainland avoid the cities and put into Kwale island, forty-five miles south-east of Dar es Salaam, before going on to the Rufiji Delta to pick up the finest quality mangrove poles in the Indian Ocean. From 1964 to 1967 an annual average of sixty foreign dhows came into Kwale while from 1968 to 1974 an annual average of only 1.3 came in. From the figures of the late 1940s (in 1946 a record of 277 dhows cleared customs at Kwale[13]), an observer might be led to think that Kwale was a big place—far from it!

Kwale is a small isolated island off the mainland of Tanzania. I counted 110 houses in the main village of which eight were permanent buildings and there are perhaps 300 people resident on the entire island.[14] There is no regular motor boat traffic to Kwale, and if one wants to go there from Dar es Salaam one must take a vehicle, preferably with four-wheel drive, south on the main Kilwa road and then branch off on the sandy track leading to the port of Kisiju. There I had to negotiate a place to sit on a local *mashua* which was already full with passengers, beans, potatoes and smelly onions on its way to Koma island. As soon as the captain saw that I was a European he attempted to charge me triple the normal fee, but I finally got him to halve this price.

Kwale is a strange place and the annual arrival of foreign dhows is the only event to disturb its torpor. The place seems very conservative, perhaps because, as an island, it has been cut off from the main stream of activities found on the mainland. As soon as I landed on the beach, the Chairman of the local branch of TANU whom I was told was illiterate in both English and Swahili, encouraged me to leave although I had all the proper forms and permissions to be there. Some months before, I learned, the Chairman had told the newly arrived school teacher to leave because there was no proper accommodation for him. The Chairman and most of the inhabitants appear to want no changes in the status quo. Since Independence there has been hardly any investment put into the island and even the government buildings have been neglected. In 1961 the District Officer stationed on the mainland wrote:

> I visited the Customs House but the airy verandah has now been blocked off with corrugated iron, placed there by a previous occupier to prevent the wind and sand from blowing in ... Water is still supplied to the island by wells ... All yield salty or brackish water ... I visited the local authority bush school, a rather pathetic mud and daub hut with a makuti roof ... Women are shy and do not come out and wander about during the day.[15]

The affairs of Kwale have hardly changed. The Customs House needs repairs, and the school still has not been completed. The two wells on the island indeed produce a brackish concoction, so drinking water must be brought in from

Kisiju by dhow at a cost of Shs. 0.70 a gallon. Women are still not to be seen during the day except at the wells.

What the District Officer did not mention which I think is most unusual is the division of the island into two parts. The people live on one side, cultivating small amounts of maize, millet and peas and grazing their cattle and goats; on the other side there are no houses whatsoever and no domestic stock allowed. Approximately down a centre line of the island stands a strong fence. On the people's side the landscape is bleak and interrupted only by the odd baobab tree. Opposite is a paradise of leafy trees and bushes, a lush green rice crop, a pond and thousands of singing birds. I can think of no better example of conservation in East Africa. It also provides a stark contrast between where man and his domestic animals have eroded the landscape and where the natural vegetation has been protected.

After putting into Kwale (the most convenient East African Customs House) to have their craft registered and cargo inspected, the foreign dhow crews sail down to the Rufiji Delta. In the delta there is no customs officer, and the forester who is responsible for the Rufiji is stationed many miles away at Utete and is rarely seen in the delta because of the difficulties in getting there. I first visited the Rufiji in 1966 when I drove down from Dar es Salaam to visit the historic ruins at Kilwa Kisiwani. On the way back the ferry across the Rufiji got stuck and we had to spend the night in the old, gigantic German *Boma* (fortified building) at Utete. The vehicles on the main road cross the Rufiji by ferry at Utete which is quite far upstream. In 1974–5, when I was doing research, I naturally wanted to go down to the delta. During certain times of the year, it is possible to drive to some of the villages there, but you need a four-wheel drive vehicle or a lorry. I tried for months to hire a suitable vehicle from various government and private car-hire firms in Dar, but was continually told that the Land Rovers and Toyotas were under repair or that someone else had booked them months earlier. In the end, I decided that it would be more romantic (and at that point the only practical way) to take a boat through the delta. It would also give me the opportunity to glimpse the activities going on along the waterway. I hired a small motor boat from Mafia and planned to leave early one morning in order to have the whole day in the Rufiji and be able to return back at night before the mosquitoes and sandflies would descend on me. Since the Rufiji is a huge area (the German Cruiser *Konigsberg* hid herself in the delta for months from the British in 1915), I had to make up my mind precisely where to go. The delta is shaped like a hand with five main finger-like tributaries pouring mud and fresh water into the sea. There are many large villages in the Rufiji, such as Mohoro, Mbwera and Kikale and I had to choose one or two which would be most relevant to the dhow trade. I decided to go to Simba Uranga, right on the eastern edge of the delta, because it is well known throughout the Indian Ocean for its quality mangrove poles, and to Salale, the main town for mangrove exports and the former headquarters of the Forest Department. As the figures show (see Table XI), the number of foreign dhows which went to Salale to pick up poles declined from the early 1960s although no similar trend is to be seen in the pole exports.

I had great difficulties in hiring a boat to go up to the Rufiji for two reasons. There are very few power boats in reasonable order anywhere in Tanzania and the owners of those that are available are afraid to have them go to the Rufiji because of all the hazards of navigation, especially sandbanks. Finally, though, I persuaded A. J. Klosser, a long-term resident of Zanzibar and Mafia, to accompany me in his 23-foot motor launch to the Rufiji. The night before we left I had to go to the police station on Mafia island and tell them that the boat would be moving before dawn from the eastern side of the island to the western. If I had not warned the police, we might have been arrested because there is a night curfew on the movement of all boats.

TABLE XI
FOREIGN DHOWS COMING INTO SALALE, AMOUNTS AND VALUES OF MANGROVE POLES EXPORTED ABROAD
(SELECTED YEARS)

Year	Number of foreign dhows	Number of poles exported	Value to cutters (£)
1945	13	18,000	700
1946	62	67,000	2,500
1947	73	79,640	3,787
1948	135	180,000	12,800
1949	76	100,000	6,000
1950	89	133,000	7,500
1966	7	82,000	5,000
1967	4	59,000	3,000
1969	11	84,140	N/A
1970	16	160,000	N/A
1971	28	303,400	N/A
1972	4	48,740	N/A
1973	8	84,400	N/A
1974	6	81,140	N/A

Source: Dhow Imports and Exports for the Rufiji area, 1945–50, Rufiji District Office, 274, 4/10 Customs, Tanzania National Archives; Tanzania Forest Department Annual Report 1966; and Transire Notes, Kwale Customs House.

On 3 February 1975, the boat left Utende at 5.45 a.m. although I did not board until some two hours later when it arrived on the western side of the island. It was a long journey north-westward to the Rufiji. February is a hot month in this part of the world, and the reflection from the sea turned us the colour of scalded lobsters half-way through the trip. Because of the millions of tons of silt built up into huge banks, we could not proceed directly west but had to move northwards about five miles off the coast and concentrate on looking for an entrance into the delta. We found a way in at around 11.40 a.m. by which time the sea was becoming slightly rough due to a strong wind blowing. Once we were into the delta, it became calm again and on all sides we were surrounded by mangrove trees, but we did not come across any dhows or people. In fact, during the journey to Salale, which is nine miles up the Rufiji and approximately one hour's travelling time, we saw only three *mashuas*.

Arriving at Salale at one o'clock, I first glimpsed from the boat the old Forestry Department building and soon learned that no forestry officers had used it at all for years. Part of it now serves as a government dispensary; the rest has been allowed to deteriorate into ruins. I began to wonder whether this state of affairs was an indication of the entire settlement. I had looked forward to getting to this historic spot and had felt so fortunate and happy about finally accomplishing my goal that I refused at first to accept the fact that Salale's renown was now little more than a faded memory. Not seeing piles of mangrove poles stacked and ready for the dhows, I quickly dismissed their absence by rationalizing that, of course, from interviews and papers I had read I should not expect to see them—the people in the Rufiji have to be prodded into cutting the mangroves and, unlike Lamu and Ngomeni in Kenya, they did not cut the poles in advance and wait for the foreign dhows to come. They were poorer people and needed to be encouraged with food and money before they would even start their cutting. I had also read that sometimes the foreign dhows spent up to a month in the Rufiji getting the people sufficiently worked up to go out and slog around these swamps. I tried to reassure myself that that was what was going on now.

I quickly walked the three-quarters of a mile or so from the Forestry Department to the end of the town and counted fifty-three buildings along the way, of which only three were made of stone. To my dismay, I learned that in the entire village there were only six adults and a few children. Since the 1950s, Salale has continuously declined in significance and is now almost a ghost town. I interviewed the sole adult male who was present to try to obtain some sort of explanation. With the decline of the foreign dhow trade from the 1950s, and especially since the late 1960s, the Arabs, Indians and Goans resident in Salale have moved on; some to Dar, the rest elsewhere in search of more lucrative business pursuits. Swahilis alone remain in the village now, and there is little alternative work for them other than trying to farm. Since Salale is poor agriculturally (the land is too sandy), many have moved into *Ujamaa* villages far away. Others go to such places as Paje every year in early February to plant crops, mostly rice, returning to Salale after the August harvest. That is why I found so very few inhabitants when I was there. I was told that in August, however, the population expands to close to 150.[16] There is some copra grown on the outskirts of Salale and the women of the village cultivate a little cassava and gather cashew nuts. A few fishermen catch prawns down the river. The two shops re-open in August. Before the inhabitants head away for the season, a few individuals cut mangrove poles for domestic use and those that are left over are transported by dhow to Kisiju, then to Dar by lorry.

Cutting mangrove poles for foreign dhows has declined from the early 1960s (see Table XII) and the trade is unlikely to recover in the near future, if ever. In 1974, the last year for which I have statistics, six Iranian dhows came to Salale in March to get some poles. What happened is not completely clear, but the story goes that they were so harassed by the Tanzanian officials that they declared that they would never return. When these dhows pulled into Kwale, the captains went through customs. Since they were planning to spend several weeks in the Rufiji, they left their documents behind at Kwale for safe-keeping. They then proceeded down to Salale, and followed the accepted custom of paying the cutters before they went out to get the mangrove poles. As a consequence a lot of Tanzanian shillings were suddenly in circulation and the authorities descended on the foreigners, demanding to know where they got their Tanzanian money. The captains said that they had legally exchanged their currency at Kwale, but they had no papers with them to prove that they had done so. The authorities were not satisfied, and although they allowed the

Fetching water from Kwale Island, Tanzania

Iranians to carry on their business, they did not make it easy for them. Eventually, the dhows sailed away with 80,000 poles, but the crew's tales of harassment and hardship made the rounds of the coffee houses in Arabia and the Persian Gulf, inevitably adding another nail to the coffin of the Tanzanian foreign mangrove trade.

TABLE XII

MANGROVE POLES CUT IN TANGANYIKA (MOSTLY IN THE RUFIJI) AND EXPORT VALUES FOR SELECTED YEARS, 1921–1971

Year	Small poles cut	Large poles cut	Poles exported (almost all large)	Export Value* (£)
1921	148,790	497,520	46,183	1,304
1925	2,249,541	361,675	109,561	3,818
1930	4,486,000	1,130,700	93,791	4,694
1931	4,005,914	2,042,206	86,944	4,265
1935	4,885,088	1,135,053	69,020	1,364
1941	3,984,529	1,162,335	49,600	1,403
1945	2,942,089	1,300,000	173,820	6,782
1948	5,623,300	1,791,900	364,180	14,965
1950	N/A	N/A	565,560	6,310
1955	N/A	N/A	155,500	N/A
1960	N/A	N/A	754,000	38,650
1962	N/A	N/A	323,751	16,242
1963	N/A	N/A	214,514	12,270
1964	N/A	N/A	85,937	4,849
1965	N/A	N/A	80,475	6,607
1966	N/A	N/A	152,310	9,018
1967	N/A	N/A	72,563	3,504
1970	N/A	726,160	N/A	N/A
1971	N/A	464,020	N/A	N/A

*including exports to Zanzibar
Sources: Forest Department, Dar es Salaam; *Blue Books*; Forest Department Annual Reports, Tanzania National Archives.

Disappointed by the pathetic conditions of the once famous Salale, we left there at three o'clock in the afternoon. Even nine miles up the Rufiji, the river is quite wide. It is not as dark muddy brown as the Sabaki River, near Malindi, in Kenya, for there is not so much thick vegetation washed down it. At the entrance to the Simba Uranga tributary, however, there is a large mudbank. The water is shallow here, and if there is a wind it becomes very rough indeed. It took us an hour to reach the village of Simba Uranga, and to our amazement and horror we found ourselves rocked and rolled by huge waves coming in from the ocean and breaking over the mudbank. It was suddenly so rough that we knew there was a real danger of capsizing if we tried to get out to the sea and had to resign ourselves to getting the boat into safety and staying where we were until morning. On shore, I decided I might as well first of all investigate Simba Uranga. It was practically deserted, too. There were three adult men

Simba Uranga, at the mouth of the Rifiji River, Tanzania

and a handful of women and children there; the others had gone to Paje to farm. The people called themselves Kianyagatwa, but the younger ones only spoke Swahili, and did not speak any tribal language.[17] The twenty-five or so houses there were simple, temporary structures with walls made out of woven coconut palms and *makuti* roofs supported by mangrove poles. The people have always been known to be poor there, but their standard of living has been reduced to bare subsistence level since the decline of the foreign dhow trade.[18]

After dark, I returned to the boat to join Klosser and our crew of three. Between us we had hardly any food since we had all expected to be back in Mafia that night. As I was munching a piece of stale bread Klosser had handed to me, the three men from Simba Uranga whom I had met earlier came up to our boat and asked us how we came to be in the Rufiji. I took out my file of permits, including those allowing me to carry out research in the Rufiji and specifically at Salale. But the men, who were all illiterate, were perplexed. I assured them that everything was in order and explained that my permissions had been granted through the Coast Headquarters, Dar es Salaam authorities, Kisarawe and Mafia. They continued to eye us suspiciously and perhaps the thought that we might be the dreaded South African or Portuguese spies crossed their minds. One of the men said that he was going to arrest us, although he did not say for what crime. He also did not say what he was going to do with us (there is no police station or any senior government officer for miles around), nor did he identify himself and say what was his authority. I laughed but he was not amused. Our party was all standing together and Klosser remarked: 'There are three of you but five of us; come take us'. They looked at us with great surprise at this realization and rapidly changed their minds. In fact, they actually laughed and started shaking hands and making all

114

An old *mashua* lying on the beach, and a *mashua* sailing off Utende, Mafia

kinds of friendly overtures. We shared what little food and drink we had with our new friends from Simba Uranga.

When we were preparing to snatch some sleep, the sand flies and mosquitoes began to appear by the millions. We were of course not prepared for their onslaught and had neither mosquito nets nor repellents with us. The insects seemed determined to devour whatever they could find on the boat, so I made up my mind to sleep on the beach right next to the sea. At least there was a little breeze coming off the water which should have deterred them somewhat. We built a fire out of fallen branches in order to stay warm, to keep the hippos at bay and to give us some protection from the bugs. The fire died down all too soon. Then the sandflies with their persistent buzzing, which was as bad as the mosquitoes, exasperated me. They went after all of us with, it seemed, deliberate malice. I completely covered myself with a couple of towels but the mosquitoes still managed to bite through. The ripples of the waves from the sea tickled my feet, while the dampness of the sand slowly but surely penetrated through my shirt and trousers leaving me to feel all the more wretched. After midnight, the wind ceased almost completely and it became very sticky. At 1.30 a.m. the moon came out, and to solace myself I lay on my back watching the clouds slowly cover the bright stars and listening to the waves breaking on the beach. I can understand now why all foreign dhow crews dread coming to the Rufiji.

At 5.45 a.m., not having caught anything like forty winks and being very hungry, we began to limp back towards Mafia. When we arrived at Kilindoni at 9.40 a.m., thoroughly miserable and exhausted, we found the entire town closed down because there was a political meeting and everyone had to attend it. Thus no food for us here, either. Finally, by paying three times the normal fare, we got transport to the other side of the island where I slept and nursed my wounds.

Dhow Building in Tanzania: The Mafia Archipelago

The several islands of the Mafia archipelago lie to the south of Zanzibar and to the immediate east of the Rufiji. To me, they are among the most interesting of all the places on the Tanzania coast so far as history and dhows are concerned. There are many old buildings to see on Chole island, including those that the Germans built when they had their local capital here. There are very old sites on Juani island, and on Mafia itself there are ruins dating back to the twelfth century.[19]

The people of Mafia support themselves with the products of palm trees, rice, cassava, petty trading (there are fifteen *dukas* in the main town of Kilindoni, eight of which are owned by Asians) and fishing. But because of the poor soil on these islands (especially at Jibondo) and the general unwillingness of the people to cultivate sufficient quantities of rice and cassava, the islanders have traditionally been importers of food. The people have paid for their food imports with the profits realized from coconut products (particularly copra), cashew nuts and fish; in the 1973–4 season the farmers of Mafia exported £154,223 of copra and £40,436 of cashew nuts;[20] the fishermen caught 1,115 tons of fish worth £147,000.[21]

During the past few years, due to the shortage of food on the Tanzanian mainland and a law prohibiting movement of food from one district to another without a specific permit, there has been a tremendous amount of smuggling from Mafia, Chole and Jibondo to the mainland. The most active group of smugglers are those from Jibondo island. There have been people living on this coral island at least since the fifteenth century,[22] which surprises me. Soil is imported from Mafia by dhow and is then mixed with pulverized coral and dumped into hollows. There are no wells on the island which produce drinkable water, and dhows must consequently make the journey to Mafia island (six miles away) to fetch it; rainwater is collected from the roofs of some of the houses, but the situation has improved considerably since a cement catchment was built in 1968. Another mark against Jibondo is that there is no decent anchorage and when the sea is rough it is difficult to land safely on the island.[23]

The harshness of the landscape at Jibondo seems to be reflected in the character of the inhabitants. They are very independent, tough and hard-working. The majority of them live in the only village, Mzini. They call themselves Shirazis, after the Persians who they believe settled in the area hundreds of years ago. Because of the almost hopeless conditions for farming, most of the men here are engaged in fishing, in part-time trading, and also in transporting goods to and from the mainland by dhow. They sell their dried octopus and dried fish as well as seashells in Dar and bring back from there firewood, rice and maize meal. The mainlanders are more than willing to sell their crops directly to the dhow traders because they can get higher prices for them by by-passing the Co-operative Union and they also get paid immediately in cash this way. Not all the food the dhow traders buy in Dar comes back to Jibondo: considerable amounts are sold, mostly illegally, to other traders on Mafia, Juani, Chole and even elsewhere on the mainland.

Left, Smoking a hookah pipe on board
a dhow in Mombasa

Below, Rowing out to a dhow in Old
Port, Mombasa

A carpenter working in a dhow yard at Dubai

Dhows anchored at Kuwait

An old Arab carpenter working on a dhow in Bahrain

Dhows in Dubai Creek

There are only 400 people altogether living on Jibondo and yet 120 of them are
fishermen, which means that practically every adult male must fish at some
time or another. They own 16 *mashuas*, 12 *ngalawas*, and 3 *daus*; their fishing
gear consists of 114 shark nets, 107 fish traps, 25 gill nets, and 14 harpoons.[24]
When they are not fishing, they are trading. In 1974, when there was a severe
shortage of food on Mafia island (population 18,000) and the Government was
not allowing food in any significant quantity to be brought in from the
mainland, the Jibondo traders supplied some of the needs of the Mafia people
completely illegally.

The government decree of 1975 which ordered everyone in the entire
country of Tanzania, including civil servants, to farm land, did little really to
alleviate the situation in Mafia. In fact, it was rather ludicrous then, when I
was staying in Dar, to contemplate how much it must have been costing people
such as the museum staff to take Land Rovers some five miles out of town to
cultivate little maize patches. The extra food that was produced on the
mainland as a result of this campaign did not find its way to Mafia, and the
Mafia people were expected to grow more of their own cassava and rice. Not
surprisingly, they were unable to expand output significantly and so still had to
depend on the Jibondo smugglers for most of their essential needs. Even so, the
shops on Mafia island often ran out of such things as soft drinks, sugar and
maize meal.

From the type of life led in the Mafia archipelago, it is easy to understand
why dhows perform an extremely important function. It is logical to expect to
find the centre for dhow building in Tanzania there, and so it is, at Chole, a
beautiful island opposite Utende, Mafia. I visited Chole on several occasions,

117

using, naturally enough, dhow transport. The trip, depending on the wind, would take from ten to forty-five minutes. The cost of the round trip was Shs.20.

I landed close to the ruins of the old German buildings which are surrounded by very attractive flamboyant trees with orange flowers. From there I proceeded through a fairly dense forest of tall, leafy trees where there were hundreds of colourful butterflies and moths, emerging on the far side of the island where there are thick mangrove swamps. It is here that *mashuas* are made.

The construction of *mashuas* at Chole is carried out by a co-operative in an *Ujamaa* village. I found ten carpenters working on five *mashuas*. They work daily from eight o'clock in the morning to four o'clock in the afternoon but rather than receiving a regular salary, they are paid for piece work. Generally, the future owner of the dhow will supply the wood (either from the Rufiji or Kisarawe district) and nails. A *mashua* from Chole would sell for £600 in 1975, and I was told that a *jahazi* would be £2,000, but very few of the latter are now made.[25] In the early 1970s, the Government was the main buyer of *mashuas* (for fishing boats for *Ujamaa* villages) and at that time they paid £325 for each of

The construction of *mashuas* on Chole Island, Tanzania

the twenty that they purchased. I was a bit puzzled as to why the workers chose this particular spot for their construction site since, being surrounded by mangrove swamps, it teems with flies and mosquitoes. The workers explained to me that they liked it because of the abundance of mangrove trees which they could use as props to support the dhows and that they had small plots close by where they cultivated bananas, cassava, oranges and coconuts.

The other place where I found dhows being made in the Mafia archipelago was at Mzini, on Jibondo island, where there are six carpenters and they charge just about the same price for a *mashua*. One of them told me they had built six *mashuas* last year, three of which were sold in Kilindoni and three to local people on Jibondo. In these cases, too, the buyers supplied all the wood and nails.[26]

People wanting dhows come from all over Tanzania to buy them in Mafia not only because this is the centre for dhow building in the country but also because the *mashuas* here are considered to be of good quality workmanship. However, buyers do not always have an easy time, as the following story illustrates. Three Scandinavians appeared at Kilindoni, in January 1975, with the intention of purchasing a second-hand *mashua* for £300, considerably less than what it would have cost in Dar. They were on an aid programme for Tanzania and they wanted to have a *mashua* as a pleasure craft to sail around the Dar area. Unfortunately, as soon as they arrived at Kilindoni they were arrested and put in jail. Their apparent crime was bringing a tent with them for camping without official permission and the fact that they were not carrying their passports with them. However, they finally made it known that they were V.I.P.s serving Tanzania and they were released after a few hours with apologies. At length, they chose a *mashua* to buy, but when they wanted to have a captain sail it back to Dar for them, they ran into further difficulties. The captain refused to comply since the sea was then rough; it also transpired that the *mashua*'s sails were full of holes. Eventually, the three Scandinavians had to return to Dar—without their *mashua*. Negotiations through various people continued to be carried out and further payments were made to certain individuals, with the result that weeks later the *mashua* did finally make it to Dar. But by then, the Tanzanian Government had initiated restrictions on leisure sailing around Dar, in particular forbidding craft to go to some of the islands just north of Dar. The whole affair was, for the Scandinavians, a failure from beginning to end.

Once when I was returning from the *Ujamaa* village on Chole I noticed a fisherman taking a large turtle out of his *mashua*. He put a rope around one of her flippers and dragged her on to the sand. To my horror, members of the fishing crew then took out knives and inserted them between the upper and lower shells of the poor turtle. Still alive, and with blood pouring out, the turtle tried to flip herself over and make towards the sea. Almost all the people along the Tanzanian coast are Muslims and I cannot understand why they did not slit the turtle's neck in the first place, which is the traditional Muslim practice in killing an animal for food; perhaps these fishermen knew that according to traditional Muslim practice turtle meat is forbidden. As the gruesome process continued, the turtle's flesh was cut up and set to one side and her eggs stacked in another pile. The scene became a veritable blood bath with offal spread all over the beach. Five more turtles were dragged out of the *mashua*, to be

Slaughtering sea turtles on Chole Island, Tanzania

disposed of similarly. Groups of people began to arrive and, right in the midst of all this, they began to build fires to cook the eggs. My stomach became unsettled as I waded through the blood and guts on the beach and out into the sea, which was also stained red from the turtles, to climb aboard my transport back to Mafia. The sea turtle is not protected in Tanzania, but one is supposed to have a licence to go out after these creatures. The fishermen here, if they catch turtles in their nets, will not return them to the sea; instead they bring them back with the day's catch because it is too tempting not to do so—their meat is excellent.

Before catching turtles was made illegal in Kenya in 1971, it was the Bajuns who went after them. They did so with the help of an eighteen-inch Remora sucker fish, to the tail of which they would attach a line. Then they would drop the Remora down into an area known for sea turtles. When the Remora found a turtle it would attach itself to the shell and the fishermen would then pull in the line and, with the aid of an iron grapnel, they would pull the turtle up and into the boat.[27]

The Local Dhow Trade of Tanzania

Unlike the foreign dhow trade, the local traffic for some parts of Tanzania, such as Pangani, Bagamoyo and especially Dar es Salaam, has actually increased since the 1960s (see Table XIII). Furthermore, some ports, including those in the Mafia archipelago and Kwale, are almost wholly dependent upon dhow transport for import and export traffic. The role of the dhow here is indeed quite important to the people in these areas. The only other place in East Africa where local dhow transport is as important is in the islands north of Lamu, but there the population is considerably less and the traffic is

120

consequently on a much smaller scale. Thus, so far as local dhow traffic is concerned, Tanzania stands in the forefront in East Africa.

TABLE XIII
NUMBER OF LOCAL DHOWS WHICH PUT INTO VARIOUS TANZANIAN PORTS FROM 1960 TO 1974

Year	Tanga	Pangani	Bagamoyo	Dar es Salaam	Kwale	Kilindoni
1960	N/A	19	248	N/A	N/A	355
1961	N/A	12	217	N/A	N/A	442
1962	N/A	25	202	N/A	N/A	450
1963	N/A	15	194	N/A	N/A	N/A
1964	N/A	14	179	N/A	308	N/A
1965	N/A	6	178	N/A	303	N/A
1966	N/A	13	203	N/A	287	N/A
1967	258	22	144	N/A	251	359
1968	229	29	147	924(approx.)	277	384
1969	191	15	105	821	208	368
1970	201	13	165	898	241	301
1971	173	20	214	794	207	258
1972	135	26	385	740	150	216
1973	175	51	498	1,384	360	316
1974	206	42	309	1,416	177	256

Source: Dhow Registers of Tanga, Pangani, Bagamoyo, Dar es Salaam, Kwale and Kilindoni.

Despite dependence upon local dhow transport, the Mafia group of islands, with some 19,000 inhabitants, has, ironically, the worst facilities for dhows in the country. The small jetty at Kilindoni is totally inadequate and is high and dry at low tide. Most of the dhows that come in just lie in the shallow water and porters come out knee-deep into the sea to carry off the cargo. When the sea is rough, there is total chaos: the dhows pitch miserably and some of the cargo usually falls into the sea and porters stagger around at the risk of being knocked down by the force of the waves. Passengers stumble on the rocks and occasionally are injured. Such inefficiency amounts to a lot of waste—in time and in goods.

In 1975, realizing that construction of a proper jetty at Kilindoni should receive top priority as a development project for Mafia, the District Development Officer wrote a memorandum, but the cost would be enormous: he estimated it at £350,000.[28] The advantages of a jetty are obvious: (1) loading of cargo could be carried out at any time, irrespective of tides, (2) more dhows and even steamships would be attracted to Mafia so that periodic shortages of goods would be less likely to occur, (3) imports and exports would be cheaper because less labour and time would be required in handling cargo, and (4) passenger traffic (in 1974 dhows carried 1,122 passengers to and from Kilindoni[29]) would be far more efficient with less personal injury and less risk of damage or loss of personal belongings.

Most (eighty-four per cent in 1973[30]) of the dhows which come into Kilindoni originate from Dar es Salaam. The major imports by dhow are diesel fuel, vegetables, rice, cement, soft drinks, flour and beer; the major exports, mostly to Dar, are coconut oil, coir fibre, copra, cashew nuts, dried fish, seaweed, mangrove poles, seashells and an unusual product, coconut shell flour, called in Swahili *unga wa vifuu*, which is used to make mosquito coils for keeping those vexing insects at bay.[31]

Many of the Mafia dhows going to Dar or to northern ports put in at Kwale, where they get fresh water and drop off or pick up some cargo. Kisiju is the entrepôt for goods moving between Kwale and Dar. The Kwale–Kisiju leg is done by dhow transport and the Kisiju–Dar one by lorry. Kwale is poor, and its only export is fish.[32]

Some of the dhows from the Mafia archipelago often go via Kwale to Pangani with copra. As a matter of fact, the only import into Pangani by dhow is now copra since there is a 31-mile all-weather road between there and Tanga, from whence come the town's supplies. Pangani was a place of relative importance during the German period but ever since has been in a state of decline. The town has quite a bit of charm, full of old large nineteenth-century and early twentieth-century structures. Pangani is located on the Pangani River and most of the historic buildings are on the north side, including the old *Boma* and the Customs House. There is little viable economic activity aside from the factory where coconut oil is produced (the *raison d'être* of the dhow trade to Pangani), a factory which builds small modern boats for use off Dar es Salaam and on Lake Victoria, and a freezing plant for fish, lobsters and prawns. The town used to have many Arab, Indian and European residents, but around two-thirds have now left.[33] Business enterprises have declined. In 1975 there were seventeen *dukas*, three carpentry shops, three tea houses, two tailoring shops, one bar, one radio shop, one barber shop, one bank, one photographic studio, and a single petrol station.[34] But even though the town has seen brighter days and a sizeable dhow trade in the past, Pangani is definitely worth a visit for its former architectural achievements and quaintness.

On the other hand, Pangani's neighbour to the north, Tanga, has a depressing feeling about it. I first visited Tanga in 1964 when it still had prestige, being the second city of the country and the centre of the sisal industry. But today the residential areas are mostly overgrown with weeds, the few new buildings which have been erected on the waterfront interrupt the vista, and the back of the town has turned into a slum. For a town of its size (85,000 inhabitants), the dhow trade is of little consequence. The amount of cargo coming to Tanga by local dhow is very small indeed because large ships and lorries now supply Tanga with all her needs. The few dhows that do come in bring mangrove poles, as in 1971 when twenty-five dhows put in with 23,720 poles mainly from Kilwa Masoko and the Rufiji. The only exports from Tanga by dhow are *mvule* timber (*Chlorophora excelsa*) for Zanzibar and Pemba and a small amount of dried fish. The passenger traffic is also very limited. In 1974, twenty-eight persons arrived on coastal dhows (twenty-one from Pemba), and twenty-three went out (twenty-one to Pemba).[35] It is highly unlikely that the dhow trade will pick up again at Tanga.

Forty-five miles north of Dar es Salaam is Bagamoyo, now a small town of 5,000 people, but during the late nineteenth century the most important urban centre in all Tanganyika. In 1880, there were perhaps 5,000 people living there, and after 1888 when the Germans made their headquarters for the whole country at Bagamoyo the population expanded, and by 1900 reached

Passengers disembarking from a *mashua* at Kisiju, Tanzania

9,000. The town, though twice as large, is similar to Pangani. Bagamoyo has some fine buildings, the blockhouse which was built in 1889, the Customs House (1895), and the magnificent *Boma* (1897), the latter being probably the finest German colonial building still standing in Tanganyika.[36] Bagamoyo has graciously accepted her decline in the hierarchy and is rather like the *grande dame* of an earlier age. It is by far the most attractive old town in the whole country. Few new buildings have been constructed, and the feeling is still that of a nineteenth-century town. There are hardly any motor vehicles present and most of the trappings of mid-twentieth century technology are absent.[37]

Bagamoyo's wealth in the nineteenth century depended upon trade with the interior and her link with Zanzibar town, only twenty-five miles to the northeast. In the middle of the nineteenth century, Bagamoyo's major exports, almost all of which went to Zanzibar, were ivory, slaves, salt, fish, gum copal[38] and coconut products. Some of these, such as salt,[39] fish[40] and coconut products are still major money earners for the people of Bagamoyo. Surprisingly, the number of dhows coming into Bagamoyo since the 1920s has not significantly changed. For instance, in 1925, 460 dhows came into Bagamoyo,[41] while in 1973, 498 came in (see Table XIII). Also, as in the nineteenth century, almost all of the exports from Bagamoyo still go to Zanzibar. In the 1970s, the major export was coconut fibre for making mats; up until the early 1960s mangrove poles were still also a major export, but that is no longer true. Since the 1950s, there has been a dramatic change in the destination of dhows leaving Bagamoyo; many used to go to Mafia, Tanga and Dar es Salaam, but in 1974, eighty-four per cent of the dhows went to Zanzibar.[42] The majority of the dhows which came into Bagamoyo also came from Zanzibar, but there is hardly any cargo at all except personal belongings. There is probably some minor smuggling of goods such as soap, from Zanzibar; otherwise, the traffic would not be economic.

Dar es Salaam is the major port of mainland Tanzania for the coastal dhow trade. The reasons for this are quite obvious. Dar is by far the largest city (the population in 1975 was roughly 400,000) in the country and the centre of industrial, wholesale and retail trades of Tanzania. Furthermore, Dar es Salaam is centrally located on the coast and is reasonably close to Zanzibar, the major dhow port for all of eastern Africa. Compared with Mombasa, the dhow wharf at Dar is superior. As many as a dozen dhows can unload at the same time, and lorries come right down to the wharf to pick up or drop off produce. The authorities in Mombasa have been negligent about maintaining their facilities and a great deal more labour is required to handle goods there than at the Dar es Salaam wharf.

The main explanation for the increase in the coastal dhow traffic lies in the growth in trade to Zanzibar since the death of the leader of Zanzibar, Abeid Karume. During Karume's time there were shortages of food and other staples in Zanzibar and Pemba, but since 1972 the government of Zanzibar has been more lenient in allowing Tanzanian dhows to bring in goods from the mainland. Over three-quarters of the 1,487 coastal dhows which departed from Dar es Salaam in 1974 went to Zanzibar or Pemba. There are no statistics on the value or quantity of the goods which went out of Dar, but the most common commodities in 1974 shipped to Zanzibar, in order of the number of dhows carrying them, were cement, onions, potatoes, chicken food, timber,

Town centre of Bagamoyo,
Tanzania

The Administrative
Headquarters at Bagamoyo,
built in 1897 by the Germans

soft drinks, beer, beans and wheat flour.[43] None of these products are produced in Zanzibar, but they are manufactured or grown on the Tanzanian mainland. A soft drink factory is now being constructed near Zanzibar town, and the Zanzibar Government is making a major effort to encourage farmers to plant more food crops. However, it is doubtful if Zanzibar will become self-sufficient in food for decades to come. Since the mainland produces many of the food requirements of Zanzibar, the dhow trade from Dar es Salaam and Tanga to Zanzibar will continue for many years. The dhows are quite efficient and since hardly any of them have engines, the oil price increase has made the sailing dhows more competitive price-wise than larger motor boats.

The only problem is that the mainland Tanzanian trade to Zanzibar is mostly one-way. On account of restrictions imposed by the Zanzibar Government, Zanzibar's major export, the clove, is not allowed to be exported out of Zanzibar or Pemba by dhow (this is supposed to prevent the possibility of smuggling). The islands produce little else of value, so the major 'exports' from Zanzibar port to Dar, in order of importance, are empty beer and soda bottles, empty gas cylinders, equipment to be repaired on the mainland and personal effects. The only commodities which are actually grown or manufactured in Zanzibar and are exported by dhows are betel leaves, coir, rope, copra, coconuts and coconut oil, all in extremely small quantities.

In conclusion, the foreign dhow traffic to Tanzania is almost dead, thus bringing to a close the more than 2,000-year-old tradition. The only way this trade might increase would be if the Tanzanian Government actually supported it and if the prices of the basic food commodities became as cheap as those in Kenya. Both of these phenomena are unlikely to occur in the near future. On the other hand, the local dhow trade has a promising future since fuel is so expensive in Tanzania. Certain islands, such as Pemba, Zanzibar, Kwale, Koma and Mafia, with a combined population of almost half a million, are dependent upon ships for most of their imports and exports. And the local *mashuas* and *jahazis* are quite efficient. They do not require engines, petrol or costly imported parts and can get into small harbours far more easily and safely than modern ships. Therefore, the Tanzanian Government should encourage the coastal dhow trade by building and maintaining better port facilities, by decreasing the number of restrictions on what kinds of commodities can be carried by dhows, and by giving more loans of money for equipment, especially high-quality sails, to those wishing to work these boats. Dhows are in fact a relatively efficient means of short distance transport in Tanzania and they are fully consistent with the Government's major policy of self-help and self-reliance.

Zanzibar

Mention the name Zanzibar to any world traveller or romanticist, and you will surely evoke a response. The conjuring allure of Zanzibar drew Livingstone, Burton and Stanley. And, less than twenty-five years ago, one could still be enchanted by the sight of the Sultan's barge gliding up to the palace. There is indeed a magic about Zanzibar which, curiously, its present state, so in conflict with its history, cannot dispel.

In the middle of the nineteenth century, the town of Zanzibar was the most famous in all East Africa and the centre for many expeditions leading into the dark interior of Africa. The intrepid explorers recruited their porters here and organized their supplies to the mainland. Ships from all over the world came to Zanzibar harbour to pick up the treasured cargoes of the East: ivory, cloves, copal (which was used to make varnish for horse-drawn carriages), copra (then used for making margarine), and the wild animal hides and skins (leopard coats were soon to become *avant garde*).

With the 'scramble for Africa', the power struggle between the Germans, French and the British for the control of Africa, Zanzibar inevitably stood to lose. The Germans took over Tanganyika, and the British exerted their influence in Kenya. The Sultan of Zanzibar was left with little more than nominal control of the ten-mile coastal strip of the mainland; even in Zanzibar itself he became the pawn of the British, and when he risked their displeasure in 1896 he ended up having his palace bombarded by them. Zanzibar was the world's largest producer of cloves, and it continued to attract more and more Arab, Swahili and Indian residents. Stone houses in attractive Arab style lined the seafront. The Indian population, which rose from 8,200 in 1910 to 20,000 by 1963, owned most of the shops in town and played an extremely important

Clove picking on Zanzibar island in the nineteenth century. *Source: von der Decken*

role in the commerce of Zanzibar and her sister island, Pemba, by providing capital. They also controlled the wholesale trade. Their handicrafts attracted many buyers: their gold jewellery, ivory carvings and furniture were in demand all over eastern Africa. Most Africans lived on coconut and clove plantations, many of which were owned by Arabs, but some cultivated rice and cassava on their own small farms.

There were also about 500 Europeans residing in Zanzibar; they were mostly professionals, yet quite a few worked in the administration and others were retired individuals. They particularly enjoyed the fine climate, pleasant topography of the island, serene atmosphere, the sporting life (there was even a nine-hole golf course), the modest cultural activities, including the cinema and the museum, and the opportunities to learn about different kinds of eastern food (for there were many Arab, Swahili and Indian restaurants open to them). They also introduced the renowned British club convention and, as a result, every community in Zanzibar—the Hindus, the Ismailis, the Goans, the Bohoras, the Ithnaashariyas and the Memons—had social clubs along similar lines to the British. The Arab and African clubs were mainly sporting: the Arabs would gather together to go hunting the wild pig and birds in the wilder areas of the island, and the Africans would get together for the ubiquitous football matches. The clubs did little to encourage social mixing among the various groups of people who lived on Zanzibar; in fact, there was quite a lot of racism practised as a consequence. The Government was not representative

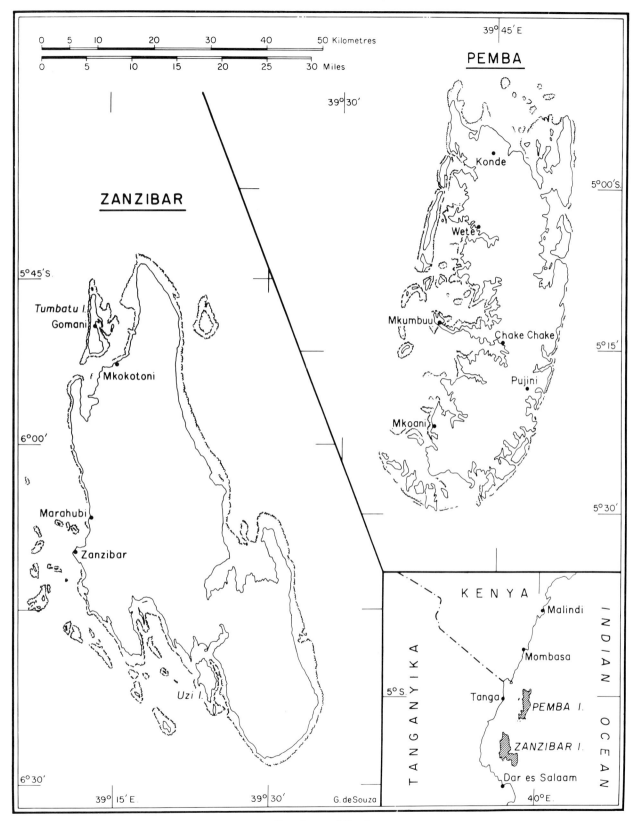

Scale:
0 5 10 20 30 40 50 Kilometres
0 5 10 15 20 25 30 Miles

39° 45'E

PEMBA

39° 30'

ZANZIBAR

Konde

5° 00'S.

Wete

5° 45'S

Tumbatu I.
Gomani

Mkumbuu

Chake Chake
5° 15'

Mkokotoni

Pujini

6° 00'

Mkoani

Marahubi

Zanzibar

5° 30'

Uzi I.

K E N Y A

Malindi

I
N
D
I
A
N

Mombasa

5° S

T
A
N
G
A
N
Y
I
K
A

Tanga

PEMBA I.

O
C
E
A
N

ZANZIBAR I.

6° 30'

39° 15'E.

39° 30'

G. de Souza

Dar es Salaam

40°E.

Zanzibar and Pemba

either, since, for example, the Sultan could rule by decree. True, too, not enough money was spent on African education, though arguably the Africans did in fact enjoy a higher standard of living here and better education than their neighbours in pre-independent Kenya and Tanganyika.

Everything changed dramatically in 1964 with the Revolution. This book is not the place to debate the pros and cons of the Zanzibar Revolution, but I will summarize the events and the consequences with references to the dhow trade. In January 1964, a group of Africans mainly from Tanganyika, overthrew violently the Sultan's Government; according to John Okello, the leader (from Uganda) of this left-wing upheaval, at least 13,000 people were killed.[1] Almost immediately, the new Government made life so difficult for the minorities that many of them left. Most of the formerly influential Omani Arabs (the Sultan's family came from Oman originally) tried to make their escape as soon as they saw what was happening, and a few were drowned in the sea in their haste to flee. A considerable number of Indian families made their way to Dar es Salaam, to settle there or to make plans for going on to Mombasa or even to Britain and Canada. The Zanzibar Revolutionary Government nationalized many of the businesses but not generally the small *dukas* and took over all the large Omani-owned plantations which were divided up into three-acre plots and redistributed to every head of family, even to the remaining Indians on the island. One is allowed to pass the plot down to other family members but not to sell it outright to another individual in order to prevent large accumulations of land by any single person. The wholesale trade was nationalized, with the not unpredictible result that shortages of goods ensued. In the mid-1960s and in 1972 the shortages became acute, and people even had to queue for food; the main staples, rice, wheat flour and sugar, were rationed to one pound per

Women covered in their *buibuis* queuing up for cloth in Zanzibar town

person per week, and this continued up to 1976 in the towns. Zanzibar's losses through emigration were severe: the best-educated people left, including numerous Africans, and the Government lacked the skilled manpower necessary to run both the administration and nationalized enterprises.[2]

The foreign policy of Zanzibar was more radical than that of the mainland. Hundreds of Chinese (the exact figure is classified, but it was probably around 700) were brought in as doctors, technicians, military advisers, and agricultural experts. About 200 East Germans, many of them teachers, also arrived; and some constructed hideous modern concrete high-rise flats, totally alien to the local culture, on the outskirts of the stone town of Zanzibar for the poorer people. All the local newspapers and magazines which had been printed and published in Zanzibar before the Revolution were stopped. Tourism declined from between 25,000 and 30,000 visitors annually to a few hundred.[3] The Government also feared that the Omanis might try to come back to regain their power over the island, so they banned Arab dhows from coming to Zanzibar. This sounded the death knell for the overseas dhow trade. From 1964 until 1972, the Zanzibar Government was one of the most extreme in all of Africa. I do not think that there is another country on this continent which changed so radically in such a short period of time. In April 1964, the Government of Zanzibar officially merged with that of Tanganyika, forming the United Republic of Tanzania. Nevertheless, Zanzibar continued to run most of her own affairs quite separately and in practice remained a different country. Abeid Karume, a former seaman on a cargo ship who had had little formal education, became the Head of State in Zanzibar.

Karume was assassinated in 1972; I was in Mombasa when the news arrived, and there was immediate rejoicing in Old Town, where former Zanzibaris began dancing in the streets. Living conditions in Zanzibar soon began to improve. Food queues for the most part disappeared, although rationing continued. Internal security was relaxed a bit, and new projects to help the people were initiated. A new, first-class hotel, the Bwawani, was opened in 1974 with sixty-five expatriate Indian staff. Tourism began to be encouraged once again; however, few foreigners have come for a holiday in Zanzibar. Dresses showing the knee are forbidden; tight pants, shorts or bell-bottom trousers on men can lead to imprisonment, as can long hair.

Outsiders still know very little about Zanzibar today. It is cloaked in mystery and intrigue. Nothing serious has been written about the island since the Revolution. Foreign journalists are permitted to come to Zanzibar as visitors for three days, but they are not allowed to interview residents without official permission. The first person to obtain research clearance by the Government to study in Zanzibar after the Revolution was Martha Honey, an American graduate student based in Dar es Salaam, studying the Asian communities of Tanzania. In 1974 she flew over to Zanzibar from Dar each Monday and returned on Friday, during the course of several months. However, she only worked in Zanzibar town, and never went out into the countryside. I was extremely lucky to receive permission from the Zanzibar Government in 1975 to carry out field research. I have travelled all over Zanzibar and to almost every single port, from the island of Tumbatu in the north to Kizimkazi in the south. I have visited every village of importance on Zanzibar itself. In March 1976, I had the unique opportunity as the first

Esmond Bradley Martin behind a large *ngalawa* in Zanzibar town; in the background is the Beit el-Ajaib, or the House of Wonders. *Source: Linda Donley*

academic to be allowed to go to Pemba to carry out field research and to talk to whomever I wished; I did field work there in the ports of Mkoani, Chake Chake and Wete. I also visited the historic ruins of Pujini and Ras Mkumbuu, and I went to the indigenous Ngezi forest on the northern tip of the island. I was especially pleased, in addition, to be allowed to examine materials in the Zanzibar National Archives and to study other government documents and records relevant to the dhow trade.

The Overseas Dhow Trade of Zanzibar

For over a hundred years, until 1964, more foreign dhows came into Zanzibar than to any other port in eastern Africa. Most were from Arabian countries, but some Persian and Indian ships also came (see Table XIV). Exports from Zanzibar in the nineteenth century included, in addition to those mentioned in the beginning of this chapter, slaves, sandalwood, hippo teeth, cowries, mangrove poles, rhino horn and tortoise-shell.[4] Imports consisted of dates, fish, wheat, cloth (ranging from cheap muslin to embroidered silks and fine velvets), spices, and luxury items such as household commodities, cosmetics, toilet sets, carriages and jewellery. There were also some Indian slaves imported and these would be auctioned at the Zanzibar slave market.[5] There were probably more Indian girls than men brought in since they would sell at high prices as additional assets to the harems.

132

TABLE XIV
NUMBER OF FOREIGN DHOWS WHICH ENTERED
THE PORT OF ZANZIBAR FOR SELECTED YEARS FROM
1907 TO 1975

Year	Arabian	Indian	Persian	Total
1907	108	178	0	286
1909	208	159	0	367
1911	173	137	0	310
1914	81	47	0	128
1919	160	47	0	207
1924	128	31	0	159
1929	104	21	0	125
1934	178	26	0	204
1938	259	27	10	296
1941	334	39	3	376
1942	443	31	15	489
1944	518	35	11	564
1946	577	87	14	678
1947	392	50	6	448
1948	474	33	9	516
1950	385	56	21	462
1953	530	135	6	671
1955	308	114	2	424
1959	193	45	23	261
1962	106	57	17	180
1968	0	0	0	0
1970	1	1	0	2
1971	0	0	0	0
1974	1	0	0	1
1975	0	0	0	0

Source: *Diplomatic and Consular Reports, Zanzibar, Reports for the Years 1907 and 1909; Zanzibar Blue Books 1912–1947; Zanzibar Port and Marine Annual Reports: 1948–1962*; Dhow Registers, Zanzibar Port.

During the dhow season, until well into the twentieth century, Zanzibar was a very dangerous place, teeming with ruffian sailors from Arabia and Oman. In the literature of the day, they were called the 'northern Arabs', and their annual invasion of Zanzibar was dreaded like the plague. The British Consul, C. P. Rigby explained why, in 1860, when he wrote:

> During the time that the northern Arabs are here, Zanzibar resembles a city with a hostile army encamped in its neighbourhood; every person who is able to do so sends his children and young slaves into the interior of the island for security; people are afraid to stir out of their houses, and reports are daily made of children and slaves kidnapped in the outskirts of the town ... Sooree Arabs have been found carrying kidnapped children through the public street in large baskets during the day, their mouths being gagged to prevent them from crying out.[6]

Even during the first half of the twentieth century from December to April each year there were sometimes as many as 6,000 'northern Arabs' in

Evening entertainment for dignitaries in the mid-nineteenth century. *Source: von der Decken*

Zanzibar. It was a lot better then, however, for the British helped the administration of the Sultan's Government to control them although, of course, there would still be street-fighting, whoring and endless thievery.

Since 1964, Zanzibar has been quiet all year round. In the late afternoon, a few Zanzibari men gather together to play draughts or cards and women do their personal shopping. The Asians go for little walks around the town, stopping to chat with their friends on the grassy open area opposite the House of Wonders. By the time dusk falls, the people are heading back to their homes for dinner. Unlike Mombasa, there is little to do afterwards. One may go to the nine o'clock cinema show or watch colour television. Both Zanzibar and Pemba have colour television, but mainland Tanzania with its fifteen million inhabitants does not even have the black and white version. Not that they are missing much! The programme begins at 7.00 p.m. every evening and ends at 9.30 p.m. and consists of short films and live performances in Swahili, English, German or Chinese. There are no more social clubs in Zanzibar; prostitution is now strictly illegal, and there is little opportunity for anyone to misbehave. The change has had its compensations: Zanzibar is probably the safest place in the world. There is hardly any crime—I have heard of a person losing a twenty-shilling note in the street and on the following day having it handed back to him.

During the decades of the 1920s, 1930s and 1940s, foreign dhows were bringing in a considerable amount of dried fish. The peak year was 1947 when dried fish imports worth £30,234 arrived from Arabia. Dried fish at that time was also coming from Aden, Socotra and Somalia by dhow. Dates from Iraq and Arabia were the second most valuable import by overseas dhows; in 1947, £21,321 worth of dates were imported,[7] which must have been a huge quantity. Major exports by dhow included cloves, coconuts, seashells, fresh

134

fruit and rope. From 1926 to 1964, dhows were responsible for carrying 11.6 per cent of the total foreign trade of Zanzibar (see Table XV). This figure is a very high percentage for the steamship era, and it is greater than the equivalent for Kenya or Tanganyika for the same period. Most of the trade was carried on Arabian and Indian dhows; Persian dhows rarely came to Zanzibar until the late 1930s, and even then their numbers were relatively small.

TABLE XV
VALUE OF THE FOREIGN TRADE OF THE ZANZIBAR PROTECTORATE CARRIED BY DHOWS FOR SELECTED YEARS FROM 1938 TO 1964

Year	Imports (£)	Exports (£)	Total (£)	Percentage of total Exports and Imports carried on dhows
1938	87,000	66,000	153,000	8.3%
1940	146,000	92,000	238,000	11.7%
1945	211,000	289,000	500,000	19.1%
1950	421,502	354,177	775,679	8.7%
1955	784,111	1,044,297	1,828,408	13.6%
1960	725,738	311,575	1,037,313	9.4%
1964	609,407	337,035	964,442	10.9%

Source: Zanzibar Protectorate, *Annual Trade Reports, 1938–1964.*

In 1946, a probable all-time record of 678 foreign dhows came into Zanzibar; this figure has never been surpassed by any other port in East Africa during the twentieth century. Although we have no extended accurate statistics on the dhow trade before the late nineteenth century, I personally doubt that even during the prosperous fifteenth and sixteenth centuries so many dhows came into a port in East Africa. Despite the lack of alternative means of transport the towns were too small to warrant larger trade fleets calling. During the 1950s, an annual average of 441 foreign dhows came to Zanzibar, which is still quite a high number. With the Revolution and the subsequent law prohibiting Arab dhows from coming to Zanzibar,[8] the foreign dhow trade practically stopped;[9] only a rare Persian or Indian dhow dared to appear. Today, more than a decade after the Revolution, there is only about one foreign dhow coming in a year direct from overseas; the dhow captains are still afraid, and, more importantly, there is nothing to buy in Zanzibar due to all the government restrictions on the importation and exportation of commodities.

Dhow Building at Mkokotoni and Tumbatu
The island of Tumbatu is the centre of dhow building in the Zanzibar archipelago. Tumbatu also happens to be the most difficult place to visit in the Zanzibar state. The authorities are not keen, to put it mildly, for people to visit this island. I think that there are two reasons for their attitude: the people on Tumbatu opposed the Revolution and the Karume Government therefore

Anti-colonial poster on
government building in
Zanzibar town

An archway in Zanzibar
glorifying the Afro-Shirazi
Party and the Revolution

allocated little money for any development projects, with the result that these
islanders are now the poorest that I have seen anywhere in Tanzania.

Mkokotoni is the village on Zanzibar island just opposite Tumbatu island.
When I first went there to get a boat to go across to Tumbatu I was forcibly
stopped from boarding, although I had permission from the authorities in
Zanzibar town. The police had no objections, but the local administration and
security were adamant that I should not try to cross over to Tumbatu. Three
days later, after a letter was sent up to Mkokotoni explaining what I wanted to
do, I tried again. The authorities on this occasion did not physically try to stop
me, but word had obviously been passed around that I was not to be given a
ride on any of the nine *ngalawas*, seven *daus* or six *mashuas* in the harbour. I tried
negotiating, fruitlessly, for more than an hour. Then I gave up and walked half
a mile northward to the well from which dhow men come to draw water to take
back to Tumbatu since no drinking water is available there. Here, I did
manage to get on a *dau* to Tumbatu, loaded completely with barrels of water
and passengers.

Tumbatu is a fairly large island, but unlike the island of Uzi farther south,
the soil here is poor. Many of the 8,000 inhabitants have farms on Zanzibar
island and commute by dhow to cultivate them. The main village on Tumbatu
is Gomani, the scruffiest place under the Zanzibar Government. When I
arrived, all the inhabitants came out to see me; wherever I went I was trailed
by hundreds of adults and children shabbily clothed in brownish rags.[10]
Gomani is an unattractive, congested village with no charm. The streets are
narrow, and the houses are constructed only out of mud and wattle. There are
two shops both government-owned and stocked with few commodities. About
the only modern thing I saw was a colour television set in the Afro-Shirazi
Party Headquarters (the only political party in Zanzibar). Gomani, of course,
has no electricity, and the battery to power the set had died some time ago. The
people of Tumbatu survive economically by fishing (I counted twenty-two

136

daus and four *mtumbwis* off Gomani), by selling maize, beans, sweet potatoes and peas to traders at Mkokotoni, and by building dhows. The dhow yard is on the edge of the village of Gomani, and, at the time I was there, four *daus* were being built by five carpenters.[11] The total cost for a twenty-two-foot *dau* is Shs.5,000 (nominally Kenyan and Tanzanian shillings exchange at parity) including a sail. Usually three carpenters work on one *dau*; in about three months they can complete one and each carpenter receives about Shs.110 per month. However, their income depends on the number of *daus* ordered, and it is not full-time employment for the carpenters. Last year, there were ten *daus* built at Gomani. Apparently, it is now rare for the carpenters here to make *mashuas*. A Tumbatu *dau* owner will use his craft for fishing or for transport; if he uses it to transport passengers and cargo over to Zanzibar island, he could earn up to Shs.900 in a good month, after paying his crew.[12]

Carpenters at Mkokotoni are still making large sailing craft. I saw one thirty-three-foot *jahazi* being constructed by an old master carpenter called Haji Haji. He told me that the ship would cost £1,500 and that it would take him six months to complete it. The owner had purchased and delivered to him local wood from Zanzibar, and he had also provided the nails. Haji Haji and the two assistants working under his direction will receive together £500. The owner of this *jahazi* lives in Mkokotoni and plans to trade between Zanzibar and the Tanzanian mainland.

The Zanzibar Coastal Dhow Trade

Since the middle of the last century, Zanzibar has been the major clove producer in the world. The clove came to Zanzibar probably from Mauritius sometime before 1818, but it is indigenous to the Moluccas. Since 1900, cloves and their by-products have accounted for approximately ninety per cent of the total value of exports from Zanzibar and Pemba.[13] Most of the cloves which Zanzibar produces today are exported to Indonesia where they are mixed with tobacco for cigarettes; other clove exports go to western Europe and North America where they are primarily used for flavouring. There are now about three and a half million clove trees on Pemba and one and a half million on Zanzibar.[14] Many of the clove trees on Zanzibar were planted immediately after the hurricane of 1872 and are now getting old. There are also some other major problems with the cloves. About forty per cent of the trees are affected by die-back, a type of fungus which can be cured by applying a solution of copper sulphate. A more serious disease is 'Sudden Death'; little is known about this disease except that it is currently believed to be caused by moisture stress to the tree itself during periods of drought or during prolonged rains. Furthermore, the Government has difficulties in getting enough labourers to pick the crop; an agricultural expert estimates that at least twenty per cent of the clove buds are left behind on the trees.[15] It is sad that Zanzibar is faced with these serious setbacks to its clove production, especially now when the clove has been going up in price on the international market: in 1975, it hit an all-time high of £1,430 a ton. No Zanzibar farmer is allowed to sell his cloves privately; he must, by law, sell them to the Government, and he only receives eleven per cent of their worth.

The coastal dhow trade was closely involved with the clove trade from the middle of the last century up to the Revolution in Zanzibar. Until 1936, dhows brought the majority of the cloves down from Pemba to Zanzibar for packaging for the overseas market; afterwards, steamships were primarily used.[16] However, dhows continued to transport pickers to Pemba. Many of the pickers, prior to the Revolution, came from the Tanzanian mainland for the seasonal job, which lasted from August to December. We know that even as early as 1909, over 2,800 passengers, many of them pickers, went to Mkoani, Chake Chake and Wete on Pemba,[17] and this, of course, entailed a good many dhow trips.

After the Revolution, no Tanzanian mainlanders were allowed to be imported to pick the cloves; the Government employed only Zanzibaris for this job, and in 1975 it recruited 1,200, who were transported to Pemba on government-owned steamships. The coastal dhow trade thus lost a considerable amount of business. And coastal dhows were furthermore prohibited from carrying clove buds, the most valuable part of the crop, under any circumstances. Their only permitted role in the clove trade now is that of transporting the clove stems which are bulky and of relatively little value, to Zanzibar town where a distillery makes clove oil from them. In 1975, for example, dhows from Chake Chake and Wete exported clove stems worth £1,338 and £2,678, respectively to Zanzibar.[18] No clove stems are sent out of Mkoani.

Because the Government pays such a small percentage of the value of the cloves to the people who grow them, the growers inevitably would like to sell them elsewhere for higher prices. These they can get in Kenya and on the Tanzanian mainland, but to get there they have to smuggle the cloves and any-one caught is liable to receive the death penalty. Most of the smuggling is carried out by people in Pemba who sail across at night in their dhows to the southern coast of Kenya. Occasionally, the Zanzibar authorities catch them in

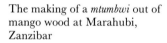

The making of a *mtumbwi* out of mango wood at Marahubi, Zanzibar

the act, and then the Government treats such an incident as a major crime against the Zanzibar state.

Although the Zanzibar Government has stifled the role that the coastal dhows used to play in the clove business, the coastal dhow trade still thrives. One of the important commodities still carried by the coastal dhows is livestock. Zanzibar and Pemba are importers of cattle, sheep and camels since so much of their agricultural land is used for growing coconuts and cloves. They make more money by growing these, and it has been economical for them to import their meat. From 1913 to 1921, an annual average of 1,861 cattle, 21 camels and 9,388 sheep and goats were imported into Zanzibar by dhow. About sixty per cent of the cattle came from Kenya, and half of the sheep and goats were imported from Italian Somaliland.[19] After World War II, the number of imported animals increased: from 1946 to 1949, an annual average of 2,460 cattle, 10,577 goats, 1,458 sheep, 70 donkeys, and 2 horses were imported, but, unfortunately, there is no information on how many of them came in by dhow.[20] During the 1950s, roughly the same number of animals were imported, but by then most of the animals came directly from Tanganyika.[21] Since the Revolution, cattle have continued to be imported from Tanzania; in 1975, 6,735 were imported to be slaughtered on the island for local consumption.[22]

Since the death of President Karume in 1972, and the subsequent easing of import restrictions, the number of dhows coming to Zanzibar has increased from 1,046 in 1972 to 2,122 in 1975 (see Table XVI). In this latter year, 29% of the dhows came in from Dar es Salaam, 19% from Mkoani, 11% from Bagamoyo, 11% from Tanga, 7% from Chake Chake, 6% from Mombasa, and 17% from other ports. These dhows bring in soft drinks, mangrove poles, spare parts, onions, potatoes, soap, cement, chicken feed, iron sheets, beer, rice

Men unloading cargo at Zanzibar port

and maize meal from Dar es Salaam; mangrove poles and empty drums (for coconut oil) from Bagamoyo; timber and plywood from Tanga; and podo wood from Mombasa.[23]

TABLE XVI
NUMBER OF COASTAL DHOWS WHICH ENTERED THE MAJOR
PORTS OF ZANZIBAR AND PEMBA FOR SELECTED YEARS
FROM 1905 TO 1975

Year	Zanzibar Port	Chake Chake	Wete	Mkoani
1905	N/A	1,283	819	0
1907	4,650	N/A	N/A	N/A
1910	3,589	451	759	592
1914	3,281	426	519	N/A
1919	4,434	331	566	683
1924	4,652	N/A	N/A	N/A
1929	3,590	N/A	N/A	N/A
1934	2,907	N/A	N/A	N/A
1938	2,489	N/A	N/A	N/A
1943	2,273	N/A	N/A	N/A
1945	2,347	N/A	N/A	N/A
1947	2,723	N/A	N/A	N/A
1950	2,881	N/A	N/A	N/A
1955	2,935	N/A	N/A	N/A
1959	3,651	N/A	1,057	N/A
1961	2,504	N/A	N/A	N/A
1962	N/A	N/A	667	N/A
1964	N/A	435	N/A	N/A
1966	N/A	231	N/A	352
1968	1,000	98	N/A	199
1970	N/A	106	80	442
1972	1,046	76	N/A	212
1973	2,009	99	N/A	287
1974	1,251	94	192	299
1975	2,122	72	243	297

Source: Report on the Administration of the island of Pemba for the year 1906, Residency F10, Zanzibar Archives; *Diplomatic and Consular Reports, Zanzibar, Reports for the Years 1907 and 1910*; *Blue Books 1914–1947*; *Zanzibar Port and Marine Annual Reports 1950–1962*; Zanzibar, Chake Chake, Wete, and Mkoani dhow registers.

The average Zanzibar cargo dhow is sixteen tons in size and has a crew of seven. Almost none of the dhows have engines. The average crew member has never been to school, but he does have a small farm. He works on a dhow every month of the year, unlike his peers in Lamu who usually do not sail at all during the strong winds of the south-west monsoon. The Zanzibar crew member is not paid a salary; he receives instead half of the net profits from a voyage, which amounts to about Shs.100 a month for him. Before the Revolution, most of the cargo dhows were owned by Indians in Zanzibar and Pemba who also controlled most of the wholesale and retail trades, but now, as far as I could ascertain, only three of the local dhows are owned by Indians, all of whom live in Zanzibar. Today's dhow owners are former crew members and captains, but they usually own only one dhow rather than a fleet. They supplement their cargo transport income by carrying passengers; the charge from Zanzibar to Pemba or Dar es Salaam is Shs.20 one way.[24]

The major exports transported by coastal dhows from Zanzibar are: coconuts, Zanzibar-manufactured soap, personal effects and empty beer and soda bottles to Dar es Salaam; and coconuts, chicken feed, copra, coconut oil and building materials to Pemba. The value of exports by dhow from Zanzibar is considerably lower than imports, but exact figures are not available. In 1975, 58% of the dhows went from Zanzibar to Dar es Salaam, 21% to Pemba ports, 11% to Mombasa, 7% to Bagamoyo, and 3% to other destinations.[25]

Although the coastal dhow trade over the past few years has seen an increase, the number of dhows moving in and out of Zanzibar is about half of what it was after World War I. Moreover, there has been a sharp decline in the number of cargo dhows registered in Zanzibar and Pemba: from 541 in 1892 to 63 in 1975 (see Table XVII). In Zanzibar the only places where dhows are still being built are Tumbatu where ten *daus* were made in 1975 (mainly for fishing purposes), and Mkokotoni with six *daus* and perhaps two *mashuas*. On Pemba the construction of *jahazis* and *mashuas* totalled six.

TABLE XVII
NUMBER OF CARGO DHOWS (EXCLUDING CANOES)
REGISTERED IN ZANZIBAR AND PEMBA FOR VARIOUS YEARS
FROM 1892 TO 1975

Year	Number
1892	541
1908	350
1912	293
1933	210
1935	187
1943	117
1950	130
1959	115
1962	97
1975	63

Source: Zanzibar Government, *Annual Reports for 1909–10, 1912*; *Annual Reports on the Port and Marine Department for the Years 1933, 1935, 1943, 1950, 1959, 1962*; and survey on registration taken by the author in 1975.

The Pemba Coastal Dhow Trade

Post-revolutionary Pemba has bad connotations in the western Indian Ocean. All visitors have been officially discouraged from coming here. Karume ordered all overseas dhows to keep away from Pemba, and out of fright they complied with his wishes. Stories of what could happen to clove smugglers terrified Tanzanian mainlanders and Kenyans, who presumably thought that they might be suspects if they went too close to the island. There was speculation in the early 1970s that there was a Russian or Chinese base being established there and, although the rumours proved to be false, all over eastern Africa people were wondering what could possibly be going on that necessitated keeping outsiders away from Pemba.

In fact, very little was going on in Pemba between 1964 and 1972, aside from some local, vocal opposition to the new Government. During Karume's reign, some of the wealthier individuals on this island had their land and shops taken away from them without compensation and they objected. Karume obviously did not want the islanders to have the opportunity to make contact with outsiders who might have possibly backed their objections to his Government. Karume was also annoyed by the repeated attempts of Pemba people to smuggle cloves to mainland Tanzania and Kenya: his Government estimated that as much as a third of the annual clove crop was being sold illegally. These deviationist activities led Karume to lend little support to investment in Pemba.

This policy was reversed by the Zanzibar Government immediately following the death of Karume. After all, forty-six per cent of the population lives on Pemba, and more cloves are produced here than on Zanzibar. The Government has possibly now gone a little too far in the opposite direction. For instance, since there is a Japanese fun fair in Zanzibar, a similar one must now be constructed on Pemba (no matter that the Zanzibar fun fair operates only three or four days a year); there must now be new hotels in Pemba since an international hotel has opened in Zanzibar—in this case, however, they did realize that a huge edifice was totally irrelevant and contented themselves with building three small hotels, all of which were opened in 1974 (two were entirely empty when I went to Pemba, and it appears that government officers and teachers are the only people ever to use these hotels). Almost incredibly, the Government invested a million pounds in a new airport at Chake Chake because a new control tower was being built at Zanzibar airport; and new schools and modern flats have also recently been constructed on Pemba island, along with a very sophisticated street-lighting system and a good road network linking the towns together. Colour television now operates on Pemba too. Concurrent with the new development projects on Pemba is a professed change in attitude towards visitors. Theoretically, visitors are now allowed to go to Pemba. Examples are given of the two Egyptian school teachers who were brought in to teach at the Fidel Castro High School in 1976. However, there are still no tourists going to Pemba. The Tanzanian Friendship Tourist Bureau (Zanzibar's state-owned and controlled tourist agency) simply does not issue passes to Pemba. I was, therefore, amazingly lucky when I was granted permission to go to Pemba to do field research.

Pemba is a potentially rich island, having better soil and higher rainfall than Zanzibar. It is the major clove-growing island in the world, with 59,000 acres under this crop. Additionally, the Pemba farmers have planted 27,000 acres of cassava, 20,000 acres of coconuts, 20,000 acres of rice, 7,200 acres of sweet potatoes, and small plots of other food crops grown for family consumption.[26] Pemba's agricultural wealth has traditionally accounted for her major exports. In 1906, cloves and clove stems earned the island £142,767 income, and a further £27,323 was earned from other products, most of which were exported to Zanzibar by dhow. In that year, the main imports were rice (£47,067), piece-goods (£15,609),[27] groceries (£6,413), sugar (£4,097), paraffin oil (£3,541), and a few other minor commodities giving a total import bill of £127,647. Many of the goods were imported by the 500 or so Indian shopkeepers, the majority of whom were financed by large Indian firms in Zanzibar town.[28]

Working on Pemba in an attempt to gather contemporary statistics on the

The traditional way of getting coconuts on Pemba

The creek at Chake Chake,
Pemba

dhow trade was quite an experience. The Government gave me an assistant
who was with me the entire time. Even so, the police often stopped our vehicle
to check on where we were going and what we were doing. While in Zanzibar,
most drivers of private vehicles and taxis need special written permission each
time they wish to travel outside Zanzibar town; this procedure is not required
in Pemba, perhaps because there are so few instances of private individuals
travelling by vehicle around the island. Except for the main tarmac road
connecting Mkoani, Chake Chake, Wete and Konde, the roads are still poor in
comparison with Zanzibar. When I went to visit the historic ruins of Ras
Mkumbuu and Pujini, the tracks were so bad that even with a four-wheel drive
vehicle we had to get out and walk long distances. Regrettably, neither of these
sites is adequately protected; the main fourteenth-century mosque at Ras
Mkumbuu is completely covered with trees and scrub vegetation. Pujini is an
unusual ruin. It was a small settlement or establishment surrounded by huge
earth-filled ramparts, unlike anything else in eastern Africa. It is thought that
the walls may have been built not only for defensive purposes but also for
keeping out the sea. Inside are the remains of two large buildings which, when
I was there in 1976, were unfortunately in the process of being destroyed by the
local people who were taking the stone and lime for use in their own building
projects. James Kirkman wrote in 1964 that Pujini may have been built by
people from the Maldive islands in the sixteenth century.[29]

The urban settlements of Mkoani, Chake Chake and Wete are depressing.
Before the Revolution they were active trading centres, but now with only
sixty-six Asians[30] on the entire island (twenty-six of whom live at Chake
Chake),[31] the shops have very few goods to offer for sale and they are mediocre

144

even in comparison with those on Zanzibar island. The only town on Pemba which has any charm, and a decadent one at that, is Chake Chake. It is picturesquely situated on an escarpment overlooking a creek where, at high tide, *ngalawas* and *mtumbwis* sail in. There are some fine old buildings in Chake Chake, including an eighteenth-century Mazrui fort. In the main part of the town there are eighty-one tiny shops, selling little more than sugar, rice and personal commodities.[32] Such luxuries as newspapers and soft drinks are rare. The modern additions to the three main towns are all identical. Each one now has a dual carriageway, lined with tall street lights, leading into the centre. They all have identical eight-room hotels, whose floor mats are all in the same colour. There is also one small bank in each town.

Zanzibar at least has three cinemas which run regularly, but on Pemba all the movie houses are closed. I was told by an official that they had run out of spare parts for the projectors. At present there is little life left in the Pemba towns and the people have allowed lethargy to become their dominant trait. Nobody seems interested in initiating anything, not even a lively conversation, and after eight days on Pemba I was glad to return to Zanzibar.

Today Pemba is still dependent upon the dhow trade for survival and, although there are many restrictions on the movements of dhows (they are not allowed ever to travel at night for fear that they might then engage in smuggling), £550,066 worth of goods was transported by dhow in 1975 (see Tables XVIII and XIX). Since the Revolution, the number of dhows coming into Pemba from Zanzibar has severely decreased. The main reason is that the Asians, who owned many of the dhows, used to help transport cloves down to Zanzibar and to bring back provisions to stock their stores. Nationalization of the wholesale trade put many of the Asians out of business. Those who survived with their little retail shops encountered strong opposition from the Government, and they were also faced with restriction on what they were allowed to import from Zanzibar to sell. Those Asians who owned dhows had, by the early 1970s, either sold them or handed them over to their crew. In 1976, there was not a single Asian living on Pemba who continued to own a cargo dhow.

TABLE XVIII
PEMBA'S MAJOR IMPORTS CARRIED BY DHOW IN 1975

Commodity	Wete	Chake Chake	Mkoani	Total
Beans	£97,300	£ ..	£51,180	£148,480
Diesel fuel and oil	11,200	12,522	21,948	45,670
Spare parts & tyres	..	35,670	3,290	38,960
Fertilizer	13,550	4,175	8,937	26,662
Building materials	20,287	..	6,155	26,442
Cement	25,860	..	..	25,860
Noodles	6,240	6,083	5,147	17,470
Steel drums	15,900	..	..	15,900
Beer	..	..	13,753	13,753
Misc.	50,360	39,721	69,055	159,136
Totals	£240,697	£98,171	£179,465	£518,333

.. insignificant

Source: Transire Notes, Wete, Chake Chake and Mkoani, 1975.

TABLE XIX
PEMBA'S MAJOR EXPORTS CARRIED BY DHOW IN 1975

Commodity	Wete	Chake Chake	Mkoani	Total
Empty bottles, drums, cylinders, etc.	£ 678	£ 705	£3,917	£5,300
Canoes	..	..	4,527	4,527
Clove stems	2,678	1,338	..	4,016
Beans (re-export)	3,775	..	..	3,775
Wood & mangroves	921	519	1,003	2,443
Motor cars & spares	..	785	1,615	2,400
Empty bags & sacks	..	..	1,523	1,523
Personal furniture	..	421	1,015	1,436
Misc.	1,625	1,837	2,851	6,313
Totals	£9,677	£5,605	£16,451	£31,733

.. insignificant

Source: Transire Notes, Wete, Chake Chake and Mkoani, 1975.

As far as the ports are concerned, Pemba is fortunate in having two good deep-water ones. The best is at Mkoani with a relatively good jetty. Wete does not have as deep water but its pier is modern. There is a third port at Chake Chake, but it is hopeless except at high tide when a *mashua* can just get in. There are no ports on the eastern side of the island and consequently few government checks; this is, naturally enough, where some of the smuggling is carried out.

Imports account for ninety-four per cent of the value of all goods carried by dhow to or from Pemba. The most valuable single import is the red bean (*haragwe* in Swahili) which comes via the port of Tanga from up-country Tanzania. During the clove growing season, it is imported in large quantities to feed the clove pickers. Diesel fuel and oil are imported in drums from Zanzibar. Other imports consist of machinery, fertilizer, building materials, vegetables, and some unusual items, such as Chinese-made noodles from Zanzibar, a dark brown coarse sugar which is called jaggery, and clove mats. Whereas in the past many of the products going to and from Pemba were carried by mainland Tanzanian dhows, the dhow trade today with Pemba is handled almost entirely by dhows from Zanzibar.

Exports by dhow from Pemba are of relatively little value. Again, it is empty bottles, cylinders and drums which make up most of the bulk. The only true exports from Pemba by dhow are small wooden canoes for fishing, clove stems, coconut products, mangrove poles, firewood, livestock, salt and palm fibres.

At Chake Chake in 1975, half of the dhows sailed to Mkoani, while most of the others went to Zanzibar and Tanga; from Wete, 33% of the dhows went to Zanzibar town, 32% to Tanga, 20% to Mkoani, and 15% to Mombasa.[33] Although the Zanzibari dhows do venture into the waters of the neighbouring territories, as shown by the above figures, despite less restrictions on the part of the Zanzibar Government, Kenyan and mainland Tanzanian dhows are reluctant to take up their reciprocal role. The atmosphere around the lush green island of Pemba is heavy with suspicion and apprehension.

Kuwait

The Lure of the Gulf

In the course of several years' research on the East African coast, I became more and more curious about the foreign dhow trade. The questions that arose in my mind for which I could not find answers began haunting me. Exactly where were the mangrove poles going and how were they being used? Why were *booms* coming such long distances with so little cargo? Why were Iraqi dhows no longer coming to Africa? What effect has the gigantic oil revenue had on recruiting new crew members in the shaikhdoms? Where were the dhows being built now? What was the dhow trade like between Arabia and India? What about rumoured gold smuggling between Dubai and Bombay?

In East Africa, all academics need to have government clearance before attempting to carry out research. What was the procedure in such countries as Kuwait, Bahrain and the United Arab Emirates? I was told that the Arabs were hospitable to foreigners, but would they allow me to do fieldwork in their countries? I talked to several people who had spent time in the Gulf, but none of them knew what research possibilities there would be on the dhow trade. The only thing I could do was to go over there and find out first hand.

On 17 October 1972, Chryssee and I flew to Kuwait from Kuala Lumpur, via Ceylon and Bombay, a ten-hour flight leaving us exhausted. We arrived in the middle of the afternoon at an airport surrounded by sand, sand, sand. We sped through customs formalities and found a taxi driver waiting outside, dressed in the traditional long white robe, almost identical to that worn on the coast of Kenya, and a *kaffia*, the flowing white head scarf encircled by a black braided band called an *aqal*. He spoke a little English and had no trouble at all fitting our numerous pieces of luggage into the boot of his big

American car. We headed towards an international hotel in the middle of the city. When we had unpacked and changed into light-weight clothes, we slipped into the coffee shop of the hotel for something cool to drink. I noticed that all the curtains were drawn and that there were very few people at the tables. It seemed rather odd until I realized that we had arrived during the month of Ramadhan when Muslims fast from dawn to sunset. Since Kuwait is predominantly Muslim, it is considered rude for non-Muslims and any other individuals who do not strictly observe the fasting hours to be seen smoking, drinking or eating in public. Due to the long hours of fasting during Ramadhan, the people tend to become irritable and to lose physical condition. This is true everywhere in the Muslim world when Ramadhan is observed. It is understandable, too, that as a result business slows down and less work is done—frankly, many become too weak to do a full day's job. When dusk descends, one is allowed to partake of a meal, and during the late afternoons while we were in Kuwait, ambling through the streets, we would catch whiffs of the pleasant aroma of meat roasting on skewers over charcoal; families and friends would gather together, eagerly awaiting sunset so that they could break their fast.

Being most anxious to find out about the chances of studying the Kuwaiti dhow trade, I approached several people. Without exception, each one said I should go immediately to the Ministry of Information and ask to see a high official. I was hesitant to do this, for so often government bureaucracy can be awkward. Also, I bore in mind that in East Africa a foreigner wanting to carry out research is supposed to have the necessary clearance even before he enters the country. However, there had been no way to find out the procedure beforehand so far as Kuwait was concerned, so I took what I thought might be a risk and walked into the Ministry with Chryssee. I simply stated that I would like to see someone in an authoritative position who would be able to tell me about research possibilities. Immediately, Chryssee and I were ushered into the Permanent Secretary's office. Affably, the Kuwaiti asked what he could do for us. I quickly explained that I was studying the dhow trade of the western Indian Ocean and would like to do some research in Kuwait. 'I will see that everything is done to help you with your project,' he assured me with a smile, after only a few minutes' conversation. The brief meeting was terminated and I was sent to another office where I was introduced to a senior press officer who happened to be a Palestinian. His English was excellent and he showed an amazing interest in my topic. He had been working for the Kuwaiti Government for fifteen years and was concerned that whenever Kuwaitis returned from abroad they were distressed that so little was known about their country. He had numerous scrapbooks filled with clippings on almost everything that has been written on Kuwait in the major newspapers of the world. Hatim Abdul Ghani certainly took to his role as Kuwait's propagandist with enthusiasm and verve. 'What books do you have on Kuwait?' he asked me. When I truthfully replied that I was sadly lacking any, he put into my arms a stack of recent publications. He then asked if I would need an interpreter for my work and I replied that I would be most grateful for the use of one but that I wished to pay for this service. Mr Ghani would not allow me to do so: it was a pleasure for the state of Kuwait to help me in my research. 'You must also have a car and driver while you are here,' he added. I told him I did

Dubai Creek at Sunset

Left, Police Fort in the United Arab Emirates

Below, A fine example of Mogul architecture in Karachi

not think it was necessary; after all the dhow port is right in the middle of Kuwait City. 'How are you going to get out to the dhow building yard which is twelve miles from town?' I replied that I could easily take a taxi, but he insisted that I take a Ministry car instead. I was overwhelmed by the generosity of the Ministry of Information. Never before had I been treated like this by any government. I reminded Mr Ghani that my book would not appear for a few years as I was not a journalist but a geographer and that it would take time for me to compile my information on the dhow trade, which I believed was the most romantic aspect of the Gulf today. Having had many apprehensions beforehand, I was completely taken aback by the outcome of my approach to the Government. I knew, of course, that Kuwait was very rich, although I was there in 1972 before the four-fold increase in the price of oil. But this could not explain it all. I asked Mr Ghani why they were going out of their way to help me so tremendously. He said that I was one of the very few visitors not interested in the oil business but in another aspect of Kuwait's economy and culture, which was greatly appreciated, and that, furthermore, I was the first person in several years to come to the country to study the dhows. Armed with an interpreter, a car, a driver, and some fifteen pounds in weight of reading material in English and Arabic on Kuwait, I felt I was floating on clouds when I left the Ministry!

This incident was not an isolated one. In the other shaikhdoms I visited —Bahrain, Qatar, and the United Arab Emirates—I met with enthusiasm for my project and was often given an interpreter and sometimes a car and driver as well. The warm hospitality of the Gulf continually astounded me.

What a contrast was this to my trip to Pakistan. Upon completing my work in the shaikhdoms, I flew into Karachi. The immigration officers at first would not let me into their country because during the few months I had been abroad, they had changed their law and required a visa, which I did not have. I explained that when I had gone to a Pakistani Consulate I had been told that visas were not necessary for nationals of my country and that in the course of my travels I had not learned of the change. I was told that Chryssee and I would be put on the next plane leaving the country—whichever direction it was going; they could not have cared less what expense it would personally entail me. I asked to use the telephone and called a friend of mine in Karachi for help. I learned that the immigration people at the airport had the authority to grant me a temporary visa on the spot but refused to do so until I bribed them. I would not go along with that. After hours of haggling, we finally were allowed into Pakistan for forty-eight hours, but our passports were taken from us at the airport. The problem seemed insoluble: the following day was a holiday and I had been ordered to leave Pakistan the day after that. I became so angry that I demanded to see the chief immigration officer of the country. Surprisingly, I did indeed get an appointment with him at his house. My Pakistani friend and I explained the predicament. Then I added that if he so desired, my wife and I would leave the country on the next available plane for Nairobi, but that we were not going to be told to depart by a corrupt and uneducated minor official. The immigration officer was neither confounded nor astonished by my straightforwardness. He said that we could stay in Pakistan for as long as we liked and he would personally see that our passports were duly stamped and delivered to us at our hotel. He apologized for the

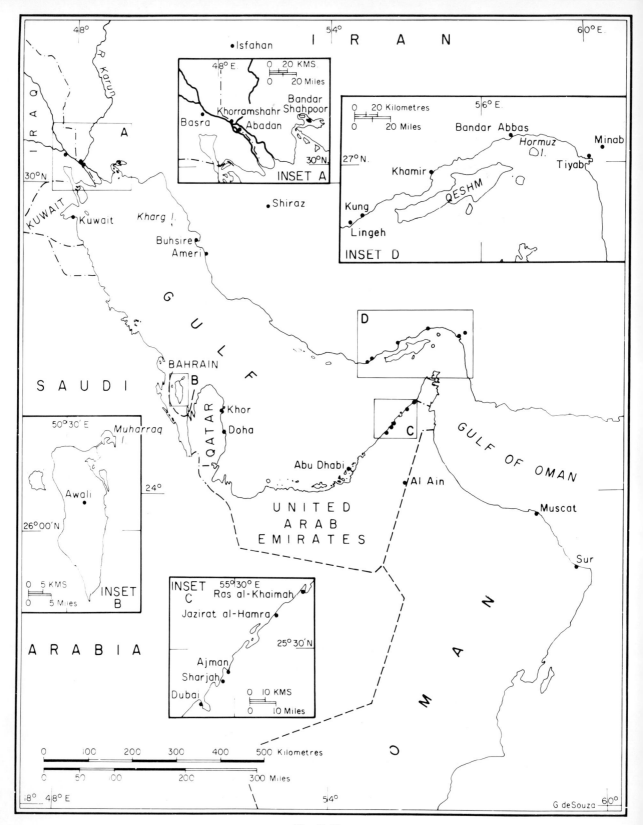

The Gulf

behaviour of his subordinate at the airport and explained that the Government gives low pay and low priority to immigration officers; corruption is a way of life in Pakistan and that while he personally deplored it, he was just one person. At this time, political and economic conditions were in an appalling mess because the eastern part of the country had broken away and become independent under the name of Bangladesh. Consequently, I was not allowed into the port of Karachi; I could not take photographs of the seafront even from a distance, and I was also prohibited from photographing any dhow. Chryssee and I visited Lahore, Peshawar, the Khyber Pass and Swat but had to avoid all the ports. This was a great disappointment but totally beyond our control.

Characteristics of the Gulf Shaikhdoms

Kuwait and the wealthier Arab Shaikhdoms are spectacular. I have travelled in about eighty countries, but I have never found any political units like these. First of all, in such places as Kuwait, Abu Dhabi and Dubai, the majority of the population consists of foreigners; in Kuwait fifty-three per cent of the population was foreign according to the 1965 census. This demographic phenomenon has produced peculiar effects. Although all the ministers and most senior government officers are nationals of the country, there are many Palestinian and Jordanian high officials and advisors and they are the ones most people meet. Many of the skilled jobs are held by foreigners. The medical doctors are mostly British, Lebanese, Pakistani and Indian; the better restaurants tend to be owned and managed by Lebanese; the more expensive hotels are staffed by Egyptians and Palestinians; the top petroleum geologists and chemists are British and American; the teachers are British, Egyptian, Palestinian and Jordanian; and many of the merchants are Indian, Lebanese and Syrian. At the other end of the social ladder are the labourers who are Iranians, Indians, Pakistanis and Omanis. Most of the middle and upper income families have servants, but Kuwaitis themselves are generally unwilling to take on menial jobs, so these are mostly held by Indians and Pakistanis. In many cases they serve as nannies to the children and since the Indians and Pakistanis do not speak Arabic, they talk to the children in English. Consequently, the wealthier Kuwaiti youth speak both English and Arabic, the former with a distinct Asian accent.

A second unusual aspect of the Gulf states is the almost total absence of taxation. In most of the wealthier shaikhdoms there is no income tax, capital gains, value added tax or death duties. Import duties rarely rise above five per cent *ad valorem*. Furthermore, the dinar is a hard currency and there is no exchange control. This situation, coupled with relatively high salaries, is what attracts many foreigners to the shaikhdoms.

The shaikhdoms offer most of the amenities of a comprehensive welfare state, but they are not socialist. All education from early schooling to the completion of a university course is free to all residents. In Kuwait, the most populous Gulf shaikhdom, there is an average of one teacher to every twelve pupils. In addition, medical care is paid for by the State, and in Kuwait there is available one hospital bed for every 150 residents. Should a Kuwaiti patient have a medical problem that cannot be dealt with locally, he may be flown abroad for treatment, also at the Government's expense. Elaborate loan schemes have been enacted to allow citizens to construct new houses or to start business enterprises. The Governments of Kuwait, Qatar and Abu Dhabi are immensely wealthy; *per capita* incomes in these places exceed those of the United States and Switzerland. In Kuwait it is in excess of $12,000 per annum.

Another important characteristic of most of the shaikhdoms is the high percentage of population living in urban areas. About eighty per cent of the people in Bahrain, seventy-five per cent in Kuwait and sixty-five per cent in Qatar are urban dwellers. Urbanization and modernization have moved at a fantastic rate in the Gulf, perhaps the fastest for any area of the world. New immigrants have come into the towns and cities, and many of the traditional nomads with their herds of livestock and the pearl fishermen have given up their old occupations, becoming also urbanized. It is almost incredible how quickly some of the cities have grown in the past few years. For example, the town of Abu Dhabi was simply a village in the mid-1960s; in 1975 it was a cosmopolitan capital with the majority of the country's populace in residence there.

Concurrent with the rapid population increases (from 1905 to 1965 the population of Kuwait increased a phenomenal 1,234 per cent[1]) has been the introduction of massive development projects which have changed the shaikhdoms from traditional pastoral, fishing and petty merchant societies into modern economies. Regrettably, the Arabs have moved so quickly into the era of technology that they have failed to preserve much of their past. From 1920 until the 1950s, the city of Kuwait was entirely surrounded by a wall, but now only a few gates remain. While I was in Dubai, bulldozers were working until after dark knocking down beautiful old stone houses with magnificent wind towers. In Dubai and other places I visited, the Arabs could not understand why I spent so much time photographing their old houses and fine wooden doors; it is sad that their new education system has failed to make them appreciate their own rich culture. I also found it distressing that when I was in the Gulf there were so few first-rate museums. Furthermore, the Arabs in the Gulf have made little effort to collect Muslim treasures; on the other hand, the Egyptians, Syrians, Iraqis and the wealthy Persians have not only collected and purchased Islamic art but some western works of art as well.

A final characteristic of the shaikhdoms is the almost total absence of manufacturing and agricultural sectors. Almost everything has to be imported into this part of the world; only oil is produced in abundance. There are two main reasons for this state of affairs. The Arabian side of the Gulf (except for parts of Ras al Khaimah and Oman) does not receive sufficient rainfall for growing crops nor is there enough vegetation to support a large livestock industry. Secondly, the population of the shaikhdoms has not been large enough to warrant modern consumer goods industries, and the Governments have found it cheaper and more convenient to import goods. Only if the shaikhdoms were to unite their efforts together and thereby provide a larger market could they render it economically feasible to establish some industries for the local consumers. The other form of industrialization, producing for export, would be technologically feasible since the petro-chemical complex of activities could be set up, but the shaikhdoms would need to rely once more on foreign expertise. The lack of manufacturing and a sound agricultural base has been beneficial to the dhow trade: the Arabian side of the Gulf is dependent to a large extent on the dhows to import foods and primary products from Iran and to re-export imported luxury goods from Europe to Iran and India. Were the shaikhdoms to become self-sufficient, the dhow trade would decline drastically.

The Early Economic History of Kuwait

In the early nineteenth century, Kuwait was a small port. One of the first descriptions of Kuwait, given by a European, was Captain Hennell's, in 1839:

> Kuwait . . . has an excellent harbour . . . without, however, any other advantage. The country around is a salt and sandy desert . . . except a few bushes which mark the wells, of which the water is particularly salty and bad.
>
> Although wanting in almost every advantage, the town presents a singular instance of commercial prosperity. Its population consists of nearly 25,000 inhabitants who possess 31 *Buggalows* [a large type of dhow now extinct] and *Bateels* [a medium-sized dhow distinguished by elaborately decorated bow and stern, which is also now extinct], from 150 to 300 tons burthen, which trade constantly with India; 50 smaller boats are employed in the coasting commerce of the Gulf and about 350 boats are engaged in fishing on the pearl banks. It can produce 6,000 men capable of bearing arms.
>
> The energy and courage of the people, who are closely united . . . render them respected and feared by all the maritime tribes.[2]

Captain Hennell was alluding to the fact that the traders of Kuwait were actively involved with the smuggling of arms to Turkish Iraq and disposing of the loot captured by the pirates of the Gulf. During World War I, the British Royal Navy blockaded the port to prevent arms from reaching Iraq, and even up to the late 1960s the independent Government of Kuwait maintained a camel corps to frustrate the smuggling of goods into the country, especially alcoholic beverages (which were prohibited in 1964).[3] The history of the Arabian side of the Gulf during the nineteenth century is, in fact, dominated by plundering and smuggling.

Throughout the nineteenth century, Kuwait remained a relatively small shaikhdom, eclipsed by Bahrain and other ports in the Gulf. From 1896 to 1915, under Shaikh Mubarak, Kuwait prospered financially. By 1904, the town of Kuwait had expanded to 35,000 inhabitants, including 1,000 Persians, 150 Jews and 4,000 Africans (of whom 2,700 were slaves). Curiously, the Jews were 'notorious chiefly for the distillation of spiritous liquors which some of the Mohammadan population consume secretly in dread of the Shaikh.'[4] Seventy-five hundred men of Kuwait worked on the 461 pearl boats, and about 3,000 of them sailed each year as far as the Ceylon banks to dive for pearls.[5]

The dhow trade was a significant factor in Kuwait's wealth at that time. There were thirty-six ocean-going vessels at Kuwait: twenty *booms*, eleven *baghlahs*, and five *shewes* (similar to a *sambuk*, but much smaller). The total value of all goods imported by sea in 1905–6 (the first year for which we have statistics) was £321,262 of which £136, 658 came in on dhows. The major imports by dhow consisted of £30,000 worth of rice from Iraq; £30,000 of tobacco from Iraq, some of which was re-exported; £23,300 of dates from Iraq; £18,300 of wheat smuggled from Persia for re-export to Iraq and the Arabian coast; and £13,300 of barley from Persia and Iraq. The exports by dhow were only a fraction of the imports: £13,300 of tobacco which was a re-

An Arabian *baghlah*, scarce
even when this photograph
was taken in 1939.
Source: Alan Villiers

export, £10,000 of wheat also a re-export, £8,300 of dates, another re-export,
£6,600 of pearls to India, and £6,600 of ghee to Bahrain. The only locally
produced export was ghee because Kuwait had few natural resources apart
from fish and pearls. The ghee was sold by the Bedouins to the merchants in
Kuwait town. The Bedouins also supplied dried curd, and camel dung for fuel.[6]

A minor import by dhow at this time, but one which became extremely
important after World War II, was fresh vegetables from the Shatt-al-Arab
region of Iraq. In 1904, fifty *belems*, small trading craft from Basra, Iraq,
brought in fresh vegetables and wood.[7]

The only industry in Kuwait at the turn of the century is one which still
exists: the construction of dhows. In 1904, twenty to thirty-five vessels were
made. The timber, coir, rope and fibre were all imported from Calicut on the
west coast of India; the wooden ribs came from Karachi. About 300 carpenters
were employed in dhow building.[8]

From 1918 to 1937, Kuwait's prosperity declined because first the
Royal Navy blockaded the port to prevent the smuggling of arms, and later,

154

from 1923 to 1937, Ibn Saud of Arabia enforced a strict blockade of Kuwait so that guns would not reach his opponents. In the following year, oil was discovered in Kuwait but because of the World War no oil was exported until 1946. From 1946 to the present, Kuwait has been one of the major oil exporting nations of the world. Despite the consequent development of Kuwait into one of the most prosperous welfare states, all within a generation, the dhow trade has surprisingly continued, and there is even sufficient demand for these vessels to keep going also the dhow construction business.

The Dhow Trade of Kuwait in the early 1970s

In 1968, Captain Alan Villiers, the greatest authority in the world on sailing craft which fall into the category of dhows, wrote the following words in his preface to his new edition of *Sons of Sinbad*, the finest single narrative of the experience of travelling by dhow:

> I did not see or hear of any Kuwait vessel which took dates to East African ports, for this trade had apparently passed to European hands . . . On the waterfront was one last boom, hauled ashore on the sand, not working but put there as a memorial to the great sailing days of the Shaikhdom's city-port, now gone forever.
>   By the 1960s, the old Arab Indian Ocean trade was done for anyway. The 'emergent nations' of East Africa had managed what the Europeans never tried to do, to bring Arab influence and trade to a halt. The age-old migrant traffic was virtually at an end.[9]

Alan Villiers was too pessimistic. Since 1968, as shown above, a few Kuwaiti dhows have continued to make their way to Mombasa. And, despite their decline in East African waters, they are still to be seen in considerable numbers from Khorramshahr in the west to Oman in the east. The real change has been the addition from the early 1950s of auxiliary engines to the *booms*. Dates are still coming into East Africa by dhow from the Gulf, and many dhows, especially those from Dubai, are going to India. Although it is true that the dhow trade between Kuwait and East Africa is dying, the dhow trade from Kuwait to other ports in the Gulf is brisk indeed. Moreover, large dhows, mostly *booms*, are still being made in Kuwait; unexpectedly perhaps, more were constructed there in 1971 than in 1904.

I was disappointed not to be able to obtain statistics on the numbers of dhows which came in and out of Kuwait during the early 1970s. As far as I am aware, such statistics do not even exist as government officials only keep records of the movements of modern steamships. I could not even find a register of Kuwaiti dhows. Instead, all I could do was to make a count of all the cargo dhows in Kuwait's port when I was there. This single count gives an estimate of the dhow activity; the trade is not seasonal in the Gulf as, in contrast to sailing conditions in East Africa, the monsoon winds are of relatively little importance. I was told, however, that the dhows are slightly less numerous in the months of June, July and August because (1) it is much hotter, (2) the Gulf's waters are rougher in these months, and (3) many of the wealthier Arabs depart for Beirut and London for the holidays, reducing the demand for some produce usually transported by dhow. I counted the number of dhows in port in each of the places I visited in the Gulf for comparative purposes; these figures are shown in Table XX.

TABLE XX
DHOWS IN VARIOUS ARABIAN GULF PORTS IN OCTOBER AND NOVEMBER 1972

Port	Cargo Dhows	Passenger Dhows	Fishing Dhows*	Total
Kuwait City	137	0	16	153
Bahrain				
Manama	47	18	0	65
Muharraq	51	0	20	71
Qatar				
Doha Old Port	28	0	7	35
Doha surroundings	7	0	10	17
Khor	0	0	22	22
Doha New Port	16	0	10	26
Abu Dhabi				
New Port	8	0	0	8
Al-Batine	0	0	16	16
Next to club	0	0	11	11
Ras al Khaimah				
Ras al Khaimah	1	0	26	27
Jazirat al-Hamra	0	0	2	2
Ajman town	4	0	35	39
Sharjah	2	0	20	22
Dubai				
Dubai side	21	0	0	21
Deira side	183	0	20	203
Totals:	505	18	215	738

*In excess of 20 feet in length
Source: Survey taken by the author.

Kuwait is the second most active port in the Arabian Gulf, although Muscat, which I was unable to visit, would probably be at least as active. There were 137 cargo dhows in port while I was there in October 1972, which is a tremendous number compared with the ports of East Africa. A majority of these dhows are *booms*, which have their home ports in Iran and have Iranian crews.[10] I spoke to a customs officer who estimated that between 5,000 and 7,500 dhows come into Kuwait, but I think he may have exaggerated the figures; to me, an annual average of 4,000 is more probable.[11] This is almost double the number of dhows coming into Zanzibar, the busiest port in East Africa. Also noteworthy, is the fact that these dhows are much larger than the *jahazis* and *mashuas* of East Africa, and their carrying capacity is much greater.

Most of the imports by dhow to Kuwait originate from the Iranian ports of Khorramshahr and Abadan. These dhows bring in alfalfa for feeding Kuwait's domestic livestock, gravel for construction purposes, fruits, dates, salt, ghee, other food products and lime. The voyage from Abadan to Kuwait takes only about twelve hours, but the crew will usually spend four days in Kuwait, unloading, and loading new cargo.[12]

Since official documents do not appear to be kept on the dhow trade, I do not have exact figures on the value of the cargo. By interviewing dhow crew,

Alfalfa from Abadan being
unloaded at Kuwait

however, I was able to ascertain many facts which yielded a general picture of the dhow business. The following are some typical examples. One Persian dhow from Abadan brought 1,500 bags of stone chips (gravel) for making mosaic floors. The value of the cargo was $2,340. The dhow owner earned $234 for transporting these goods from Abadan to Kuwait. Two other dhows each carried four tons of salt from Abadan, which was sold for only $140. A *boom* from Khorramshahr transported $18,700 worth of ghee which the captain had purchased for $14,000; the dhow owner thus grossed $4,700 for a twelve-hour journey. Even with wages for the crew of ten, the petrol expense and the four-day stay in Kuwait, the profit was high.

The money to be made in transporting goods between Kuwait and other Arabian Gulf ports is much more than transporting them to East Africa. Furthermore, sailing in the Gulf is less risky than the long and quite often hazardous voyage across the Indian Ocean. For these reasons and also on account of government restrictions in Tanzania, few dhows from the Gulf even consider making the journey to East Africa. I interviewed almost three hundred crew members in the Gulf, not one of whom had been to East Africa.

Some of the Persian dhows return empty from Kuwait back to Iran because, here too, there are restrictions on what may be imported. Other dhow owners take advantage of the tremendous profits to be made from smuggling luxury goods on to quiet beaches at night in Iran: such goods legally on sale in Iran carry a tariff in excess of fifty per cent. The legitimate cargo from Kuwait to Iran is mostly limited to cars (which are transported to Khorramshahr or Abadan for $85 each), scrap iron and the re-export of some manufactured goods.[13]

Dhow owners earn additional income by transporting passengers between Kuwait and Iran. The charge for legitimate passengers is $12 one way, without food, but the illegal movement of persons is a much bigger business. *Booms* pick up Iranian passengers and drop them at night on remote beaches in Kuwait or even on the outskirts of the city. The numbers of people involved in this traffic are indeed great. Before 1947, there were only 1,611 Iranians in Kuwait; in 1957, there were 15,143, ninety-six per cent of whom were men. Between 1957 and 1965, the immigrant community had increased by more than two-and-a-half fold. Many of these came in illegally by dhow from Iran, Oman, India, Pakistan and the poor Arab shaikhdoms. In 1965, this caused such concern on the part of the Kuwaiti government officials that 14,400 iranians were deported. Almost all of them returned home by dhow. In 1963, there were 34,875 illegal immigrants in Kuwait's labour force, among whom 30,542 were Iranian.[14] The smuggling of people occurs throughout the Gulf; it is not a problem unique to Kuwait. The immigration authorities in Qatar and Abu Dhabi are continually expelling people, and the dhow owners make a good living from transporting these unfortunate people back and forth.

After having visited Iran, Pakistan and India, I fully understand why so many nationals of these countries are attracted to the wealthy shaikhdoms. Living conditions for the poorer people are appalling, especially in Pakistan and India. Around Bombay I saw people living in drain pipes, cardboard boxes and even with no shelter at all—camped on the pavements of the streets. Modern hygiene does not exist in some parts of Bombay. When I went to have a look at the main dhow harbour of Bombay, people were using the beach as a public latrine. Pakistan is hardly any better. In the dry areas around Karachi the people eke out a pathetic existence. To the west of Karachi and stretching across the border into eastern Iran are thousands of Baluchis, a pastoral people, herding livestock. In the nineteenth century, Baluchis were brought to East Africa as soldiers. Today many Baluchis have made their way to the Gulf. Many of them inhabit shacks on the outskirts of towns; others live in tents. They have neither electricity nor running water and their living standard is practically as low as it is in Pakistan; the Gulf Governments do not seem to take much care of the Baluchis and tolerate them because they undertake menial tasks that no one else will do. In the Iranian ports there are also many poor people, but during the last decade development projects in such places as Abadan, Bandar Abbas and Bushire have improved their lot.

It is, of course, the high salaries which attract immigrants to the shaikhdoms in the first place. They earn roughly double what they would get paid for the same job in their home countries. Furthermore, they are earning dinars, a hard currency which they can, and often do, exchange on the black market, receiving double the official rate from Indians and Pakistanis who desperately want hard currency. When they do so, they are in effect quadrupling the salaries that they would earn in their homelands. However, almost as important to these immigrants as the money are the services offered by the Gulf welfare states: the immigrants can get free and high quality medical care and free education for their children. The fringe benefits are also appealing. For example, there is no such thing as a pay telephone in Kuwait: all local calls are free. One just picks up a telephone and calls whomsoever one wishes. Additionally, shopping is far superior in the Gulf than in Pakistan or India. Almost every single commodity is available in the shaikhdoms from an air-conditioned Cadillac to an electric toothbrush.

The Governments do have problems with the poor immigrants. Many of them live in segregated communities. The Baluchi slums are often filthy, constituting a health hazard to everyone. Near the Beach Hotel in Abu Dhabi, some of the Indians and Pakistanis go down to the beach to defecate instead of using modern public toilets. Surprisingly, there is little if any friction among the immigrant colonies and the other residents of the Gulf countries. This is quite an achievement since foreigners often make up over half the total population.

Chryssee and I found working in Kuwait a delightful experience. People answered our questions readily and in the dhow port we both took hundreds of photographs, of the dhow men as well as of the sailing craft. I did not, however, try to take pictures of women as I felt it would have been in poor taste to photograph those who still cherish their privacy. During interviews, I was often treated to anecdotes. One in particular I well remember. It was the story of a Kuwaiti who had sold his rather ramshackle house in town. He was paid a very exorbitant price for it by the Government, which in turn would have the building torn down and the space made available for some shop or business. The Government has done this on many occasions: it gives the opportunity to Kuwaitis to invest the money from the sale into business and to build better accommodation for their families. In this instance, the Kuwaiti found it difficult to believe that the Government actually had opened a bank account for him with the money deposited in his name. He went to the bank and said, 'I want my money.' The bank clerk asked him how much of it he wanted in cash and the reply was simply that he wanted it all. He was told therefore to go home and bring back some bags into which the money could be put. He did so and watched carefully while the $300,000 was counted out. Kuwait's largest currency note is a ten-dinar bill (worth about $30). When the money was finally all stacked up, the Kuwaiti said, 'Fine, now put it all back. I just wanted to make certain that you were really keeping all my money for me.' If the house that this Kuwaiti built with his new capital was typical, it would not be what we would call attractive. The new houses in Kuwait are often quite large, but on only small plots of land, and inevitably have enormously high surrounding walls. The architecture is usually modern Lebanese in inspiration. A curious characteristic of all the new houses is the huge water tank on top of the roof with a long pipe stretching from it. Every night trucks that look like old-fashioned street cleaning vehicles go around to the houses and refill the tanks. There is no piped water in some of the residential areas of Kuwait.

It is in the early evening that many people do their shopping in Kuwait. The luxury shops are all open then and Chryssee especially enjoyed following some of the women into the various boutiques. Many of the Kuwaiti women are in purdah, but their black robes are not all-concealing and we guessed that more often than not the shop clerks recognized their customers. Even members of the Shaikh's family partake in evening shopping excursions. We laughed to ourselves while watching one lady who obviously was a rather important personage seated on a little chair in a shoe shop trying on every available style. There must have been close to fifty pairs of shoes out of their boxes on the floor beside her. The salesman was very pleased to show her all that he had to offer. Whether or not she did decide to purchase any of them, we never discovered. Once when passing by a lingerie shop that looked almost identical to one in

Paris's Faubourg Saint Honoré, Chryssee saw in the window some exquisite underwear that caught her fancy. She waltzed inside, and a Kuwaiti man seated on a fake Louis XV gilt chair snapped his fingers. A Lebanese man came dashing towards her and the Kuwaiti gestured that Chryssee was to speak to him. She pointed out what she wanted to purchase, and the Kuwaiti's black eyes danced with amusement, highly approving Chryssee's choice. She asked how much it cost and the Lebanese had to go back to his books in the back room to check. So that there would be no mistake, he carefully printed the numbers on a piece of paper. She bought her new lacey treasure and while the salesman was wrapping the parcel the Kuwaiti 'supervised', making sure that everything was done just right. He stood up from his chair and bowed to her as she left. Finding the arrangement a little odd, Chryssee later asked a few questions about the running of shops in Kuwait and learned that frequently Kuwaitis put up money for the capital to start a business with a foreigner. The foreigner actually does the running of it but even though he is a partner in the operations he remains in a subservient position to his patron.

The evening that we were due to leave Kuwait, we saw a notice in our hotel about a special display of Bulgari jewellery that would be open to the public the following day. I thought it would be interesting to see the creations of the most famous Roman jewellers and led Chryssee by the hand to the roof-top private dining-room in the hotel where the show was to be held. I saw someone who looked as though he might be in authority and told him that we would be leaving Kuwait in a couple of hours but would appreciate, if it were possible, seeing the jewellery. The man was in fact one of the Bulgaris himself and very charming indeed. He told us that he was giving a private viewing party that night for some Kuwaitis and that he was just then supervising the arrangement of the jewellery. We were welcome to look around at the items already in their cases. Chryssee was awed by a superbly designed diamond bracelet and asked

Mr Bulgari its price in dollars. 'Madame, your eye has caught the best piece of jewellery here, but it is expensive: $165,000.' I quickly turned Chryssee around to look at some costume jewellery set out on little trays. Mr Bulgari told me that he was eagerly looking forward to his party in the evening. He was curious to see whether the Kuwaitis would like the sophistication of the craftsmanship of his jewellery and whether they would want to purchase some of the pieces. It would have been fun to have had a secret window from which to watch the *crème de la crème* of Kuwaiti society at the party to view the jewellery.

The Law Pertaining to Kuwaiti Dhow Voyages

The respective roles of the *nahoda* (captain of a dhow), the *mukaddam* (head crew member) and the men of the crew are not as haphazard as they may look to the novice watching their activities. There is a strict code of behaviour and responsibilities for everyone aboard a dhow. I found a document translated from Arabic into English in 1913 which states precisely the conduct that is expected to be upheld by Kuwaiti dhow men. For how long this has been accepted, I do not know, but it certainly appears to be the product of a long tradition of dhow trading, and the explicit instructions cover almost every contingency. Below are a few excerpts:

> If any member of the crew disobeys or acts contrary to the orders of the *mukaddam*, the *nahoda* shall be empowered to impose a fine or to deduct a portion of his earnings. Such fine or deduction shall be distributed to or may be applied to the accounts of other sailors. On the contrary, if any sailor does more work than what he is supposed to do and more than what other sailors have done, the *nahoda* shall have the right to reward any such sailor, and such award shall come out of freight and passage account . . .

> Whatever remains after paying all expenses for food, harbour dues and other necessary expenses shall be divided into two equal parts. One part will go to the dhow owner and the other shall be divided amongst the sailors . . .

> If a dhow is sailing for Basra from Kuwait and a member of the crew becomes sick on the way, the *nahoda* shall take him to the nearest doctor for treatment . . .

> If a crew dies in the port of Basra while a dhow is sailing outwards, he shall receive full share for the outward trip. If he dies while the dhow is returning home, his share will be for both outward and homeward trips.

> If a crew deserts his dhow while in India, Yemen or Zanzibar, he shall not be entitled to any share. He will on the contrary be liable to pay all the money that was advanced to him on account of that trip . . .

> No bazaar-man shall hinder or stop any sailor whose dhow is about to sail even if such sailor is indebted to him, particularly when the sailor has already taken an advance for the purpose of sailing in a dhow . . .

> When a dhow arrives at Kuwait and if all the work in the dhow has been completed, the *nahoda* shall present the accounts to the members of the crew . . .

> When a dhow picks up any article at sea such as ambergris, etc., one-fifth of its value shall be credited to the account of the dhow and the remaining four-fifths shall be divided amongst the persons in the dhow.[15]

Dhow Building in Kuwait

Despite the fact that Kuwait is today one of the most modern and wealthiest countries in the world, boat building along traditional lines remains an active

Dhow building yard at Dawha, twelve miles outside of Kuwait City

enterprise. Only maintenance work is carried out in the port area; the dhow yard at Dawha, twelve miles west of the city, is the construction site.

Since it was Ramadhan when I was in Kuwait, little activity was going on at Dawha. There were only a few people present when I made my visit, and these included a couple of carpenters and some guards who told me that the building of dhows is carried on throughout the year, except while Ramadhan was being observed. They even worked regularly during the summer months when the mean monthly temperature exceeds 30°C. About thirty-five dhows are built each year (slightly more than in 1906) but twenty-five less than in 1939;[16] in 1963 forty-five were built.[17] The customers are not only Kuwaitis but also Iraqis, Iranians and Saudi Arabians.

The cost of a large *boom* is roughly $27,000. In addition, the buyer must pay for an engine: British and German ones are imported to Kuwait for installation on dhows, and a big one costs approximately $20,000. For a medium-sized *boom*, which costs about $20,000, the buyer will usually pay $3,000 in advance, followed by another $3,000 after each stage of construction. Five to six carpenters will take between four and five months to complete an average *boom*. Their salary is two and a half dinars a day, or $7.80. Thus the carpenters receive a total of about $5,800 per ship. Many of the carpenters working at Dawha are from Iraq, since Kuwaitis find other jobs which pay higher salaries. Following traditional sources of supply, the wood and nails for Kuwaiti dhows still come from India. While I was in Kuwait, twelve dhows were then under construction.

As I drove back late one afternoon from Dawha to Kuwait City on the modern highway, I remember how pleased I was that despite the fact that one would think the odds were high against the dhow trade, this ancient means of transport not only survives but thrives in a society which has seen one of the most spectacular *per capita* income increases in world history. Surely it is the versatility of the dhows that has gained for them a new lease of life in the Gulf. But, as I passed by the port once again, was it not slightly ironic to watch four gaudy new Chevrolets being loaded onto a *boom* for transport from Kuwait to one of the United Arab Emirates so that their owners (who would fly over on the next plane) could enjoy showing off their new acquisitions to friends living there?

Bahrain

Bahrain in the Nineteenth and Early Twentieth Centuries

The State of Bahrain, as the country is now known, consists of a group of islands twenty miles east of Saudi Arabia. By far the largest of these islands is Bahrain itself, containing the capital (Manama), the majority of the population, the main port of Mina Suluman, and the oil field of Awali. The second most important island is Muharraq, which is now connected to Bahrain by a one-and-a-half-mile long causeway. What distinguishes this island group from others in the Gulf is the lush tropical vegetation. This is due to underground fresh water springs which have been tapped for centuries by the people of Bahrain to cultivate date palm trees, vegetables and citrus groves. In the sea around Bahrain are the richest natural pearl beds in the world, and in the early nineteenth century the principality of Bahrain was so renowned for its pearls that the towns of Manama and Muharraq ranked among the most important ports in the Gulf. For 1824, we have statistics expressed in German crowns on the trade of Bahrain; the crown was equivalent to the Maria Theresa dollar. Of the total value of exports of 1,651,900 German crowns, 1,500,000 consisted of pearls going to Arabia, India and Turkey. The other main exports were dates, tortoise-shell, Bahrain canvas, and shark fins to India; and to Persia and Iraq, Bahrain canvas, mats, date syrup and dates. The total value of imports was 807,300 crowns, which showed a huge surplus of trade in Bahrain's favour. The most valuable imports consisted of dates and grain from Basra, the Persian coast and Muscat (400,000 crowns) and coffee from the Red Sea and Muscat (93,000 crowns). India supplied Bahrain with cotton (100,000 crowns), rice (89,000 crowns), sugar

Fruit and vegetable stall in
Bahrain

Iron smelting in Bahrain

products (17,000 crowns), and timber for boat building (17,000 crowns), plus a wide variety of minor commodities including pepper, cinnamon, musk, tumeric, camphor, sandalwood and tamarind.[1]

According to contemporary accounts, Bahrain continued to prosper financially throughout the nineteenth century, markedly so after the pirates in the Gulf were subdued. However, disturbances occurred between the local people and the more recently arrived Arabs known as Uttobees, who became the new ruling class. When Captain Hennell visited Bahrain in 1839, he reported that:

> The only towns of any size are Manama and Muharraq, near the harbour . . . No fixed taxes are taken from the inhabitants, but whenever the Shaikh requires money, he levies forced contributions, particularly on the Bahreinees (or aborigines of the island), who, being descendants of the old Persian settlers, and consequently Sheeas in their religious tenets, are greatly oppressed.
> The Uttoobee Chief can muster a greater number of vessels than any other power in the Gulf. He has 12 large *Buggalows* which are never employed in trades, and in case of emergency he prohibits the departure of merchant *Buggalows* which traffic with India: these consist of 25 . . . In addition to the above, 12 *Buteels* and *Ghoonchas* are engaged in the Indian trade . . . The boats employed in the pearl fishing may be reckoned at about 800.[2]

In this same year, $800,000 worth of pearls were exported along with dates and bullion. The principal imports came from India and comprised rice, cotton, cloths and spices worth in total $600,000, of which three-quarters were re-exported to other places in the Gulf.[3]

At the beginning of the twentieth century, Bahrain was still the commercially dominant trading centre on the western side of the Gulf. Bahrain was also the major agricultural producer of the region. The farmers grew vegetables for home consumption (only a very few were exported), lucerne, and many types of fruits, such as lemons, oranges, bananas, dates, almonds, apricots, figs, melons and grapes. The stock raisers were justifiably proud of their Saluki greyhounds and white donkeys. According to Lorimer, the Bahraini donkey was the finest in the world; he also noted that, 'the females, being less noisy than the males, are sold at higher prices and a good one sometimes fetches as much as 500 rupees'.[4]

The population in 1905 was estimated by Lorimer at 99,000, including, '5,000 free negroes and 6,000 negro slaves'.[5] The 917 Bahraini pearl boats were responsible for the employment of 17,500 people; several thousand other people were involved in the dhow trade. In 1905, there were one hundred dhows (mostly *booms* and *mashuas*) which sailed overseas to Arabia, India and East Africa. Additionally, during the 1903–4 season, 200 were employed as carpenters to build 130 boats which sold for between 300 and 8,000 rupees each to buyers in Qatar and Oman.[6]

The Pearl Industry of the Gulf

The major source of wealth for many of the shaikhdoms of the Gulf, including Bahrain, during the nineteenth century was pearls. Diving for pearls in the Gulf has been going on for centuries, and Pliny refers to Bahrain in the first century A.D. as being famous for the vast numbers of its pearls.[7]

An Arabian dhow using wooden sweeps to keep the lines clear and to help prevent accidents; photographed in 1938. *Source: Alan Villiers*

From the early 1830s to the end of the century, the output of the pearl industry of the Gulf was worth about $1,750,000 a year on average, although there were great annual fluctuations.[8] The peak period for pearl fishing in the Gulf appears to have been in the first decade of this century when the pearl catch was annually worth $7,000,000.[9] In the late nineteenth and early part of this century, when the captains had collected a quantity of pearls, they would bring them to Bahrain and other Gulf ports for purchase by Hindu traders.[10] According to Colonel Miles, who was resident in the Gulf from 1867 to 1879, the Hindus paid low prices for the pearls, which the Arabs readily accepted because they did not know their true value. This seems to me to be a strange form of economic behaviour. After receiving the money from the traders, the captains would deduct the ships' overhead costs, and then divide the proceeds remaining; the captain of each boat would receive 20%, the ropemen 20%, the divers 30%, and the last 30% would be set aside to provision the boat for the next season.[11] By the 1940s, Arab brokers themselves would sail out to the pearl fishing grounds and try to buy the pearls off the pearl fleet so as to resell them to the Indian traders in the ports. Armed with a magnifying glass, a hand balance, weights, and a set of brass screens, the Arabs would grade the pearls on the boats and take them back to the ports for sale. When the pearls reached Bombay (as soon as air transport became available, the pearls would be flown to India rather than taken by dhow or steamship because insurance was thereby possible), Indian workers skilfully pierced the pearls and set their prices according to size and colour, then they sent them to Paris, the capital of the pearl jewellery business for centuries.[12]

In the late nineteenth century, the number of pearl fishing boats may have reached a maximum of 5,000, employing up to 75,000 men,[13] but the annual average number was probably around 2,700 boats of which 900 worked out of

Pearl divers with nose pegs in the Gulf in 1939. *Source: Alan Villiers*

Bahrain, 700 from the Trucial Coast, 600 from Kuwait, 200 from Qatar, 200 from the East Arabian ports and 200 from Persia. By 1946, the number of boats had declined to 530, carrying almost 10,000 men, of which Bahrain still led with 150 boats.[14] In the early 1970s, I was told that less than a hundred boats were still involved in pearl diving, and of these, only four were from Bahrain.[15]

Although the Japanese developed the cultured pearl in 1921, it was the World Depression of the 1930s which dealt the first blow to the pearl industry. Real pearls were suddenly too much of an extravagance for anyone. Then, after the Depression, the market was flooded by cultured and artificial pearls which were extremely difficult to recognize as 'fakes'. Even middle-class women began wearing pearls, and the value of a pearl as a precious ornament fell dramatically. In 1926, the Persian Gulf pearl industry was still worth probably more than three million dollars, but twenty years later, the value had declined to an estimated three quarters of a million dollars. In the early 1970s, pearls did not even merit mention as an export from Bahrain in the annual *Statistical Abstracts*. It was very fortunate for the economy of Bahrain that oil was discovered there in the 1930s and that some of the former fishermen and pearl divers found employment in the oil industry.

168

The life of a pearl diver was an appallingly dangerous occupation. Although the diving season lasted only about four months, it was an endurance test that only those who were fit at the beginning could survive. Furthermore, the divers were exploited by the captains and owners of the dhows who controlled their finances. Once a diver took an advance from his employer, he might become indebted to him for the rest of his life. In certain shaikhdoms, his debts in some cases did not even terminate with his death but were passed on to his brothers or sons. Because the diving season was so short, the diver often had to borrow money at high interest rates to see himself through to the next season. Some divers, however, did find alternative employment during the rest of the year as fishermen or farmers.

The divers usually departed for the pearl beds in early June and stayed out on the dhows for up to three weeks at a time with few if any breaks in the work routine unless they became too ill to go down to the depths necessary to find the oysters. First thing every morning, the divers would sip a little tea or coffee, but they would not be able to consume a proper meal because it would nauseate them when they went below. Using only a noseclip (no goggles), the divers, guided by ropes, dived as deep as seventy-two feet and stayed down for as long as ninety seconds at a time. They collected the oysters as quickly as they could and placed them in a bucket that they tied around either their waist or neck. An average dive would last a little over one minute, and then the diver would return to the surface, empty his bucket, tread water for another two minutes, then go back down again. After about ten dives, he would return to the boat to rest for a short spell. On a typical day, the diver would make forty dives and be under water for approximately a total of one hour. Many divers suffered from trachoma which impaired their vision; this made it all the more difficult for them to locate the oysters. Towards the end of the season, the divers would become emaciated and physically debilitated. Even in the evenings they could only eat very small amounts of food, usually nothing more than a handful of rice and some dates. Death rates were high:

> Occasionally they have to go ashore to bury a diver who fails to complete his 3,000 dives. It is not surprising that there are one or two empty stations in each boat; their occupants lie huddled corpse-like under their cloaks in some part of the ship, too sick from scurvy or plain fatigue to dive. After they have been at it for many weeks, the divers are apt to get convulsive shivers when they come out of the water for their rest, even though the temperature may be 110°F.[16]

The divers were also threatened by jelly-fish, needle urchins, sharks and the dreaded saw fish, known to cut a diver in half. The survivors at the end of the season would look more dead than alive, the effects of malnutrition having taken their toll, rheumatism having taken hold of most of them and suppuration of the eardrums being also a common complaint. And for what reward? Only one oyster in three contains any pearl at all and sometimes few oysters were found; in a poor season the diver may have only received $25 for three to four months' gruelling work. Moreover, that $25 might have to be spread over an entire year if the diver had no other source of income. On average, however, in the late 1940s, a diver would earn $47 in a season. For the nineteenth and early twentieth centuries, we can make a rough estimate of how much the average diver earned by dividing the gross value by three (the other two-thirds represents expenses including the non-diving crew and the portion that went to the dhow owner) of the pearls by the number of crew. In 1835, the average diver probably earned roughly $33 a season, and in 1905, $61. These figures indicate that the divers made more money relatively in the nineteenth century and early part of the twentieth than in the 1940s. However, on the other hand, in the nineteenth century, there were few other opportunities for the divers to find alternative employment, but by the 1940s, some of them were able to supplement their incomes by working for the oil companies.

Today, pearl fishing in the Gulf is almost at an end. In the past, some of the pearling boats doubled as cargo dhows in the off-season, but during the past forty years, hundreds of these *sambuks*, *mashuas*, and *batils* have been beached and allowed to rot because they are really too small to be economical for cargo transport. Had it not been for the discovery of oil in Bahrain, one wonders what would have happened to the dhow trade. The development of the petroleum industry in Bahrain has brought forward other economic sectors and modernization in recent years has led to an expansion of dhow fleets once again. Large quantities of food are imported by dhow from Iran,[17] illegal immigrants are brought into Bahrain by dhows from India, Pakistan and Iran, and dhows are also used to export from the shaikhdoms manufactured goods and gold. Oil has saved most of the Gulf ports from deteriorating into forgotten backwaters with thousands of unemployed persons.

Bahrain in the early 1970s

Since Bahrain is not one of the Gulf's major oil exporters, the *per capita* income is considerably lower than that of Kuwait, Qatar or Abu Dhabi. As a result, there are fewer foreigners in Bahrain.[18] In 1971, the total population was 216,078, of whom only 17% were not citizens. Of the foreigners, 28% were Omanis, 17% Indians, 14% Pakistanis and 13.5% Iranians. Many of these people were employed at the lower end of the economic ladder in such jobs as construction work (4,765 foreigners in 1971), wholesale and retail trades (2,855), transport (2,382), and domestic help (1,709). The more skilled foreign workers came from Britain (2,901 in 1971), other European countries (301), the U.S.A. (272), and the Lebanon (280); the majority of these were employed in the petroleum industry and the professions. Strangely, the number of foreigners declined from 1965 to 1971 by 504, although the total population of Bahrain increased by over 34,000; part of this is due probably to return migration following the new found prosperity. This is a most unusual phenomenon and completely contrary to what has occurred in Kuwait, Qatar, Abu Dhabi and Dubai.[19]

When I was in Bahrain in October 1972, I spent all my mornings in the dhow port, with Chryssee, taking photographs and interviewing dhow captains and crewmen. We usually lunched at the Delmon Hotel and then in the late afternoon, when the heat subsided, we would walk around the capital of Manama which has a population of about 90,000. Manama has charm: most of the buildings are old and have not given way, as in Kuwait, to modern edifices. The streets are narrow, unplanned and, in the early evenings, crowded with strollers and the Bahraini white donkeys, their long ears flopping at almost right angles to their head. The donkeys are mostly used for hauling water barrels from the public wells to the poorer private houses. There are also many birds of prey kept for falconry in Bahrain and some are chained to posts in front of simple, Arab-style houses. Their masters can often be seen pulling up their straight-backed chairs to the birds, whom they treat as pets, and talking to them in caressing tones while they feed them bits of meat. Around one corner, one might find a Somali-run restaurant providing services to some of the Somalis who left Aden when the Government there became socialist, or one might see a huge *boom* being constructed right in the middle of the street. Sometimes, Chryssee and I drove out to the oasis to spend the late afternoon amongst palm trees, more donkeys and lush patches of cultivation.

Dhow Building in Bahrain

In the main towns of Manama and Muharraq, dhows are built everywhere: on the beaches, in the middle of the street, next to one's house, in a dhow yard or in one of the many anchorages. When I was there, I saw eleven large dhows and three small ones in the process of construction around Muharraq, and nine large and three small dhows in Manama. It takes from four to five months to build a large dhow and only a month or two for a small one. Grossing up these construction rates, perhaps forty large dhows were built in Manama and Muharraq in 1971 and forty-eight small ones. Most of the large dhows are not being built for Bahrainis but for Saudi Arabians, Qataris, Omanis and other businessmen from Abu Dhabi and Dubai. The large dhows are used for carrying cargo and the smaller ones are employed as fishing craft; in 1971, there were 1,309 fishermen in Bahrain, of whom 273 were foreigners.[20]

One day I visited the Doy Boat Yard, one of the oldest boat yards in Bahrain, now jointly owned by Khalil Aldoy and his brother. Mr Khalil Aldoy was present at the time and he was very helpful to me in explaining the dhow construction business. Next to his yard, he has a long shed where he stores large quantities of teak wood from India, the purchase of which either he or his brother negotiates in Calicut. The wood is brought to Bahrain by Indian dhows together with dates for sale in the shaikhdoms. Some of these Indian dhows go to Dubai to buy gold bars with the Bahraini dinars they have earned and then smuggle the gold back to India.

Mr Aldoy builds all types of dhows. He showed me one ship which would cost $47,000. A typical dhow costs $305 (100 dinars) per one-and-a-half feet without an engine (a foot in Mr Aldoy's yard is still measured in the traditional manner as the distance from one's elbow to the end of the longest finger on the hand). The engines are usually installed in Bahrain and are mostly of British and American makes.

The Aldoy brothers could build more dhows if they had more carpenters, but there is a shortage of skilled local workers. Recently, carpenters and joiners have been attracted from Iran and Oman even though they are paid slightly less than their Bahraini counterparts. In 1968, Mr Aldoy paid his best carpenters $6 for a full day's work from early morning until dusk, with only one hour off for lunch; but in 1972, the carpenter's wage had doubled. Khalil Aldoy is confident that his dhow construction business will continue to flourish for many decades. He believes that there is a long-term demand for new dhows as these vessels have to be replaced at least every thirty years, even if well maintained. He may well be right for the short haul traffic within the Gulf where other craft are unlikely to compete. Moreover, Arabs from the emirates,

Oman and Saudi Arabia enjoy coming to Bahrain to have their boats built as they like the traditional atmosphere still to be found there and they also find Bahrain cheaper than most other ports on the Arabian side.[21]

The Dhow Trade of Bahrain

Bahrain is the third most active dhow port on the Arabian side of the Gulf. The imports into Bahrain by dhow are similar to those which come into Kuwait: large quantities of vegetables and fruits such as water melons, onions, potatoes, dates and lemons are brought in from Iranian ports, especially from Bushire. Iran also supplies a considerable number of live animals, mostly goats. Other major imports carried by dhow are rice from Karachi, tobacco from Oman, and general provisions from the major ports of Iran.

Most of the cargoes carried by dhow out of Bahrain are actually re-exports, not goods produced in Bahrain. These commodities, consisting primarily of manufactured goods from Europe and the Far East, are sent to various shaikhdoms, Saudi Arabia and Iran. This dhow traffic is likely to continue for many years to come. Although the Bahrainis do produce some fresh vegetables and fruits, there are certain times of year when this produce is in short supply for domestic consumption. Lebanon supplies some fruit, but theirs is more expensive than that of Iran for the simple reason that the port of Bushire is so much closer. The dhow trade in the Gulf is an efficient means of transport. The dhows can make their trips at any time of the year and the small vessels can easily move in and out of the small ports which do not have the facilities to handle large ships. Since the trip from one side of the Gulf to the other takes less than a day by dhow, the fruits and vegetables need not be kept in cold storage which would greatly increase expenses. Furthermore, many small merchants prefer dealing with the dhows as compared to modern steamships because there is less bureaucracy and red tape; payment, too, is both quicker and simpler. In some of the Iranian ports a modern freighter may only come once in a month (as opposed to dhows moving in and out of Bahrain hourly), making it costly for the small merchants to store large shipments of food coming in by this means. One can feel fairly certain that even though some of the more traditional aspects of the culture of Bahrain may soon disappear, the dhow trade stands every chance of continuing to prosper, being practical and having a sound economic basis.

Qatar and Abu Dhabi

Qatar and Abu Dhabi were hardly known outside the Arab world at the beginning of this century, and even during World War II they remained minor settlements. For purposes of contrast and comparison, I have linked these two small emirates together in this chapter. Oil was first discovered in Qatar in the late 1930s, but it was not until 1949 that it began to be shipped out. The first oil tanker left Abu Dhabi in 1962. Today these countries have become two of the wealthiest in the world, and their desolate, arid and sandy terrains are the sites for the construction of what are supposed to become the most modern capital cities to be found anywhere. 'Speed of Progress' is Abu Dhabi's motto, according to the label on post card packets sold there, but in the Government's haste for neoterism there is no room for aesthetics; you shuffle through light, moving sand, knee-deep in places, to get from one building to another (there are no sidewalks because everyone drives); the buildings themselves epitomize the worst of Middle East taste, and inept, shoddy and careless workmanship.

The Development of Qatar

Qatar is a peninsula jutting northwards into the Arabian Gulf, covering an area of about 4,000 square miles, fifteen times larger than the state of Bahrain. Qatar has always had a small population; in 1904 there were 27,000 settled inhabitants, including 4,000 African slaves, 2,000 free Africans and 425 Persians. Most of the men at this time derived their livelihood from the sea in one manner or another. The pearl fleet of 817 boats, 350 of which were based at Doha, employed 13,000 men, while 215 fishing craft and 140 cargo boats employed several thousand more people. The cargo dhows took the local pearls to market in Iran and India, and they also brought into Qatar imported provisions such as grains, cotton piece goods, dates, coffee and sugar, mostly from Lingeh and Bahrain. Some of the other men of Qatar made their living from breeding and exporting camels, and it appears that Qatar was the main market for camels on the Arabian side of the Gulf.[1]

The capital of Qatar, Doha, was a small town of 12,000 people at the beginning of the twentieth century. It was an unattractive place: 'The lanes are narrow and irregular, the houses dingy and small. There are no date palms or other trees, and the only garden is a small one near the Fort.'[2] There was only one well in the town, and the water from it was brackish. Most of the people were employed as pearl divers, fishermen and as crew for the cargo dhows; there were some Bahraini blacksmiths, carpenters and petty pearl dealers.

By the early 1970s, Doha had completely changed in appearance: most of the older buildings had been replaced by modern structures. Major tarmac roads, including a four-lane highway, and a corniche motorway around the bay on which the capital stands, had been constructed. There are now modern hospitals, schools, the al-Montazah Park, the Musherib Gardens and a public library. It must be admitted, none the less, that although Doha is now a modern cosmopolitan city of 100,000 people, of whom over one-half are foreigners, the place does not possess much charm or individuality. In my opinion, Doha is not a particularly interesting city. Kuwait is at least as modern as Doha and has a certain dynamism in its atmosphere. One has the impression that Doha is only following unimaginatively and not very enthusiastically the footsteps of other newly-rich Arab oil nations, while Kuwait fairly scintillates with experimentation in social welfare and with a population actively eager to partake in new developments.

Qatar had a troubled history in the nineteenth century, dominated first by the Bahrainis and then by the Turks. Because of Qatar's relative weakness and inability to safeguard her own interests, a group of notables approached the British Government and asked for protection. This led to a treaty in 1916 by which Britain promised to protect Qatar from any other outside power, and Qatar agreed in turn to undertake no negotiations with any other country without British consent.

In 1935, the Anglo-Persian Oil Company obtained permission from the then ruling Shaikh of Qatar to conduct a geological survey of the region. Because Qatar has the same geological characteristics as the oil-rich al-Hasa province of Saudi Arabia, oil explorers had become extremely interested in gaining concession rights shortly after World War I. A year after exploration in Qatar was begun, oil was found at Dukhan, on the western side of the peninsula, in October 1938. Due to British dominance in the company which secured from Anglo-Persian the development contract, the first three wells had to be plugged as a defence measure when World War II diverted British energies elsewhere. Field activities in Qatar did not resume until 1947, and, when two years later oil began to be exported, Qatar's economy was revolutionized.

The British Labour Government decided in 1968 that it could no longer afford its commitments in the Gulf and announced its intention of withdrawing troops from there by the end of 1971. This prompted Qatar, Bahrain and the Trucial States (which later became the United Arab Emirates) to open discussions aimed at developing a federation of the Gulf states with a united foreign policy. However, there were difficulties in agreeing among these shaikhdoms about the terms of union. Qatar decided to become an independent nation on its own, on 3 September 1971. It is, with its population of 150,000, one of the smallest countries, but on the other hand, it ranks with the richest. In 1971 the *per capita* income of Qatar was about $2,000, roughly the same as that of Austria or New Zealand.

Qatar's wealth has typically attracted many thousands of immigrants from the other shaikhdoms, Iran, Pakistan and India, seeking a higher standard of living. Dhows have been the commonest means of transport for these people. Before the road was improved between Doha and Salwa on the Saudi Arabian border, almost all the illegal immigrants came in by dhow, many from Dubai. Over the past few years, though, the Qatari authorities, realizing that about half of the country's population is already foreign, have severely clamped down on immigration by patrolling the waters off the peninsula.[3] In the early 1970s, dhow owners charged 1,000 rupees, about $110, to a Pakistani who wanted to be transported from Karachi to Qatar. Usually, illegal immigrants are dumped on secluded beaches at night to avoid detection. A Pakistani in Qatar told me that he is able to increase his official salary by not repatriating his money: he instead deposits his Qatari currency in a Doha bank and then gets it transferred to a European bank in a friend's name, who will pay him double the amount in Pakistani rupees for the hard currency. Since there are many wealthy Pakistanis who are unable to obtain foreign exchange legally for their trips abroad, a rather high percentage of immigrant labourers is able to take advantage of this method of exchange.

While the Qatari Government tolerates the presence of over 50,000 foreigners, it does not encourage them to seek citizenship. In fact, Qatar is one of the most difficult countries in the world in which to obtain naturalization rights. The law states that the applicant and members of his family must have

The *Huda*, the huge quasi-dhow of approximately 650 tons under construction in Qatar in October, 1972

been lawfully and habitually resident in Qatar for a period of not less than ten years in the case of an Arab and not less than fifteen years for a non-Arab. No more than ten persons are granted citizenship in any one year and priority is given to those people having technical qualifications.[4]

The transport of legitimate cargo is not just a front for dhows involved in the smuggling of people into Qatar; it, too, is a profitable enterprise, as Qatar is dependent upon dhows for its supplies from Iran, Dubai and Bahrain. Similarly to other Gulf states, Qataris find shipping by dhow economical and practical. In 1971, 1,130 dhows (of which 386 were Qatari-registered craft) came into Doha, 31% having departed from Iranian ports, 29% from Dubai, 18% from Bahrain, and 9% from Abu Dhabi (see Table XXI). The usual food items and fodder for domestic animals are imported from Iran, especially from Bushire, while all types of general cargo are sent out.

TABLE XXI
ORIGINS OF DHOWS COMING INTO DOHA, QATAR IN 1971

Coming From	Qatari Dhows	Foreign Dhows	Totals
Iran	14	336	350
Dubai	231	101	332
Bahrain	36	169	205
Abu Dhabi	87	17	104
Kuwait	5	40	45
Saudi Arabia	4	23	27
India	0	24	24
Muscat	6	9	15
Sharjah	2	5	7
Somalia	0	7	7
Iraq	0	7	7
Ras al-Khaimah	1	3	4
Pakistan	0	3	3
Totals	386	744	1,130

Source: Port Department, Doha

Few dhows are constructed in Qatar these days. I saw only one fishing boat and one huge quasi-dhow being built in Doha while I was there. This latter ship of 650 tons was being constructed in the shape of a dhow, but there was going to be no mast on it. A wealthy Qatari named Al-Saleh Fatha commissioned a Lebanese carpenter to create this very large craft with a refrigeration unit for fresh vegetables and fruit to be transported from Iran to Doha. When I saw this ship (she has been named *Huda*, after the owner's daughter), it was only partly completed. Another three months of work would be required on it. At a total cost of $250,000, it is probably the most expensive dhow-type vessel ever built.

Not all the towns in Qatar are modern. I visited the port of Khor, twenty-eight miles north of Doha. In 1905, Khor possessed a pearling fleet of eighty boats, ninety cargo boats and thirty fishing craft.[5] Khor is still a major fishing port for Qatar. One day in October 1972 I counted twenty-two fishing boats after lunch when most of them were in, but there are no longer any cargo or pearling boats. Khor is a charming Arab port with a population of around

1,000. The architecture and way of life in Khor is probably quite similar to what Doha was like in the late 1930s. When I was at Khor one afternoon, I watched the fishermen sitting on the sand, shaded by the shadows cast by the tall, graceful minaret of a mosque, repairing their nets in exactly the same manner as their forefathers had done for innumerable generations. I was pleased to be in a port which had not become so modern that one would hardly know what part of the world one was in.

The 'Boom Town' of the Gulf

I doubt if there is any country in the world whose rate of growth has been as spectacular as Abu Dhabi's in the mid 1960s. Despite the fact that the first oil was exported from Abu Dhabi in 1962, the era of startling development did not begin until the accession of the present ruler in 1966. Abu Dhabi had a population in the early 1960s of 30,000, on the island of Abu Dhabi and on a long coastal strip bordered by Dubai, Oman, Saudi Arabia and Qatar, covering an area of some 32,000 square miles across a bleak desert, the largest area in the United Arab Emirates. Most of the economically active population in the early 1960s was still engaged in traditional pursuits: subsistence agriculture and small-scale fishing. Incredibly, there were hardly any indigenous traders, who were so common in other shaikhdoms.[6] Donald Hawley, who was the British Political Agent in the Trucial States from 1958 until 1961, described what it was like to travel to the town of Abu Dhabi and what one could expect to find there:

> . . . Before the advent of oil, the approach to the town of Abu Dhabi, which is on an island, was appalling. High winds drove in the sea over miles of saltflats and only one narrow track, glistening with thick white cakes of salt, was passable. A square fort guarded a causeway—replaced by a bridge in 1968—connecting Abu Dhabi island with the mainland, and even the causeway was only built in the 1950s. Earlier, visitors had to drive through the shallows of the sea to reach Abu Dhabi. The town itself was a place of palm-frond houses, *barastis*, built on white sand among palm trees. A small market with tiny shops stood in higgledy-piggledy fashion between the simple houses, and the streets were narrow and roofed with palm-fronds. Little was to be bought.[7]

Choose statistics from any sector illustrating the level of development of the various countries of the Gulf, and, every time, Abu Dhabi will head the list as the most primitive of the larger shaikhdoms until just ten years ago. There was not a single hospital in the whole country, and even in 1966 there was only one medical doctor.[8] During the 1960–61 school year, there were only eighty-one students, all boys, enrolled in government schools in all of Abu Dhabi.[9] After 1962, as the oil revenues began to expand considerably, the ruler, Shaikh Shakhbut, remained unwilling to spend the money on an adequate scale to improve his people's standard of living. Development plans were drawn up by many advisers, but by 1965 only $4,900,000 had been spent—some of which went towards consultants' fees. In Donald Hawley's words, 'development in Abu Dhabi was less rapid than its sudden oil wealth had led people to expect. The ruler Shaikh Shakhbut ibn Sultan was affected by a noble but untimely nostalgia for the traditional Arab way of life.'[10] Even before he was overthrown in a family coup, he had become a legendary figure: it was believed that he stored bags of money under his bed. But when he went to visit a new oil rig, he appeared in a Cadillac, accompanied by a fleet of Land Rovers for his retinue. What a sight he must have made touring the gigantic, glistening rig with his followers in tow, bandoliers across their backs, parading both their firearms and falcons![11] It was indeed fortunate for his subjects that his brother Zaid replaced him in 1966; a year before, Shakhbut had irrationally refused to accept the oil company's offer of an increased share of the royalty.

Immediately following Shaikh Zaid's acquisition of the leadership of Abu Dhabi, modernization and expansion of Abu Dhabi town began. In 1966, ocean-going vessels landed 36,748 tons of cargo, but in the following year, 144,185 tons were unloaded; eighty-two per cent of the total imports by weight consisted of construction materials.[12] In 1969, 272,336 tons of cargo were unloaded—a sevenfold increase in three years![13] By 1972, the town of Abu Dhabi was a jarring sight: tremendous carriageways, coming to an end abruptly, sometimes at an intersection with a tiny narrow alleyway; buildings half erected and seemingly abandoned temporarily by workmen who had found some other task more urgent to complete; the shell of what we learned was to be a new Hilton Hotel looming precariously skywards. Movement by foot from one place to another was quite an undertaking: not only did we have to tread through miniature sand dunes, we had also to thread our way through construction sites laden with iron piles and discarded equipment, building materials, and heaps of scaffolding.

Although there are no income taxes, corporation or capital gains, the prices for office and hotel accommodation are very high. I was told that the Shaikh and his family owned much of the land in the city centre, which they often lease to business enterprises for a short period, usually eight years. The lessees build their premises on the land but because they are not certain whether or not they will be able to extend their leases afterwards, they want to recover their building expenses within the period of their initial lease. Whatever structures they have constructed on the land revert back to the lessor at the termination of the lease.

Along with the development of Abu Dhabi into a modern capital city, Shaikh Zaid improved the education system and social services of the state. The number of government schools expanded from three in 1963 to twenty-four in 1970, and the number of students increased from 281 to 6,972 over the same period.[14] From one medical doctor in 1966 there were twenty doctors and sixty nurses in the Emirate two years later.[15] Abu Dhabi's growth and modernization in turn attracted a huge influx of foreigners. The 1968 Census showed that out of a total population of 46,375, only 20,352 were native Abu Dhabians; that is to say that fifty-six per cent of the population consisted of foreigners. In 1971, the population had increased to 100,000 with still a higher percentage of foreigners. The largest numbers of aliens were Omanis, Jordanians, Palestinians, Pakistanis, Iranians and Bahrainis. On account of the rapid transformation of Abu Dhabi, there was a severe shortage of skilled local manpower. For instance, in the 1970–71 school year, the Government employed 439 teachers, only four of whom were citizens.[16] It appears that Abu Dhabi, like many of the other wealthier shaikhdoms, will have to rely on foreigners for skilled labour for many years to come.

Most unfortunately, there are no statistics available on the dhow trade of the early 1960s, but it is obvious that it was much smaller than today. From 1968, when there were 810 small vessels (about ninety per cent of which were dhows) to 1971, an annual average of 990 small vessels came into Abu Dhabi. The most common ports from which the dhows came were Doha, Dubai, Bahrain, Ras al-Kaimah, and others in Iran (see Table XXII).

TABLE XXII
SMALL VESSELS ARRIVING IN ABU DHABI IN 1969, 1970, AND 1971

From*	1969	1970	1971
Qatar	261	121	131
Dubai	183	101	195
Bahrain	177	121	144
Ras al-Khaimah	171	69	149
Kuwait	146	77	69
Iran	98	131	118
Saudi Arabia	89	71	51
Iraq	41	18	19
Das Island	40	89	178
Sharjah	8	10	8
Jebel Dhana	6	8	15
Aden	4	2	1
Oman	2	3	5
India	0	3	7
Pakistan	0	0	5
Others	0	1	5
Totals	1,226	825	1,100

*The source does not specify whether this is the last or original port of call.
Source: Government of Abu Dhabi, Statistical Office, *Statistical Bulletin, 1971.*

The dhows brought in food from Iran (in 1971, $140,000 worth of food was imported into Abu Dhabi but not all of it was carried by dhow) and general cargo from the other main ports. Most of the Abu Dhabi dhows had foreign crews consisting of Omanis and men from the poorer shaikhdoms. Hardly any true exports, except fish, go out of Abu Dhabi. The fish are obtained from the fifty-four Abu Dhabian fishing boats. Often the fishermen stay out in the Gulf for as long as three or four weeks and sell their fish in Saudi Arabia, Abu Dhabi or other ports, depending on where the price is found to be the highest. Most of these fishing boats are called *lanchas* by the Arabs and are rather small vessels, about forty feet in length, with a transom stern. The largest fishing fleets come from the poorer shaikhdoms, such as Bahrain, Ajman, Ras al-Khaimah and Oman, where there is less opportunity for alternative employment.

Some of the costliest vegetables grown in the world travel by dhow from a little island named Sadiyat to the town of Abu Dhabi. It is an important experiment in hydroponics (the growing of plants in chemical solutions without soil), initiated by Shaikh Zaid and the University of Arizona in the late 1960s. Shaikh Zaid decided to do this because Abu Dhabi's vegetables were being imported and he wanted to have a local 'food factory', as the project is called in the press. It was a very expensive undertaking, requiring a desalination plant for water (first a fairly small one was built which produced 2,000 gallons a day; now there is another one in its place which makes 50,000 gallons but which in 1972 cost $2.50 for every 1,000 gallons), greenhouses (which have had to have evaporated cooling during the seven-month-long hot season, because of humidity during the day, and the almost constant temperature at night on the island), and expert advisers (this is the first time hydroponics have been practised on a large scale in coral sand).

In October 1972, I visited Sadiyat island and I was shown around by Dr Merle Jensen and Jack Yelf of the Arid Lands Research Centre, Abu Dhabi. It was in 1969 when the project got under way, with a grant of $4,000,000 from the ruler. The forty-eight greenhouses covered an area of about five acres, and because of the cost of the greenhouses which are mainly air-inflated enclosures similar to balloons, and the expense of maintaining these facilities, those vegetables which take up the least ground space are figured to be the most economical, i.e. the cucumbers and tomatoes. In 1972, they were able to produce 600 kilos of cucumbers every other day on only a quarter of an acre. The Government wants the project to experiment with a great variety of vegetables, and at the time of my visit, mustard, spinach, lettuce, radishes, cabbages, turnips, broccoli and peppers were all under cultivation. The cost of running Sadiyat island was then $660,000 annually. Without taking into account the capital investment, there was still little hope of breaking even on running expenses. This was because of the free market in Abu Dhabi for vegetables, and when the project flooded it with more tomatoes than were demanded at existing prices the price had to fall. One solution would be to export surplus vegetables to Kuwait and neighbouring shaikhdoms, where, instead of the equivalent of about U.S. ten cents a pound being paid in Abu Dhabi, perhaps thirty cents could be raised. Of course, there would be transportation costs added on to that, but already some transportation expenses are involved in getting the vegetables from Sadiyat island to Abu Dhabi by dhow. Naturally, exports to other countries would also help the dhow trade.

Had the experiment been located in the oasis of al Ain, which is well inland and consequently cool in the evenings, there would not have been the need for expensive air-conditioning in the greenhouses which raises the overheads more than anything else. Transport from al Ain would have been no problem either, since this oasis is only ninety miles via a tarmac road from the capital of Abu Dhabi.[17] But Sadiyat was considered a more glamorous location even if less economic.

Although Abu Dhabi uses dhows, very few Abu Dhabians seem involved themselves in the ancient trade. This may be the result of the more attractive returns from other activities as much as the rejection of the traditional ways of livelihood.

Inside the Portuguese Fort in Hormuz

Two men plying a traditional *guyuck* off Khorramshahr

Dubai

The most prepossessing and intriguing of the ports on the Arabian side of the Gulf is Dubai, which is situated on an eight-mile-long creek. Since oil was not exported until 1969, the construction boom is very recent and, therefore, many of the old buildings with their imposing wind towers (which are of Persian origin[1]) and carved wooden doors still remained in 1972. Most of the population of 100,000 in 1972, when I visited Dubai, lived near the mouth of the creek, with the majority of them on the northern, or Deira side of the creek; the southern part, called the Dubai side, contains the modern Port Rashid for steamships, and is connected to Deira by a bridge. However, many people still prefer to take the picturesque and quaint wooden boats called *abras* to cross from one side to the other. The creek contains more dhows than any other port in the western Indian Ocean, except Bombay. Particularly on the Deira side, anchored dhows are crowded together awaiting the unloading and loading of cargoes. Lining the side of the creek are the old Arab buildings together with a few modern hotels, shops and warehouses. The atmosphere is very cosmopolitan with Lebanese and Pakistani merchants, Arab businessmen, Egyptian clerks, shoppers from other emirates, and sailors from all over the Gulf. The port hums with activity. There is a vitality of an earlier age present, reminiscent of Venice long ago, and, indeed, Dubai has been called the 'Venice of the Arabian Gulf' as well as the 'Pearl of the Coast'.

Dubai is also a haven for immigrants, with about seventy per cent of the population consisting of foreigners and a ruling Shaikh who understands and sympathizes with the desire of Pakistanis and Indians to escape from the dire poverty in their own homeland. Shaikh Rashid's 'open door' policy has turned Dubai into the most lenient of the shaikhdoms as regards immigration. There is even an anecdote about Shaikh Rashid's feelings: like many other Arabs, he enjoys visiting Pakistan, which is close, also Muslim, and offers better hunting grounds for falcons, and—yes—pet cheetahs, still trained even today to hunt for their masters. Once when he was in Pakistan, Shaikh Rashid received word that some authorities in Dubai had begun to oust illegal immigrants. He cut short his visit to rush home to read the riot act to his subordinates: if they could see the poverty of Pakistan, so he is reported to have declared, they would never have brought themselves to perform such an act of cruelty. It may be, however, that Shaikh Rashid is not wholly motivated by humanitarianism: he certainly realizes that the Pakistanis and Indians fulfil Dubai's acute need for cheap labour.

Although Dubai's oil revenues are recent and relatively small as compared to those of Kuwait, Qatar and Abu Dhabi, Dubai is a wealthy shaikhdom, and is one of the few which is not entirely dependent on oil money for its prosperity. It is, and has been, at least since the early nineteenth century, when the ruling family came to Dubai from Abu Dhabi, a major entrepôt. By the end of the 1870s, Dubai was the most important port of the coast. In 1906, the population exceeded 10,000, including many Persians and Baluchis; there were also sixty-seven Hindu and twenty-three Khojah traders. Steamers of the British India Company paid fortnightly visits to Dubai, and the Bombay and Persia Steam Navigation Company ships were also a familiar sight in this port where goods from all over the Indian Ocean changed hands. It did not seem to matter that the only locally produced goods were pearls, mother-of-pearl sea shells and dried fish for export; the creek itself was so easily navigable that products from Iraq, Persia, India and Africa all found their way there and became available for re-export. In 1906, there were 300 shops and 200 warehouses to serve the thousands of merchants who came annually to Dubai.[2] Dubai's past is reflected in its course of life today, which Donald Hawley so colourfully describes:

Its market, though much is now modern, preserves a way of life centuries old. Merchants sit cross-legged in small square shops, goods stacked high around them, and occasionally murmur dictations to a scribe. In the crowded streets, Arabs mingle with Persians in gold-brocaded turbans and smooth-faced Indians in *dhotis* [long white robes]. Pakistanis in astrakhan caps and handsome Baluchis jostle with Bedouin, and the dark faces of many passers-by betray their African origin. Sweating porters manhandle barrows and, until piped water was installed, donkeys laden with water-tins and jingling their bells trotted ahead of the shouting water-sellers. In the camel park, camels, temporarily abandoned by their master from the interior, sit hobbled as they ruminate and cast disdainful glances around.[3]

The present ruler of Dubai, Shaikh Rashid ibn Said al Maktum, has followed in the footsteps of his grandfather, continuing to foster Dubai's commercial well-being and taking a liberal attitude towards foreigners who wish to come to Dubai to make their fortunes, just as his grandfather made welcome the Lingeh merchants who moved to Dubai at the beginning of this century to escape from heavy taxation and harassment by the Persian government. Although Shaikh Rashid's father was technically the Head of State until his death in 1968, he himself has in effect run the government since 1941. His imaginative shrewdness has led him to turn present-day Dubai into the second greatest entrepôt in the world for gold (after Switzerland).

A man in front of a fine Arab wooden door at the main entrance to the
Dubai Museum

The time of day I preferred in Dubai was the late afternoon when the sun was setting behind the mosques; the sky a brilliant apricot colour; long shadows being cast on the creek by the dhows where the crews aboard were cooking their evening meal; and, with the approach of twilight, the windows of the houses shimmering with lamplight while the *muezzins* called the faithful to prayer once more.

The Gold Trade

In 1947 when India became independent its new Government, realizing that for centuries the Indian people had been spending millions of rupees to purchase gold, decided to call a halt to this unnecessary expense. In an attempt to conserve India's foreign exchange and to prevent rupees from leaving the country, it was decided in 1947 to prohibit the importation of gold. Soon afterwards, Dubai began supplying Indians with gold, which was freely imported into and exported out of Dubai. The Dubai Government correctly perceived that Indians would not forego their traditional luxury and would even smuggle it if need be into their country. The Government furthermore saw no reason to discourage its businessmen from pursuing their lucrative interests in the gold trade and gave them free rein to carry on. By 1966 more gold was being imported into Dubai than anywhere else, with the exceptions of Switzerland and France; in 1966, $410,000,000 of gold came into Dubai, equal to ten per cent of the total gold mined in all the non-communist countries for that year. Almost all of this gold made its way to Pakistan and India by dhow.[4] In 1970, Dubai imported amost 260 tons of gold worth $300,000,000, which represented twenty per cent of world production for that year.[5] In 1971, 215 tons valued at $360,000,000 were imported.[6] Dubai thus became the largest buyer of gold on the London market and one of the largest importers of gold in the world, though its population was only 80,000.

Almost all of Dubai's gold is flown from London on regular British Airways and Middle East Airlines flights; only a small percentage is air-freighted from Beirut. The gold is packed in wooden boxes, each containing 200 or 250 ten-tola bars (ten tolas equal 3.75 ounces), and is usually sent on consignment from London by the bullion firms and the major Swiss banks which control about two-thirds of the market. When the gold arrives in Dubai, it is transported to the various banks of the shaikhdom for safe-keeping: the British Bank of the Middle East, the National Bank of Dubai and the First National City Bank of New York. This last bank which was established in Dubai in 1964 to carry out traditional banking practices soon realized that its clients were not satisfied with simply opening chequing accounts and obtaining loans; if the bank were to do well in Dubai it would have to deal in gold, too. The officers of the First National City Bank duly applied to the U.S. Treasury for a special licence to hold gold, a rare privilege for a U.S. bank at that time, but one which it did receive.[7]

So far as the Government of Dubai is concerned, there is nothing illegal about the gold trade: there are no restrictions in Dubai on importing or exporting gold. When the gold trade suddenly became big business in Dubai, the majority of the gold merchants were at first financed by businessmen in Pakistan, Britain and Switzerland, but now most of the financing comes from the Dubai merchants themselves. When the merchants are ready to arrange a gold shipment, they go to the banks and collect up to $2,000,000 of gold in ten-tola bars to put on various dhows. A single merchant may be backed by a group of subscribers who put up part of the capital. At the end of every three months, the subscribers will be paid off, if a profit has been made. None of the gold exported from Dubai is melted down and made into jewellery; all of it remains in bars which are easy to handle.[8]

I counted 204 cargo dhows in Dubai in November 1972, 183 of which were at Deira and 21 on the Dubai side of the creek. From interviews, I estimated that about one-third of them were involved in the gold trade and almost all were going to ports around Bombay. Of the dhows involved, 45% were Indian, 33% registered in Dubai, and 22% were from Pakistan. There were more Indian dhows in Dubai than in all the other ports I visited in the Gulf. The Indian dhows used in the gold smuggling are easily recognizable as they are different from either the traditional Indian *kotia* or the Arab *boom*. They are quite small in size, being roughly forty-five feet in length, with a single mast, and having matting running around the ship in a way similar to that of the Lamu *jahazi*, which, in both instances, is used to prevent sea water from flooding the cargo. I was told that this type of vessel is called a *manji* and I did not see such a craft in Kuwait, Bahrain, Qatar, Abu Dhabi or in any of the Iranian ports. Although *manjis* are relatively small, they are extremely fast because they have very powerful engines to enable them to outrun the Pakistani and Indian patrol boats.[9] In one *manji* I even saw two engines, one to turn each propeller. I noticed that in general the *manjis* were scruffy in appearance, and that quite a few of them were having repairs made on them while they were in Dubai. The Dubai dhows which go to India are usually owned by Dubai Arabs and may have an Arab *nahoda*, but most of the crews (which average nine men per dhow) are of Indian nationality. Some of the Indian and Pakistani dhows also are owned by Dubai Arabs.[10] All the Indian dhows which come into Dubai are involved to some extent in the gold trade. When a dhow is ready to go to India, the gold bars, generally amounting to about $250,000 on the free market, are hidden amongst the planks of the vessel.[11] Upon departure from Dubai, a discreetly worded cable is sent to Bombay alerting the merchants of the probable arrival time. The trip takes between five and six days, covering a distance of 1,200 miles. The dhows do not go directly to Bombay but rendezvous with fishing boats from small villages north of Bombay. Before the gold is transferred, it is stuffed into the pockets of smuggling jackets, each of which may hold as much as 1,000 tolas; wearing the jackets, the crews of the fishing boats quietly make their way back to the Indian shore. Afterwards, the dhows may go on to Bombay or farther south to pick up silver, cloth or currency to pay for some of the gold, returning directly afterwards to Dubai. On rare occasions, Indian patrol boats may try to intercept a dhow smuggling gold. When this happens the crew will toss overboard the gold attached to marker buoys that will float just below the surface at low tide, and the fishing boats will later come to collect it. If the Indian authorities are clever and actually catch some of the smugglers, then the smugglers may attempt to bribe the appropriate officials. As far as I was able to ascertain, few dhow crew members are ever caught and imprisoned for gold smuggling. The risk is not very great.

Timing to return to shore at night, the fishing boat crews await a signal from

185

their colleagues, the flashing of headlights or a message on a two-way radio; once they know that it is safe to land, they come in quickly and hand over the jackets to someone in a car, who in turn takes the gold and drives into Bombay to leave it at a pre-arranged pick-up point. There, another person collects the gold and goes to a flat rented by another member of the syndicate. Finally, the gold will be passed on to various other people who will distribute it to buyers throughout India. The whole operation is sophisticated and very secretive. No person knows the names of the other individuals involved; not even the man who delivers the gold to the flat knows who actually rents the place. If one member of the syndicate is caught by a policeman, the chances are that he will be able to bribe him; after all, the policeman probably receives no more than $25 a month as his salary, while the gold carrier receives about $150 per transaction. Furthermore, if someone is apprehended, he is unable to implicate any other individual. All communication is carried out by two-way radios and through public telephones at specified times. It is not surprising that the smugglers seldom end up in jail.[12]

Occasionally, crew members or middlemen attempt to steal some of the gold. I was told that in 1972 there were four attempts by dhow crew members to filch gold, but such endeavours end unsuccessfully because the syndicates are highly organized. Timothy Green narrates an incident in which the captain of a Dubai dhow sold his gold directly to merchants in Bombay. He was found in a café, brought back to Dubai in a sack, and flogged in front of other dhow captains to discourage them from trying to do the same. Later, he was thrown into a Dubai prison for several months—probably on a trumped-up charge.[13]

One aspect of the gold trade puzzled me. How can the Indians pay for the smuggled gold? Until recently, the Indian rupee was the generally recognized currency throughout the Gulf, although in the more remote places, the Maria Theresa dollar continued to be legal tender. However, in 1958 the Indian Government, waking up to its losses of some $100,000,000 a year through the gold trade, gave up the prestige of having the rupee accepted as currency abroad and produced new non-convertible paper notes for legal tender in the Gulf. However, they did not prohibit the use of the coins, and clever merchants immediately took advantage of this loophole. Dhows returned to Dubai from India laden with 40-gallon drums filled with Indian coins. The banks became annoyed with handling huge sums in small coins and initiated a five per cent handling charge.[14] Then, in 1966, even the Indian coins ceased to be legal tender in the Gulf, and the gold merchants had to think of alternatives.

From 1966 at least until 1972, there were four ways for the Indians to pay for their gold. In the late 1960s, a large portion of the gold was paid for by the illegal movement of silver, which India possesses in the form of old coins and jewellery which can be melted down. In Dubai, some of the imported silver from India is made into knives, but most of it is sold on the world market. In 1968, when silver prices were high, Indian merchants paid for two-thirds of their gold by exporting silver; however, by 1971, silver had dropped to covering about one-third of the cost of the gold that they imported.[15]

The second way of paying for the gold is through Indians and Pakistanis abroad who will exchange their foreign currency for higher-than-official rates in return for rupees for their families at home. This is carried out in the same manner as described earlier in reference to immigrants in the Gulf who send their hard currency to Europe for friends who need it and in return receive payment in Indian or Pakistani rupees. Gold dealers in India and Pakistan can thereby arrange to have a pool of money set aside for them to have sent to Dubai in payment upon receipt of the gold that they order.

Thirdly, there is the possibility of obtaining hard currency illegally from tourists who travel in India or Pakistan. When I was in India in 1968 and 1974, I was continually being asked for foreign exchange by people in Bombay and other tourist centres. Openly on the streets, dealers in foreign currency would offer me rupees for cash or travellers' cheques at forty per cent higher than the official rate. There appears to be considerably less demand in Pakistan since the black market exchange is only fifteen per cent higher than the official rate.

The fourth method of payment is the most nefarious of all—the illegal export of drugs, especially opium, from India and Pakistan. This is a subject which is kept well hidden and I have not been able to get any reliable statistics on the value of this trade. It was difficult even to find people who would talk to me about it since opium and other narcotics are contraband in Dubai and in the other shaikhdoms. In the end, I did succeed in obtaining interviews with two people involved in the drug traffic. One had been jailed for a year in Kuwait for being caught smoking hashish (Indian hemp) in a private house. I also learned that a man with 250 kilos of opium had been traced by the authorities in Ajman earlier in 1972. The fact that he had this much indicates that demand does not seem to have been repressed by harsh punishments of users as well as suppliers. An opium addict who travels widely in the Middle East trying to avoid detection of his habit, explained to me that the price of opium increases proportionately with the distance from Pakistan. A kilo costs $72 in Dubai, $200 in Kuwait and $3,000 in Egypt. Dealers of opium in Dubai are

A police fort in Ajman

often users themselves, and they are mostly resident Iranians, Pakistanis and Indians; few Dubai Arabs seem to be involved.

The crew members of the dhows do not make huge profits carrying gold to India and returning with silver and other commodities. On a round trip which will take about one month (due to delays both in Dubai and in India), a crew member will make between $120 and $240.[16] None the less, this sum is a great deal more than the average wage of Indian crews on non-smuggling voyages who earn $20 a month. The crew members going to India supplement their salaries by smuggling in small radios,[17] fountain pens,[18] and other small manufactured items which are scarce, expensive and of poor quality in India. They exchange them for clothes, perfumes, records, swords and other Indian-made products which they can sell back in Dubai.

The big winners in the gold trade are the heads of the syndicates in India and Dubai. How much profit these people make is a matter of controversy among writers on the subject. Timothy Green believes that there is fifteen per cent profit in the gold smuggling, while Donald Hawley suggests that it is much higher: 'The price [of gold] in Dubai in 1967 was $35 an ounce and it was sold in India at $68 an ounce; thus the profits of such transactions were enormous, even though large sums stuck to a number of fingers on the way.'[19] It is true, as Donald Hawley states, that gold is very much more expensive in India than in Dubai, and, when I was in Dubai in 1972, I was told that at that time gold fetched on the black market in India up to one hundred per cent more than in Dubai. I would estimate that the top people in the syndicates were earning at least thirty-three per cent profit yearly. As I tend to agree with Mr Hawley's estimates, I would also point out that with the considerable outlay of capital in gold smuggling, it is not likely that the risks involved would be worth a mere fifteen per cent return. The merchants would find it far more profitable and much less complicated simply to deal in the exchange of dinars for rupees on the black market.

There is another commodity which is illegally imported into India from Dubai by dhow—watches. In 1966, Dubai businessmen imported $16,150,000 worth of them.[20] Two years later, $22,650,000 of watches were imported, mostly from Switzerland; and, in 1971, $23,347,700 was spent on imported watches in Dubai, making Dubai the third largest watch-importer in the world.[21] Tiny, relatively unknown Dubai has the dubious distinction of being probably the major country in the world for smuggling gold, silver and watches—what a gimmick for survival!

India has periodically tried to stop the illicit trading from Dubai, but without success. The main problem is that there exists a great demand for gold not only for personal jewellery but also as a means of storing one's savings against the disasters of a poor harvest or as a hedge against further devaluation of the rupee. Hoarding gold has been going on for hundreds of years in India, and rare indeed must be the Hindu family that does not start a collection of gold rings, bracelets and necklaces for their children soon after birth. The collection is perhaps more important for a girl than a boy, since women in India have not held any rights over their husband's or father's property, and gold is consequently about the only provision made for protecting a girl in the case of the death of her husband or father. Gold is thus the equivalent of an insurance policy. At the time of her marriage, the bride is showered with gold jewellery which, along with her childhood collection, she can always keep. Furthermore, a Hindu wife's prestige is measured by the amount of gold given to her by her husband and his family. This long tradition of hoarding gold is not one which will willingly be set aside.[22]

During the last thirty years, the Indian Government has made repeated efforts to stop further importation of gold. First, in 1947, the Government banned outright the importation of gold, but as the few mines in India could not possibly produce enough gold for domestic use, smuggling began again in a big way. From 1958 to 1966, the Indian Government passed various laws leading finally to the prohibition of the use of the rupee as legal tender in the Gulf, but these measures just encouraged more illegal imports of gold. At home, the Indian Finance Minister in 1963 initiated a law forbidding the manufacture of gold ornaments over fourteen carats; this precipitated a crisis. One hundred goldsmiths committed suicide, protest demonstrations were carried out in New Delhi, and a black market started for twenty-two carat jewellery. Three years later the Government admitted defeat and reversed their earlier decision.[23]

Unless India overhauls its economy to give more confidence to businessmen and also manages to reduce the traditional importance of gold to Indian brides, gold will certainly continue to be imported. Various estimates have been made on the amount of gold held by private citizens of India. In 1958, the Reserve Bank of India estimated that 3,150 tons of gold were held privately;[24] this gold was then worth $3,000,000,000 at the fixed world price of $35 per troy ounce. In 1972, I estimate that the private gold stocks in India would have reached at least 5,150 tons worth $5,500,000,000; the price then was $42 an ounce. At the 1974 world market price of around $120 an ounce, gold stocks, grown to at least 5,250 tons, had appreciated in value to $16,900,000,000—a staggering figure for a poor country. Some experts believe that private citizens in India may be hoarding as much as 8,000 tons of gold.[25] If this were true for 1975, when the world market price reached $198 an ounce, Indian gold would be worth a phenomenal $42,600,000,000.

Besides the clandestine trade with India and Pakistan in gold, silver, narcotics, pens, watches and transistor radios, the merchants of Dubai also import and export huge quantities of playing cards. In the recent past, playing cards were banned from certain places in the Gulf because of the traditional Muslim aversion to gambling. Dubai businessmen also profited from this prohibition. From 1966 to 1971, they imported a yearly average of $129,000 worth of playing cards, mainly from the United States, which they exported to neighbouring states by dhow. In terms of weight, the 1971 imports of playing cards were eighty-nine tons, an enormous quantity.[26] It absolutely amazes me how quick and perceptive the Dubai merchants are to take advantage of contraband laws. They must bless their stars for the dhows which can so unobtrusively slip in and out of shore.

The Dhow Trade of Dubai

Aside from the smuggling of goods into India, Pakistan, and other Arabian countries in the Gulf, the dhows of Dubai are also heavily involved in trade to and from Iran. Dhows leaving Dubai smuggle into the many Iranian ports consumer items such as radios, record players, cigarettes and clothes, which,

The police fort at Jazirat al-
Hamra, U.A.E.

while readily available in Iranian shops, carry a very heavy duty when sold
legally. The dhows bring back to Dubai fruit, vegetables, live animals (goats,
sheep and cows), and people. During the late 1960s and early 1970s, about forty
per cent of the dhow movements from Dubai were between the ports of Iran
(see Table XXIII).

TABLE XXIII
DHOWS COMING INTO DUBAI FOR SELECTED YEARS

		Numbers in	
Last Port	*1967*	*1969*	*1971*
Iran	1,912	1,475	2,720
Trucial States	732	724	582
India	588	474	1,208
Qatar	216	194	274
Bahrain	165	159	271
Muscat	156	154	267
Saudi Arabia	115	111	124
Kuwait	82	123	151
Aden	80	0	46
Pakistan	39	72	84
Br. al-Mahra	30	0	0
Iraq	24	68	45
Totals:	4,139	3,554	5,772

Source: *Statistics Reports, 1967, 1969 and 1971*, Dubai.

Dubai's dhows are so versatile in their smuggling activities that they are
often involved in smuggling persons from India and Pakistan to Dubai and to

190

other shaikhdoms. Officially, however, the Dubai dhows do not carry any passengers to or from India and Pakistan.[27] There are an estimated 100 licensed 'employment' agencies in Karachi whose services range from fixing jobs to smuggling job aspirants. How many unlicensed ones there are in addition is a matter of conjecture. The agencies charge from $100 to $300 to arrange the transport of a customer from Karachi to any of the shaikhdoms by dhow. Some of the unfortunate job seekers are dumped on remote sand spits without having a passport or even a single piece of identification. One Karachi bus conductor who paid $1,000 to an agent for a clerk's job in Bahrain ended up employed there as a servant to pour tea![28]

The dhows do a good business even with the legal movement of people in and out of Dubai (see Table XXIV). In the late 1960s and early 1970s, dhows brought about twice the number of passengers carried by steamships. Of the total number of passengers disembarking and embarking at Dubai in 1967, about one-third went to or came from ports in Iran; one-fifth Bahrain, one-fifth Qatar; and one-ninth Saudi Arabia.

TABLE XXIV
NUMBERS OF PASSENGERS CARRIED BY DHOW
TO AND FROM DUBAI

Year	Total Passengers
1967	60,693
1968	39,407
1969	41,064
1970	37,205
1971	38,900

Source: *Statistical Reports, 1967–1971*, Dubai.

Not all of Dubai's commodity trading is cloaked in secrecy and intrigue. There is a considerable legitimate goods trade to other countries. Moreover, some of these goods are locally produced commodities for export. In 1971, $863,942 worth of dried fish was exported to Ceylon, Saudi Arabia and other Gulf shaikhdoms; $120,710 of dates were sent to Muscat; $100,000 of shark fins were exported to Singapore and Hong Kong; and $32,560 worth of hides and skins were exported, mostly to Qatar.[29] We do not know how much was carried on dhows; obviously the shark fins went to the Far East by steamship, but probably most of the dates, the hides and skins, and perhaps a high percentage of the dried fish going to the Gulf states were transported by dhow (see Table XXV).

TABLE XXV
EXPORT OF LOCALLY PRODUCED COMMODITIES FROM
DUBAI FOR 1967, 1969, AND 1971

Commodity	1967	1969	1971
Dried fish	$984,594	$901,985	$863,942
Dates	167,598	286,750	120,710
Shark fins	9,896	29,788	100,000
Hides and skins	0	7,000	32,500
Fish manure	0	59,113	0
Totals:	$1,162,088	$1,284,636	$1,117,152

Source: *Statistical Reports, 1967, 1969, and 1971*, Dubai.

An Indian engineer checking the engine on his dhow in Dubai

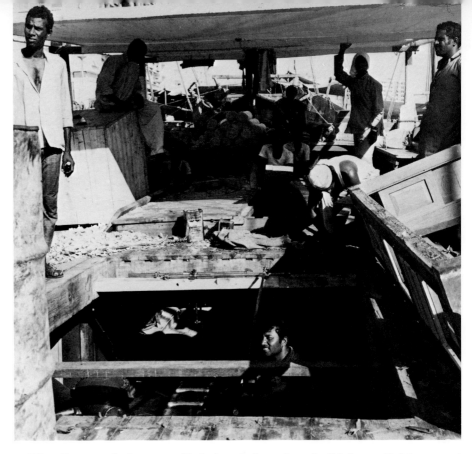

The dhow trade between Dubai and the other shaikhdoms, Pakistan and India is the most important in value in the entire western Indian Ocean. From the 1960s up to at least 1973, when I was last in the Gulf, hundreds of millions of dollars worth of gold, silver, narcotics, watches, pens, playing cards, radios and more lawful commodities passed through Dubai hands. Furthermore, illegal immigrants poured into Dubai, and there was as well a brisk business in legitimate passengers to and from Dubai. The Dubai merchants and also the dhow owners profited tremendously from handling a significant proportion of these commodities and passengers. They have shown a shrewd sense in ascertaining economic weaknesses in neighbouring countries and then exploiting them to the maximum. Often the countries issuing restrictions on imports are so disorganized in the first place that their authorities are at a loss to try to stop the widespread smuggling of goods. Although the dhow is one of the oldest means of transport, it is ideally suited for the clandestine purposes assigned to it. Dhows in the Indian Ocean number several thousand, and the ones used for smuggling can easily intermingle with legitimate cargo and fishing craft; they have also the added advantage that they can go into small ports undetected and slip silently on to isolated beaches at night. It is, consequently, even for truly determined authorities, an almost impossible task to try to control the illicit trade by dhow.

It is interesting to recall that the dhow has long figured in illegal traffic. Last century, the frustrations of the Indian Ocean anti-slavery patrols bear eloquent witness to the dhow's undoubtedly superior qualities as a conveyance of nefarious cargoes.

192

Iran

On the other side of the Gulf, opposite the shaikhdoms, lies Iran, formerly
called Persia, a large country with a great diversity of landscape, people and
culture. Almost all of the foreign tourists who come to Iran visit the historic
cities of Tehran, Shiraz and Isfahan, and some of the mountains and lakes.
Very few tourists, in fact, go to the ports on the Gulf although such places as
Bushire and Hormuz have long and fascinating histories with important buildings of architectural interest still intact. Except for a few Iranians who go to
Abadan to escape from the cold winters of Tehran, rarely anyone but a
businessman visits the main ports in the Gulf. I was amazed that when I was in
Tehran I experienced considerable difficulties in trying to find out about the
Persian Gulf port towns: travel agents did not know about the hotels in Kung
or Lingeh and were unable to give me any information at all about the
conditions of the roads connecting the various ports.

The most numerous foreign visitors to Iran are people from Muslim
countries, particularly the Kuwaitis (17,116 in the year 1971–2) and Saudi
Arabians. They are also the biggest spenders.[1] Chryssee and I saw many Arabs
in Shiraz and Isfahan during the summer of 1973; they had mostly flown over
from the other side of the Gulf, where it is much hotter, and it is in these places
especially that they enjoy the lush landscape and feel at home in the Muslim
atmosphere which is as dominant in Iran as in their own countries. They
appreciate the beautiful surroundings of tiled mosques, gigantic pigeon houses,
ancient stone bridges, magnificent palaces, elegant sculptures, blue faience
buildings, and sumptuous rose gardens.

Chryssee and I first went to Tehran, the capital, on 1 June 1973. Except for a
few eighteenth and early nineteenth-century palaces and the magnificent

An old woman in the dhow harbour of Bushire

crown jewels, we did not particularly like the city of Tehran. The city is very large and spread out over a huge area; transport is a major problem as distances are great, and the traffic, noise and air pollution are appalling. We were, however, able to do something that most tourists are not, and that was to visit the Shah's brother's palace which gave us the opportunity to see how members of the Royal Family lived. We had a letter of introduction to H.I.H. Prince Abdorreza Pahlavi, one of the three or four greatest hunters in the world today. When I spoke to 'le Chambellan de sa Majesté Impériale le Chahinchah' on the telephone, I was informed that the Prince was overseas hunting but that none the less I would be welcomed if I chose to call at his palace to view the Prince's trophies. The following day, Chryssee and I drove to the Prince's estate which enclosed several acres and many different buildings. We were greeted at 11.00 a.m. by the Chamberlain and ushered into the palace, accompanied by several guards and servants. The palace is built in eighteenth-century French style and furnished with European furniture and *objets d'art*. We saw a few of the public rooms as we were ushered downstairs into a large suite of rooms plethoric with stuffed animals and trophies from all over the world. The white walls were covered with antelope and deer heads with horns and antlers only inches apart from one another; some of them had tags hanging from them indicating that they were world record specimens. A stuffed crocodile leered at us from across one room and in another corner stood a gigantic bear on his hind legs. On a much larger scale, of course, it reminded me of trophy rooms I have seen in Texas, with one major difference: here there were six liveried servants present graciously serving us tea and dainty French cakes.

After a few days in Tehran, we decided that we should fly down to the Gulf to visit the ports of Khorramshahr, Abadan, Bushire, Lingeh, Kung,

194

Khamir, Bandar Abbas, Tiyab and Hormuz. Our first port of call was Abadan.

Abadan and Khorramshahr

The modern history of Abadan is closely associated with the development of the petroleum industry of Iran. Although oil was known to exist in Persia two thousand years ago, modern exploration did not begin until 1901 when the British financier William d'Arcy obtained a concession. Within a few years, d'Arcy discovered oil deposits at Masjid-i Sulaiman, 130 miles north of Abadan. In 1909, the Anglo-Persian Oil Company purchased d'Arcy's concession, and, shortly afterwards, the company built an oil refinery at Abadan; a pipe line carried the oil from Masjid-i Sulaiman to it.

During the first decade of this century, Abadan was only a poor village of 400 people, but the construction of the refinery there rapidly turned it into a growing city. By 1943, there were 100,000 inhabitants, 25,000 of whom were employed by the refinery; eight years later, the population had increased to almost 200,000, and the refinery had become the largest in the world.[2] When Chryssee and I visited Abadan in 1973 the population was 300,000.

Abadan is unlike any other city in Iran. One author describes it in these words: 'In many ways Abadan is a unique phenomenon in Iran, for in its origin and structure it is like a foreign body that has recently been grafted on and not perfectly assimilated.'[3] Abadan is not an attractive city. The industrial sections of it are ugly, and the residential areas are segregated by the class of people working in the refinery. Such divisions are unlike those prevalent in the older Persian cities which possess a unity based on traditional Islamic principles. Indeed, the British were responsible for the construction of the majority of the modern buildings in Abadan, but since the nationalization of the oil company

A carpenter working in the Abadan dhow port

in 1951, there are only about 600 Europeans left in Abadan, and one would like to see the Iranians take the initiative to improve this city which certainly does look like a foreign transplant.

Although Abadan is a modern city, it is the major dhow port for Iran (see Table XXVI). One might think that the older cities of Bandar Abbas or Bushire which dominated the earlier trade scene with the Arabian side of the Gulf would have been able to maintain their positions, but in fact Abadan has usurped their roles. There are two main reasons for this. Firstly, Abadan's population is more than twice as great as any other port's on the Iranian side of the Gulf, having consequently a larger demand for imports such as radios, clothes and manufactured goods from the shaikhdoms of Kuwait, Abu Dhabi and Dubai. Secondly, behind Abadan in the hills, plains and mountains and farther away in the Isfahan region are agricultural areas which produce fodder for livestock and large quantities of fruit and vegetables; these commodities are trucked down to Abadan where dhows transport them to the wealthy Arab Shaikhdoms. There appears to be an especially active trade in fodder from Abadan to Kuwait. On 5 June 1973, I saw six dhows loading up with fodder for nearby Kuwait. Additionally, a lot of iced fish is taken by dhow to Kuwait for sale. The owners of the dhows based in Abadan are Persians, but most of the crews are actually Arabs of Iranian nationality.

TABLE XXVI
CARGO DHOWS IN VARIOUS IRANIAN PORTS IN JUNE 1973

Port	Number	Port	Number
Abadan	61	Khamir	15
Bushire	48	Ameri	7
Bandar Abbas	37	Bandar-Shahpoor	6
Khorramshahr	23	Hormuz	5
Kung	17	Lingeh	3
Tiyab	16		
Total:			238

Source: Survey taken by the author at various times during June 1973.

Only seven miles north of Abadan is the city of Khorramshahr which lies on the right bank of the Karun River at the junction of the Shatt-el-Arab, next to the border of Iraq. Unlike Abadan, Khorramshahr was a major port and town at the beginning of the twentieth century. Khorramshahr, then known as Muhammarah, founded in 1812 by an Arab, had a mostly Arab population of 5,000 in 1906, and was not effectively part of Persia until 1925. It was the main port and the only important town for all of south-west Persia. During the early years of this century, about 200 dhows came into Muhammarah each year, bringing cotton goods, metals and tea from India. The chief exports were dates to India and Muscat, wool and sesame to India, locally grown opium to Muscat, barley to ports in the Arabian Gulf, and Isfahan carpets to the richer Arabian shaikhdoms. The total value of the imports carried by dhows and the 143 steamships which came into Muhammarah in 1906 was £225,000, while the exports were worth £100,000.[4]

In 1973, Khorramshahr, with its population of 100,000 had the highest percentage of Arabs living in an Iranian city, due not only to its proximity to Iraq but also to its centuries-old links with innumerable ports in the Arab

Housing for the poorer inhabitants of Khorramshahr

world. It has held tightly on to its traditional architecture, and very few of the buildings have more than three storeys. The city is attractively spread out along the Karun River and landscaped with trees, bougainvillaeas and small private gardens. Scattered throughout the city are little tiled tea houses, and inside men and even women, who are not normally in public during the day, can be seen at all hours sipping mint tea and smoking water pipes placed on square tables surrounded by cushioned benches. Wandering freely along the streets amongst the many shoppers are white donkeys, similar to the ones in Bahrain, looking for bits to nibble, and there are also rather small sheep which are often tied on a string to the door of a little shop. To reach Khorramshahr from Abadan, one can cross over the new bridge which is a reasonable distance by foot from the centre of the city or take a small pirogue called a *guyuck*. This strange craft, which I have seen nowhere else in the world, resembles a cross between a Venetian gondola and an African canoe. The *guyuck* is about twenty-five feet long. The bow and stern are pointed and shaped like torsades. The craft are painted in bright colours, red and blue predominantly. They are propelled by a man standing in the back pushing a long pole or using a small paddle. A *guyuck* can carry about twelve passengers, who pay only the equivalent of U.S. three cents for the half mile voyage across the river. When I was in Khorramshahr, I counted ninety-eight *guyucks*. Over the past few years, motorized craft have been introduced for passenger transport, but since they charge four and a half cents per person, although they travel twice as fast they have not really caught on. I hope they never entirely replace the colourful *guyuck*, but history alas is probably against me.

Although most of Khorramshahr appears to be a traditional city with an Arab flavour, the main port for large ships which is located on the Shatt-el-

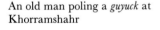

An old man poling a *guyuck* at Khorramshahr

Arab has periodically been modernized to insure that Khorramshahr remains the largest Iranian port. Khorramshahr is connected to Tehran by railway and road; its supremacy in the Iranian port hierarchy is unlikely to alter in the foreseeable future. During the early 1970s, there was considerable tension between Iran and Iraq, and the border was in effect closed. Since Khorramshahr is right on the boundary, the Shah of Iran has recently purchased many hovercraft to patrol the waters of Khorramshahr and the other main ports on the Persian side of the Gulf. In fact, Iran now has the largest fleet of operational hovercraft in the world; some of these craft can move at speeds of up to seventy-five miles an hour. When Chryssee and I hired a boat to see Khorramshahr from the water, our captain moved too close to the Iraqi border and we were chased by a couple of Iranian patrol boats. The police were very strict indeed about our movements on water, which was fully understandable as there had been some border clashes previous to our arrival and they were acting in their own best interests to guard our safety.

We saw only twenty-three cargo dhows at Khorramshahr, which was fewer than I expected. Undoubtedly, the reason for the small number was that Iraqi dhows were not allowed into the port. Dhows from Basra, in Iraq, only thirty miles up the river from Khorramshahr, used to do a considerable amount of trading here. For example, during the 1938–9 year, 6,630 dhows came into the Shatt-el-Arab, of which 2,568 were bound for Iraq and 4,062 for Persia; at that time dhows carried 21,708 tons of imports into Basra, consisting mainly of building materials, cloth and tea; the major exports from Basra were dates and grain.[5] In 1975 no Iranian dhows were allowed into the waters of Iraq and no Iraqi dhows were permitted to sail into the ports of Iran, a major blow to the international dhow trade.

I interviewed the crews of four Iranian dhows in Khorramshahr. The tonnage of the dhows varied from 100 to 140 and averaged 118; all had engines. Three of the dhows were carrying small stone chippings for construction purposes to Qatar and Saudi Arabia, while the other was transporting dates to Dubai. The crews told me that they were not paid a salary but received one-half of the profits after expenses; the dhow owner received the other half. The profits on these relatively short voyages are quite reasonable. One dhow captain said that the cargo charge for carrying small stones to Al Khubar, Saudi Arabia, a two or three day trip one way was $1,450. This was of course the gross figure from which expenses would be deducted. I would surmise that the expenses were $450 for fuel, food and other miscellaneous charges; thus $1,000 would be left to split between the crew and the owner. The owners of the dhow would get $500 and the crew of ten would split the remaining $500. The major question left unanswered is the period of time required to earn this money. Usually, a minimum of two days are required to load the stones and to prepare for the voyage.[6] Sometimes, however, the dhow owners have to wait as long as a couple of weeks to get cargo, and, occasionally, a dhow has to come back empty. Thus, it is extremely difficult to ascertain how much a crew member earns on average in a month, but I would estimate that in 1973, excluding the revenue from smuggling, a typical crew member working out of Iran would earn about $60 a month, far higher than his Indian, Somali or East African counterparts.

I was surprised that with Iran's tremendous oil wealth (petroleum exports in

1969 amounted to over a thousand million dollars), not very much of it by 1973 had trickled down to the average man in the ports. For instance, just opposite Khorramshahr on the Abadan side of the river, hundreds of people were living in poor mud-and-wattle houses with coconut-fibre roofs; there was no running water, drainage or sewage for them. We took a motorboat about six miles up the Karun River, and most of the people living along the banks appeared to be eking out a very pathetic existence among date palms and water buffaloes. After I had spent a month in Iran travelling to most of the ports in the Gulf, I came to the conclusion that Khorramshahr was not the exception but the rule. The people in the south are not prosperous, and the development of such places as Khorramshahr, Bushire and Bandar Abbas was, at least then, mostly confined to the modernization of port facilities for steamships, communications systems, and better services for the armed forces. In some of the dhow ports such as Tiyab, Kung and Lingeh, the people certainly were not living at a higher standard than their counterparts in Lamu or Malindi in East Africa where there is neither oil nor significant mineral wealth.

The official Iranian statistics confirm the maldistribution of the oil benefits. In 1967–8, 40% of the urban population had yearly earnings less than $133 *per capita*, while just under three-quarters of the urban population earned less than $265 a year.[7] The average family income in the rural areas and villages was about half that sum. During the 1960s, farm production increased at an average annual rate of only 3% (which was only slightly higher than the population growth of the country) while the *per capita* income of the whole country rose by 7.6% per year. According to two leading economists, 'the slow growth of agriculture ... continues to be a stumbling block against government efforts to raise the living standards of the rural population'.[8] The general standard of education was also low. In 1966, only 28% of the urban population, ten years of age and over, was literate, while in the rural areas the figure was 13.7%; the statistics on rural females were truly shocking: only 3.4% of those over nine years old were literate.[9] Unfortunately, I do not have any later statistics. None the less, it would seem that still today there would be a tremendous contrast between the education standards of dhow ports in Iran (except for Abadan) and the modern, wealthy ports of the Arab shaikhdoms.

On the other hand, it is only fair to add that tremendous improvements have been made in Iran since the early 1950s when Iran's economy was semi-feudal. For instance, the literacy rate rose from 7.3% to 16.5% between 1956 and 1966.[10] There have also been major developments in industry. We visited the new port of Bandar Shahpoor, sixty miles from Abadan, which possesses a huge petrochemical factory which started producing sulphur, ammonia and other chemicals in 1970. Twelve miles from Bandar Shahpoor is Bandar Mashoor, another new port at which yet another oil refinery was under construction in 1973. In creating new industries in the ports, Iran will raise the living standards of the people there, but I also believe that the country would gain from a concerted effort to improve as well the agricultural output around the port areas.

Bushire

From the middle of the eighteenth century to the early part of the twentieth century, Bushire was one of the major ports of the Gulf. The rise of Bushire was

200

the direct result of plans initiated by Nadir Shah. He wanted to build a great naval fleet that would make Persia the major power in the entire Gulf, and he chose Bushire as the fleet's headquarters because vessels drawing as much as twelve feet of water could come right up to the buildings on the quay at high tide. Nadir Shah was obsessed with his idea and even considered bringing timber all the way from the shore of the Caspian Sea to Bushire by forced labour. Although his wild schemes never materialized since Nadir Shah's reign came to an abrupt end in 1747 when he was assassinated,[11] enough had been done to generate considerable international interest in Bushire.

In 1763, the East India Company transferred its principal factory from Bandar Abbas to Bushire. In the early nineteenth century, Bushire became the seat of the British Political Resident in the Persian Gulf, and soon afterwards other foreign governments set up consulates there. In 1829, Captain George Brucks described Bushire in these words:

> [Bushire] is a town of considerable importance, being the port where all the British and foreign trade with Persia centres. It is walled in, and about two miles in circumference . . . Caravans arrive and depart daily. There is no water in the town that is drinkable—all is brought from places about 2 to 3 miles distant. The Shaikh or governor . . . is despotic in the extreme, and having 4 ships, besides several large *Buggalows*, of his own, he engrosses most of his freight, as he will not allow the merchants to ship their goods on any other vessel until his are loaded.[12]

A Persian in the dhow port of Bushire

In the early twentieth century, Bushire still retained its role as the main port of Persia. From 1901 to 1903, £701,000 worth of commodities were brought in, consisting of cloth, sugar, tea, grain and metals. Exports during the same period were half of the value of imports; the single most valuable commodity was opium which was sent to India; other items included gums, carpets, wheat, almonds, and hides and skins. The only locally manufactured item at that time was the copper coffee pot, quantities of which were sent all over the Gulf.[13]

The home fleet of cargo dhows in 1903 comprised fifty-five *mashuas* of ten to fifteen tons with crews of six to seven men who sailed between Bushire and the deep-water harbour three miles from the town; fifty *sambuks*, *booms* and large *mashuas* of thirty to forty tons which made voyages to various ports in the Gulf; four *baghlahs* of fifty to sixty tons; and twenty still larger vessels which visited Karachi, Bombay and Zanzibar.[14]

At the beginning of the twentieth century, Bushire had 1,400 houses (as compared with only 400 a century earlier[15]) with a population of 15,000. Almost all the inhabitants were Persians, but there were 600 Jews, 240 Arabs, 52 Europeans, 35 Armenians, and 20 Goans.[16] Bushire continued to prosper until the ports of Khorramshahr and Bandar Shapoor were modernized, allowing much larger ships to dock there. The final blow to Bushire's predominance was the completion of the Trans-Iranian railway in 1938 which connected Khorramshahr with the Caspian Sea; later a branch line was built between Ahwaz and Abadan, leaving Bushire comparatively isolated from the big cities of the interior, especially Tehran.

The population of Bushire had peaked at around 60,000 but in 1957 had declined to 14,000.[17] With the discovery of oil three miles south of Kharg island and in other areas near Bushire, and the development of Kharg into one of the biggest oil ports in the Gulf, Bushire began to revive. In 1966, the population was still under 30,000 but by 1972 it had increased to 45,000. A further impetus to the expansion of Bushire in the late 1960s and early 1970s was the decision to build an air base there for the most advanced American jets, and a modern naval station.

I found a kind of derelict charm about Bushire. At least half of the houses in the older part of the town were collapsing and consequently uninhabited. Most of the old buildings are double-storied, constructed out of local grey stone, a conglomerate of shell and coral, and tan bricks.

The wealthier merchants of an earlier era built three-storied houses with wooden balconies. The roofs were held up by mangrove poles, many of which were imported by dhow from East Africa. I was told by dhow owners and merchants that in the early 1970s hardly any mangrove poles were being imported at Bushire, but that most poles from East Africa went to Oman.

There is one unusual feature of the old Bushire houses. In some of them, the second storey protrudes into the street; this upper part of the building, supported by mangrove poles placed at an angle of forty-five degrees to the ground floor, practically touches the second storey of the house across the street. I imagine that the reason that these houses were constructed in such a fashion was to give pedestrians protection from hot sun as well as to allow for more space upstairs.

The buildings on the waterfront are the most grand, but many of them have been knocked down to make more room for the new port and the new tarmac

202

road. There appears to be no plan to save any of the old buildings of Bushire; in fact, the people seem to be encouraged not to maintain the elegant old houses but to build instead new modern ones outside the old town. Most of old Bushire in 1973 was in a shambles and none of the money that had been invested in Bushire was being used to preserve any of the historic landmarks. Even the huge Anglo-Persian mansions with pillars, lattice windows and attractive Arab-type doors, which had been occupied by wealthy and influential people in the nineteenth century, were falling down.

The covered market, or bazaar, was the finest I visited anywhere on either side of the Gulf. Again I was to be disappointed: most of it was not in use when I was there because a new market had recently been built. I distinctly remember ambling through that great old bazaar, covered with a roof made from thousands of mangrove poles, and seeing scores of small shops on both sides of the passage. Not much light penetrated through the mangrove pole slatted roof, but that which did created parallel shafts of brightness. The only sounds to be heard were made by the creeking of the old doors to the little shops, which swayed back and forth in the breeze.

Outside the old covered market are narrow streets with small food shops lining the sides. These are all run by men (as are the ones in the new market), and they are filled with many types of vegetables and fruit, including watermelons, cantaloups, onions, lettuce, carrots (there is a tasty local drink made from carrot juice and fresh milk), grapes, citrus fruits and tomatoes; most of these come from around Shiraz, 100 miles to the north-east. Such high quality produce constitutes an important dhow export to the Arabian shaikhdoms. Occasionally, a crowded lane will open on to a little square with a large tree in the middle under which people gather to chat in the shade. Under a tree in one of the busiest sections in town, I saw a woman sitting on the ground, smoking a water pipe. I approached her, and with her permission granted via sign language, I took her photograph. All of a sudden, a policeman appeared and arrested Chryssee and me. At that time I did not know why we were being arrested since there was a language barrier (he did not speak either French or English), and we were escorted to the police headquarters to be interrogated. Our cameras were immediately seized and we were ensconced in a tiny office with bars on the windows and the door closed. After waiting for what seemed an intolerably long time, the officer in charge came in. He asked us what we had done, in English, and I simply stated that I was taking a picture of a woman in the street when the policeman came. The ignorant policeman, close on the heels of the officer, barged into the room and started screaming at him, claiming that we were spies and were taking photographs illegally. This I gathered in translation, so I asked the officer if one needed a permit to take photos in Bushire and he replied in the negative. In the end, the officer reprimanded his subordinate, apologized to us for any inconvenience, returned our cameras and film, and released us. That was the only really awkward incident I had with the authorities in Iran. I found that the Iranians were not only extremely courteous generally but often eager to help me in my study of the dhow trade.

For several days, I worked in the Old Port of Bushire where there was an average of thirty-one dhows in the harbour. Additionally, there were five cargo dhows in the new port and twelve in the customs area, but I worked in

A woman smoking a hookah in the main street of Bushire; the authors were arrested by the Persian police for taking this photograph

neither of these places as to do so I needed to have an official permit. I discovered two main generalities which apply to the dhow ports of Iran. Firstly, there is very little dhow trade among the ports of Iran. The dhow captains find it far more profitable to go directly to the wealthy Arab shaikhdoms (which in some cases are closer than other ports in their own country) than to try to find cargo to carry, say, from Abadan to Bandar Abbas. Since most of the major Iranian ports are connected to one another by road, there is little demand for dhow transport. Road transport in Iran is not only faster but also cheaper. Secondly, few foreign dhows come to Iran because there are so many restrictions and there are high duties on manufactured goods as well. As it is, Persian dhows tend to take out far more goods than they bring in, and some of the commodities which are imported are brought in clandestinely to avoid the taxes. Iranian dhow crews are more successful smugglers than foreigners since they know the local language, topography and customs better.

At Bushire, some of the dhows have been used to ferry cargo from large steamships that are unable to get into the port. In 1973, the dhow owners received $2.50 a ton to transport cargo from a large vessel to Bushire, a distance of about five miles. Two round trips a day can be made while ships are in, earning a gross revenue of about $200.[18] The harbour was being dredged in 1973, as ships with draughts of more than seventeen feet could not come into the port, and it may be that the ferrying business was only a short-term phenomenon.

The average dhow in Bushire Old Port was sixty-eight tons, which, relative to other Gulf ports, was small. Most carried fruit and vegetables to the Arab

204

shaikhdoms, from Kuwait in the west to Oman in the east; almost none of the Bushire vessels go any more to the Hadhramaut or Aden. Dhows from Bushire commonly take live camels to Bahrain, Qatar and Dubai. These voyages are quite profitable; in a week's round trip, the dhow owner and crew can gross as high as $800, perhaps making a profit of as much as $500.[19]

How much the Iranians smuggle in from the Arabian side of the Gulf is anyone's guess. The import duties are so high that there is a great incentive to smuggle in any manufactured goods. For example, in 1973, a new American Chevrolet with air conditioning which would cost $4,000 in the States was worth $20,000 in Iran, because of taxes. The Iranian authorities are diligent in trying to stop illegal traffic into the country. When we drove down to Ameri, a village on the Gulf, thirty-five miles south of Bushire, our vehicle was stopped several times by the police to check whether or not we were smuggling anything. We saw seven cargo dhows off Ameri, a poverty-stricken place with mud-and-wattle houses encircled by a few date palms. The economy of Ameri is based upon dates, sheep and goats. The vegetation from Bushire down to Ameri was so sparse that one wonders how people survive economically. No agriculture is possible except under irrigation. We thought it was highly unlikely that the seven dhows we saw off Ameri were bringing in or taking out quantities of goods legally because Ameri is too poor. It seemed reasonable to suspect that the captains had brought their craft to this quiet spot to unload smuggled goods from the Arab shaikhdoms.

Bandar Abbas

Before the rise of Bushire, Bandar Abbas was the main Persian port. With the decline in the early seventeenth century of the Portuguese stronghold and port of Hormuz, following the defeat of the Portuguese at a fishing village called Gombroon opposite the island of Hormuz in 1615, one of the greatest rulers of Persia, Shah Abbas, decided that his chance had come to rid his Kingdom completely of Portuguese interference. He built up Gombroon and gave it his name, so that from then on it has been called Bandar Abbas. From there in 1622, a combined fleet of Persian and British ships launched an attack on the Portuguese, decisively defeating them at Hormuz and so ending the Portuguese dominance of Persian waters. The following year, the East India Company moved their factory from Jask to Bandar Abbas where it stayed until 1763, when it was once again re-sited. Until the end of the seventeenth century, Bandar Abbas flourished with both the English and Dutch importing and exporting large quantities of goods. During the first half of the eighteenth century, Bandar Abbas' prosperity was interrupted by attacks from Baluchis and Afghans, and in 1759 the French bombarded the English factory; in the same year, the Dutch pulled out completely, followed by the English, four years later.[20]

From 1759 until the end of the nineteenth century, Bandar Abbas was in economic decline. In 1793, the Sultan of Muscat took over Bandar Abbas, and the town remained under the political control of Muscat until 1868. Captain Brucks visited the town in 1831 and was dismayed by its appearance. At that time, Bandar Abbas had a population of 4,500, mostly Arabs and Persians, who exported tobacco and dried fruits and imported 250,000 rupees worth of goods, many of which went into the interior of Persia.[21]

In 1904, Bandar Abbas had a winter population of about 10,000; during the summer months many of the people withdrew to cooler areas. They were mainly of mixed Persian and Arab stock and they spoke a patois made up of Persian, Arabic and African words. The trade was similar to that of Bushire's, but vegetables and fruits surpassed the value of opium. In 1903–4, exports were worth £130,000 and imports £390,000.

Some of this trade was carried on the forty-six cargo dhows, which were based in 1903 in Bandar Abbas, including three enormous *baghlahs* with an average tonnage of 417 and an average crew of thirty-eight.[22] These *baghlahs* must have been the largest dhows in the Indian Ocean at that time.

Until the mid-1960s Bandar Abbas remained a backwater because the harbour was too shallow for modern cargo ships; steamships had to anchor about a mile out and barges were used to go and collect their cargo. Furthermore, fresh drinking water was (and still is) a problem; the wells produce a salty mixture which is not palatable. In 1955, Bandar Abbas was a small port of perhaps 20,000 people making their living from fishing and cultivating dates, fruits and vegetables. The town and most of its inhabitants were poor. There was no electricity and no running water.

The remains of a dhow at Suru, Bandar Abbas

In the mid-1960s, the Shah of Iran began to implement his policy of protecting the oil producing areas of the Gulf by building large military bases

in Khorramshahr, Bushire, Kish, Bandar Abbas and Chahbahar, near the Pakistani border. In the Shah's words:

I began thinking about it [the feasibility of Iran's becoming the strongest military power in the entire Gulf] in 1959 or 1960 when I concluded that the U.S. could not go on playing the role of international gendarme forever . . . Then came the British decision in 1968 to phase out of the Gulf in 1971—and the obvious power vacuum that would ensue . . . We have not only national and regional responsibilities but also a world role as guardian and protector of 60% of the world's oil reserves . . .

Chahbahar is being turned into an army, navy and air force base and will be the largest any power will have on the Indian Ocean guarding the approaches to the Persian Gulf. Bandar Abbas in the Strait of Hormuz, which is now [1973] almost completed, will protect the world's most important oil lane.[23]

Major developments at Bandar Abbas began in the 1960s, with the construction of a new jetty which was completed by 1967. Next came a new port, huge military installations, modern housing, a new piped water supply, and improved roads. The military complex planned for Bandar Abbas alone cost $200 million.[24] On account of all the economic activity, the population of the town expanded from 34,627 in 1966 to 47,000 in 1973.

Although in 1973 much of the modernization of Bandar Abbas had already been achieved, some of the old residential quarters had hardly been touched. Electricity has been supplied to some of the houses, yet the atmosphere is one of the early years of this century, and most of the older buildings are still used. The fishermen and dhow crews live in one of the oldest areas, Suru, which is situated a couple of miles from the new commercial part of Bandar Abbas. Suru has many old mud and brick houses with simple wooden doors. Most are only single-storied and not kept up as well as they should be, though their surrounding walls, at least six feet high and made of clay and straw, are still standing. Inside, there is usually a garden of date trees and flowering bushes, a secluded place where the family might take tea together. A few of these old houses have *badgirs*, tall rectangular ventilating chimneys, somewhat similar to the wind towers in Dubai, Sharjah and Ajman. The chimneys catch the wind and force it down into the main room.

The sandy beach in front of Suru was filthy. I saw smashed dhows, the remains of fish guts, dead cats, diseased dogs and other eyesores. At the eastern end of Suru's beach was an open fruit and vegetable market with dirty wooden stalls tenanted by flies and frequented by stray cows. Such an untidy seafront was not unique in Iran; the same is to be seen at Kung and Lingeh.

The Suru people are impoverished and seemingly cling to old customs which are especially obvious in their dress. The men wear the typical long robe which is common throughout the Indian Ocean and adorn their heads with a type of *kofia* which is often hand embroidered. The women wear a most unusual leather face mask called a *borka*. I had not seen anything like it in East Africa. I asked about it and learned that there are three reasons for it. Primarily, it is worn, as veils are elsewhere in the Muslim world, to seclude the woman's face from men's wandering glances, but it also protects the woman from the hot sun and against sunburn. Finally, the inside of the mask is covered with a black wax which is believed to improve the texture of a woman's skin.[25]

207

In Suru and in the adjoining old section of Bandar Abbas, where the majority of the fishermen and dhow crews live, I saw many fishing boats, and, in addition, ten cargo dhows in the water east of Suru, and thirteen cargo dhows on the beach on the western side of Suru. These latter were being repaired, and one of them was foreign. Some of the fishing boats are *booms*, and at certain times of the year the fishermen catch prawns; at other times the *booms* are mainly used to carry cargo to places such as Dubai and Ajman. The major exports from Bandar Abbas by dhow are prawns, goats, camels, vegetables, fruits and small stone chippings. Much of the traffic is to Dubai, which is 150 miles away. Imports from Dubai consist of clothes and manufactured goods.[26] Each cargo dhow is owned by an individual; however, no one person appears to own a fleet.

At the new port to the west of Bandar Abbas, there were fourteen cargo dhows. All the dhows from Bandar Abbas which were going to foreign ports had to depart from the new port and come into it on their return. Before this new port was established, dhows simply anchored off the jetty leading from the middle of the commercial section of the town. No dhows at all were using the jetty while we were there as it was undergoing long-needed repairs.

The dhows supplement their earnings by carrying passengers, and crew members get extra income by bringing in personal goods from the shaikhdoms which they sell to merchants in the Bandar Abbas bazaar. Legally, each crew member may bring in 5,000 reals (in 1973 worth $72) of personal goods to Iran duty-free from five trips abroad a year. Since duties are so high in Iran, the average crew member probably does quite well in importing, even legally, goods from the shaikhdoms. Because dhow crew earn their livelihood by foreign travel, they are not liable for the 10,000 real exit tax which other Iranians must pay each time they depart from the country.

On account of extensive smuggling of goods into Iran, security is very tight at the new port of Bandar Abbas. One morning while I was there, I saw a dhow which had just come back from Dubai, full of Persian passengers; each traveller had paid the equivalent of $3.70 for the trip. As soon as the dhow anchored, the customs people went onto the vessel and thoroughly inspected everyone's luggage and even the clothes on the passengers' backs. All the men were furthermore forced to lower their trousers to make certain that they were not hiding anything underneath. On another occasion, I saw a dhow, again having come from Dubai, full of Persian undesirables who had been deported by the Dubai authorities for a variety of crimes. For twenty-four hours these passengers had to wait until the police came and took them away in a special van. They would be tried in a court of law and, if convicted for the crimes attributed to them by Dubai, imprisoned in Bandar Abbas.

One afternoon we decided to take a trip to visit a port to the east of Bandar Abbas. We chose to go to Tiyab, a village fifty-two miles away. On route, we stopped at Minab, a town of 7,000 people. It is known for its date palms, which number several million in an oasis that is considered to be one of the best agricultural areas in all Iran. Some of the fruit (especially citrus) and vegetables that are exported from Bandar Abbas by dhow are grown here. Beyond Minab, the tarmac road came to an abrupt end, and we continued along salt flats, feeble paths and then on to desert sands with no markings whatsoever. The landscape was desolate; even though we had a short wheel-based Land Rover, we none the less got stuck while attempting to negotiate an irrigation canal. Eventually, we arrived at Tiyab. What a disappointment! Tiyab is without a doubt the dirtiest settlement I have seen anywhere in the Gulf. The flies swarmed around us in thousands as soon as we alighted from the vehicle and never for a moment forsook our presence.

Tiyab has about 1,200 people living along one side of a muddy creek, several miles from the sea. The houses are most primitive; some are made of mud-and-wattle but others are constructed only out of straw. The inhabitants throw their refuse almost anywhere. It was worse than anything I would have imagined in Iran, for despite poverty, Iranians are a reasonably clean people. Tiyab was a disgrace. I examined the main shops in the village and found that they offered very little indeed aside from locally made mats, chewing gum and candy; very little food was available aside from melons.

Tiyab is almost entirely dependent upon dhows for survival. Since the road is quite literally non-existent in parts between it and Minab, almost all of Tiyab's exports and imports are carried by dhow. Although the place is relatively small, there were twenty-three cargo boats based at Tiyab. During my visit sixteen (including four *booms*) were in the harbour. The inhabitants survive on the export of palm fibre, palm fibre mats and dates, all of which are produced at Tiyab, to Bandar Abbas, Qishm, Hormuz and Dubai. There is also a long-distance trade with India. The dhows take dried dates to the west coast of India and return with cloth, tea, ginger, sandalwood, black pepper and, significantly, mangrove poles. Tiyab is one of the few places in the western Indian Ocean still importing mangrove poles for the construction of houses. Since Tiyab is so dependent on dhows for its survival, one would presume that the village would have a decent harbour, but this is not so. The dhows can only get near Tiyab at high tide and the harbour consists of a narrow channel furrowed from the mud; there are no port facilities at all. I had to wade through muck and mud knee-deep to get out to the dhows. In June, July and August, the dhow captains do not like to travel much because of the heat and relatively rough seas. During these months, many of the Persian dhows are under repair, and these are the reasons for which I found most of Tiyab's fleet present while I was there.[27]

Khamir, Kung and Lingeh

To the west of Bandar Abbas are two towns which I had heard were important dhow ports: Kung and Lingeh. However, absolutely no one with whom I had talked in Tehran knew anything about these places, and none of my friends who are interested in dhows had ever visited them. I was determined to see them for myself, despite any difficulties that might arise in trying to get to them. I was unable to charter a plane from Bandar Abbas, so I was forced to make the 155-mile drive to Lingeh.

On 20 June 1973, I left Bandar Abbas at sunrise for Kung and Lingeh. Seven miles out of town, the tarmac road ended and for the rest of the way I followed a stony, rough track that ran parallel to the coast about ten miles inland. The countryside between Bandar Abbas and Lingeh is bleak with little vegetation and few animals. I passed through quite a few villages, surrounded by the ever present date palms, goats and camels. The people led a traditional existence, unaffected by developments elsewhere in Iran.

Almost half way to Lingeh, I stopped at the port of Khamir, a small town of 3,400 people. Dominating the seafront was a new two-storied Customs House and a new jetty which were built by the Government in the 1960s to help the dhow trade. The Government's effort to boost the trade of Khamir seems to have been highly successful as the total trade had increased six times from 1970–1 to 1972–3 (see Table XXVII). In 1972, 315 dhows departed from Khamir laden with local fresh dates, fruit from Shiraz, and cotton from Shiraz and Kerman.[28] These latter goods are mostly transported some 200 miles to Khamir in lorries, but occasionally camels are used. While I was there, one camel was lying on the beach, recuperating from his arduous task.

TABLE XXVII
DHOW CARGO HANDLED AT KHAMIR PORT
(in kilos)

Year	Imports	Exports	Total
1970–1	388,701	289,279	677,980
1971–2	710,052	1,339,414	2,049,466
1972–3	915,778	3,284,099	4,199,877

Source: Customs Department, Khamir.

Most of the exports are taken to Dubai, and the dhows return with clothes, wheat and personal items. In 1973, the people of Khamir owned fifteen cargo dhows and twenty-nine fishing boats.[29] What impressed me about Khamir was the obvious prosperity of the town due to the Government's interest in improving facilities for the dhow trade. It is a fine example of how good conditions can encourage the dhow trade to the economic benefit of a small society, and I wish other governments, especially in East Africa, would follow suit.

Three miles to the east of Lingeh lies Kung. This town has the distinction of being the most picturesque dhow port in the country. Along the beach I immediately caught sight of many cargo dhows and fishing craft out of the water, with their sterns facing the sea. They were awaiting repairs. Behind them were piles of wood recently imported from India for the construction of new dhows; carpenters were carefully choosing the correct pieces of wood for the building of hulls. The owners of the dhows milled about supervising repairs to their craft and enthusiastically conversing about the new dhows being built. In the background stood buildings typical of the coast of Iran: single and double-storied rectangular stone houses painted white with simple carved wooden doors and window frames. Men in long flowing white robes sat on the steps of their houses drinking coffee and discussing the matters of the day. There were even wind towers on some of the houses, gracefully reaching skywards to trap the smallest breezes off the Persian Gulf.

Kung, more than any other port in the Gulf, resembles a Swahili town in East Africa. In fact, until quite recently, there were strong trading links between the two; many dhows from Kung used to visit Zanzibar, Dar es Salaam and Mombasa annually with cargoes of salt, salted fish and dates; these dhows brought back mangrove poles to Lingeh, Bahrain and Basra. In the early years of this century, many of the residents of Kung were fishermen and catchers of shark.[30]

In 1973, Kung was the major dhow building port in Iran; in fact it was the only port I visited in the country where more than a couple of dhows were being constructed. Not all of them would be for Iranians; I interviewed one *nahoda* from Dubai who had just had his eighty-ton *boom* constructed in Kung for $15,000. Both the engine (which would cost an additional $7,500) and the sails were to be purchased in Dubai, where they would be cheaper due to the absence of taxes. While I was looking at the new *boom*, the owner was preparing to have it towed to Dubai. I asked him why he had his *boom* built in Kung, and he replied that the carpenters and their assistants were more skilled and that they could build a large dhow quicker than the craftsmen in Dubai. Furthermore, he added, the price was less because Iranian labour was cheaper.[31]

I counted forty-five cargo and fishing dhows lying right next to one another along the beach in front of the town. What a superlative sight! Most were out of the water and propped up by poles, in the course of repairs undertaken after a busy season. Around these craft were large quantities of wood, nails, chains, wooden toilets and other dhow paraphernalia. Scores of dogs sought shade in the sand, and donkeys were being led back and forth, carrying the timber which had arrived from Malabar to different parts of the beach. The guard, with a rifle on his back, stood in front of the Customs House and tried to look important, but there was really nothing for him to do. Iranians, Arabs and people of African origin mingled about, putting off hard labour until the intense summer sun began to set. I found this milieu so enthralling that I just wandered about, mixing with the people and watching their activities for hours.

At last, I decided that before it got dark I should drive the remaining four miles to Lingeh to see what this former wealthy port would be like. At the beginning of the century, I knew, Lingeh had had a population consisting of some 5,000 Arabs, 5,000 Persians, 1,500 Africans, and quite a few Indians. The town had been well built with stone and extended for about a mile along the sea. Lingeh was a major entrepôt for southern Persia, importing large quantities of cotton piece-goods and food; the value of imports (which excludes re-exports) was £146,000 per year from 1901 to 1903. Exports comprised carpets, rose-buds, gums, flax-seed, tobacco and fruit, worth a total of £101,000 a year. Re-exports included pearls and grains. There were 455 shops at the beginning of this century, catering to people who came from miles and miles away. Some of these commodities were carried off to other ports on a resident fleet of nineteen *baghlahs* and eighty-six other large sailing dhows. In addition, there were thirty pearl boats which worked mostly on the Arabian side of the Gulf and forty-five fishing vessels.[32]

By the early 1970s, Lingeh had deteriorated so much that I could scarcely believe that only a couple of generations previously it had been prosperous and lively. The rubble from tumbled down stone buildings impeded my walk through the old part of the town, and wistfully I looked up at the abandoned balconied residences where not so long ago bejewelled and lavishly dressed ladies would have held their tea parties. Now on the seafront rested the remains of decaying dhows. I strolled aimlessly around, hoping to see some activity, but there was little going on. The main old port was equally depressing. I climbed up on to the roofs of some of the old stone buildings with mangrove pole rafters, carefully avoiding balancing against the crumbling remains of wind towers, and focused my camera to take pictures and to count the dhows in the sea before me. There were only three cargo dhows (all *booms*) and nine fishing dhows (all *lanchas*). I was told that there were more cargo dhows but that they were out trading in other ports. I could well understand why there were so few craft around: the remaining Lingeh population was poverty-stricken and even the fishermen take their catch elsewhere to sell.

Had I visited Lingeh a year or so later, there would have been hardly any vestige of its famous past visible: the old residential area was being gutted to make room for a new road and I learned that a new port would soon be constructed. The people living in Lingeh, then housed behind the old sections in a rather dirty and dusty settlement, would move back on to the seafront in the future, and into bland, modern little abodes. What a shame that modernization could not preserve some of the gracious old structures. I ambled around the remains of what had been extremely attractive houses, overlooking the waters of the Persian Gulf and was completely lost in my reflections. The setting sun gave way to twilight and I knew that I ought to head back to the car. I rounded one more corner, when suddenly my reveries were rudely interrupted and I was confronted by a large noisy monster with two bright lights shining directly into my eyes; ruefully, I recognized my monster to be a bulldozer, determinedly engaged in mowing the fine old buildings deep down into the ground. The driver could not comprehend why I was there and shook his head completely dismayed when I pointed out that I had been taking photographs of the empty town.

Before attempting the long drive back to Bandar Abbas, I visited the present residential and commercial section of Lingeh, which is located behind the old port area. Although there was considerably more going on there, this part of the town had a rundown appearance, presaging, to my mind, an even more imminent need for bulldozers. I visited the main hotel, the Koorish, to see if I could get some dinner, but it did not even have a restaurant. I saw people through the upstairs windows cooking in their rooms which looked rather foreboding. I decided to ignore my hunger and head quickly back to Bandar Abbas.

The old port of Bandar Lingeh

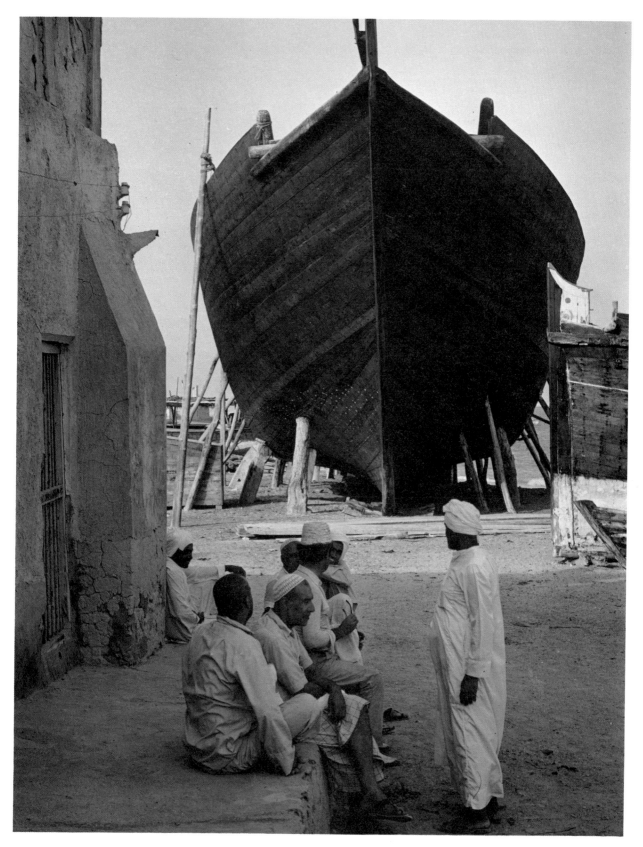

Huge dhow under construction at Kung

Right, A Bajun of Lamu

Below, A man paddling a canoe out to a dhow
in Old Port, Mombasa

Hormuz

The legendary lore and opulence of the island of Hormuz had fascinated me from the time I had first thought of studying the Indian Ocean. Chryssee, too, was enthralled with the idea of visiting the place; laughingly, she confessed she had had no idea where to look for it in an atlas when, in school, she had read Milton's *Paradise Lost* and was told to find out about the reference to 'the wealth of Ormuz'. In a nineteenth-century history book of Iran, I remembered coming across an Eastern saying that 'were the world a ring, Hormuz would be the jewel in it'. Hormuz, being less than sixteen miles from Bandar Abbas, I had no doubt that we could get a power boat and reach there within an hour or so with no difficulty at all. Such was not to be the case. Bureaucratic red tape impeded my efforts for several days: I needed to have a permit from the authorities in Iran to go anywhere near the Strait of Hormuz (for security reasons, since it guards the entrance into the Gulf), and when I made inquiries about going there, I was met with odd stares from officialdom: why would any tourist want to go to that forsaken island—there isn't even any water there, they said. I already knew that—there never had been. Since its founding many centuries ago, the island capital (there was an earlier settlement of the same name on the mainland, not far from the present Minab) has had to rely on dhows to bring over water for its inhabitants who, at one time, numbered 40,000. Trying to dissuade us from the trip, even after I finally obtained the official permission, we were informed that there were no power boats available for our transport. I sought help from a businessman who had two boats which had outboard engines, whom I had met in the old port. We haggled for hours and when he finally agreed to contemplate my proposal to hire one of his boats for a day, he set out to find his captains to discuss the matter with them. In the evening, he came back and said that both boats were broken down and he would have to get spare parts for them from Tehran. If we would wait for a week or ten days, he would try to arrange a trip for us then . . . Frustrated and annoyed, I plodded my way back to the hotel, at which point Chryssee suggested that we go by dhow. It could take hours, or if the wind stopped, all day. 'What has happened to your spirit of romance?' Chryssee chided me. I could not at the moment think of a suitable retort, so we set about looking for a free dhow the next morning. Again, I came up against the bureaucrats: a foreigner cannot just walk up to a dhow captain in port and make arrangements for going wherever he wishes by sea. But, in the end, we prevailed and armed with yet another official permit, sailed off to fabled Hormuz on one of the hottest mornings of the year, at the end of June.

We almost were not able to leave even then. Chryssee was determined to take a photograph of what was indeed an unusual sight to our eyes—live camels in the process of being loaded by a crane into a dhow at anchor in the port. Had she taken the picture, we should surely have been arrested for the Iranian Government is most adamant that no photographs be taken in any of the new ports. None the less, it was quite a spectacle. Each camel, in turn, was made to lie down. A man then proceeded to tie the two back feet together and then the front feet. He next took a heavy cloth and slipped it under the camel's belly, tying the ends to the hook of a mechanical crane. Another man, operating the crane, was given the go-ahead sign, and he lifted the camel into the air (the camel protesting with loud grunts against the indignity of his situation) and then slowly lowered it down into the waiting dhow. Someone there helped place the poor beast into a vacant space and untied the cloth. I was amazed to see how tightly they were packing the camels together aboard the dhow. Difficulties arose when it was a baby camel's turn to be moved. Half in the water, several helpers joined in to try to hold its neck while they swung the crane over to the dhow; they were afraid that the little one would break its neck in panic. He was safely transferred in the end, and would, with the others, reach Dubai twelve hours later. Despite Chryssee's insistence that a photograph of the operation, showing how a modern crane is used for the transport on to a dhow of one of the oldest trade items, would surely be one of our best, I did not want to risk a jail sentence for a permanent reminder of a bunch of howling and hysterical camels in a filthy dhow.

The dhow we had managed to hire for our trip to Hormuz was a *lancha* 45 feet long, with a crew of three, including, typically enough, a young boy to carry out the odd jobs. It took us two hours and twenty-five minutes to reach our destination, even with the help of an engine, because the wind was against us and the sea quite rough with waves breaking all around us. Fortunately, I did not have to use the primitive toilet facilities which consisted of a circular wooden container with a hole in the bottom perched precariously on the outside of the stern. If I had tried to climb into that unstable structure, I would probably have been tossed overboard by the severe rolling of the dhow. What an ignoble end that would have made to my years of research on dhows!

The history of Old Hormuz, on the mainland, goes back to the tenth century. This is the Hormuz that Marco Polo visited in 1272 and again in 1293. He was much impressed:

> Merchants come thither from India, with ships loaded with spicery and precious stones, pearls, cloths of silk and gold, elephants' teeth, and many other wares, which they sell to the merchants of Hormos, and which these in turn carry all over the world to dispose of again. In fact, 'tis a city of immense trade . . .
>
> In this country they make a wine of dates mixt with spices, which is very good. When any one not used to it first drinks this wine, it causes repeated and violent purges, but afterwards he is all the better for it, and gets fat upon it . . .
>
> The people are black, and are worshippers of Mahommet . . . In summer a wind often blows across the sands which encompass the plain, so intolerably hot that it would kill everybody, were it not that when they perceive the wind coming they plunge into the water up to the neck, and so abide until the wind has ceased.[33]

Marco Polo also mentioned the horses of Hormuz. Dealers arranged their transport on to India, especially to Malabar, whose local king imported as many as 2,000 every year:

> The reason why they want so many horses every year is that by the end of the year there shall not be one hundred of them remaining, for they all die off. And this arises from mismanagement, for those people do not know in the least how to treat a horse; and besides they have no farriers. The horse merchants not only never bring any farriers with them, but also prevent any farrier from going thither, less that should in any degree baulk the sale of horses, which brings them in every year such vast gains.[34]

Perhaps it was a just retribution that Old Hormuz was 'severely and repeatedly harassed by raids of Tartar horsemen'.[35] Consequently, the King of Hormuz, Mir Bahdin Ayaz Sayfin, in 1301, abandoned his city and founded a new capital on the island of Jirun, to which he gave the same name. The island was, of course, much easier to protect, and the new Hormuz earned a reputation for magnificence that soon outshone the old:

> Hormuz became the capital of an empire which comprehended a considerable part of Arabia on one side, and Persia on the other. At the time of the arrival of the foreign merchants, it afforded a more splendid and agreeable scene than any city in the East. Persons from all parts of the globe exchanged their commodities and transacted their business with an air of politeness and attention, which are seldom seen in other places of trade. The streets were covered with mats and in some places with carpets, and the linen awnings which were suspended from the tops of the houses, prevented any inconvenience from the heat of the sun. Indian cabinets inlaid with gilded vases or china filled with flowering shrubs, or aromatic plants, adorned their apartments. Camels laden with water were stationed in the public squares. Persian wines, perfumes, and all the delicacies of the table were furnished in the greatest abundance, and they had the music of the East in its highest perfection. In short, universal opulence, and extensive commerce, politeness in the men and gallantry in the women, united all their attentions to make this city the seat of pleasure.[36]

By the time of Ibn Battuta's visit in 1355, Hormuz had become world renowned, particularly for its 'many magnificent bazaars'.[37] Throughout the remaining fourteenth and on into the fifteenth century, Hormuz flourished and was the wealthiest and most important trading centre in the

Esmond Bradley Martin
walking towards the Portuguese
fort at Hormuz

entire Gulf. Duarte Barbosa, in the early sixteenth century, also gave a detailed description of Hormuz; some excerpts from his account read as follows:

> The inhabitants of this island and city are Persians and Arabs . . . There are among them very rich merchants, and many ships . . . Many horses from Arabia and Persia [are imports], of which they carry away to India every year as many as five or six hundred, and at times a thousand;[38] and the ships which export these horses load much salt, dates and raisins, and sulphur . . .
> These Moors of Ormuz are . . . very agreeable and polite people . . . Their food is of very good meats, very well cooked, wheaten bread, and very good rice . . . They drink wine of grapes in secret, because their law forbids it them, and the water which they drink is flavoured with pistachio nuts, and set to cool . . . And all the noblemen and honourable merchants always take, wherever they go, both in the streets and in public places, and on the road, a page with a bottle of water, which is covered underneath with silver, or with a silver cap, as much for state and show as for use and comfort.[39]

In the opening years of the sixteenth century, the Portuguese arrived in the Indian Ocean, determined to take control of the trade of East Africa, Arabia, India and the Persian Gulf for the Portuguese Crown. After conquering the major towns in East Africa, a Portuguese fleet under Affonso de Albuquerque arrived off the island of Hormuz in 1506. Arrogantly, Captain Albuquerque threatened that he would take the great city of Hormuz by force if the King did

216

not agree to become his vassal and pay him tribute. The King refused and organized his fleet of 200 ships and 15,000 men for the defence of Hormuz. But Portuguese fire power was too great and the entire fleet of the King was destroyed, and the outskirts of Hormuz burnt to the ground. The King capitulated and allowed Albuquerque to build a fort which was commenced on 24 October 1507. After the principal tower was completed in January 1508, Albuquerque sailed away to the great relief of the inhabitants of Hormuz.[40]

During the Portuguese occupation of Hormuz, from 1506 until 1622, the city remained prosperous with traders from all over the Indian Ocean coming to buy and sell their commodities there. The main fort, which still stands today, was completed around 1515, and the Portuguese also supervised the building of Catholic churches, monasteries and domestic houses in the city.

In 1622, the Persians under Shah Abbas finally gathered enough courage and strength to expel the Portuguese from Hormuz, but they lacked the warships necessary for such an effort. By chance, an English fleet was then in the Gulf, and the commander of the Persian troops persuaded the English to join them, by suggesting that they might lose some of their trading privileges in Persia should they refuse to do so. On 9 February, a combined Anglo-Persian fleet set sail from Bandar Abbas. The following day, the Persians landed on the island and forced the Portuguese into their fort. However, they were unable to dislodge them, and their huge army of 45,000 men soon ran out of food and water on the desolate island. By April, the Portuguese also had run out of provisions, and many of the defenders became so ill that on 23 April the Portuguese garrison of 3,000 men surrendered. The English allowed them to proceed safely to Muscat and Suhar. During the siege, the English had only lost twenty dead, but the Persians one thousand. Hormuz was then looted by both the English and the Persians. Shah Abbas decided to abandon the island and developed instead Bandar Abbas to become the major port of Persia. By 1627, only five years after it had been sacked, Hormuz was in a rapid state of decay. The city never recovered its former glory and prosperity.[41]

In the early years of this century, Hormuz was little more than a sadly neglected village. During the cool season when the iron oxide and salt mines were worked, the population increased to 1,200, occupying some 200 houses, but during the torrid summer months over one-half of the people left for Minab, where they found employment picking the dates. It is hard to believe that 400 years earlier, some 40,000 people lived on this island.[42] In 1905, most of the inhabitants were poor miners, fishermen and sailors. They had fifteen dhows, including their fishing boats, which accounted for 172 jobs.[43] About the only reminder of the grandeur that Hormuz had once known was the presence of the enormous Portuguese fort, but even that imposing edifice was partly in ruins due to the removal of stones from it for the construction of small houses.

When we pulled into the small jetty at Hormuz, we found ourselves right in front of the impressive castle-like Portuguese fortification, but before we could explore it we were told in no uncertain terms that we would have to report to the local police station. There, the policeman, suffering from the scorching heat of the midday summer sun, gave a cursory glance at our permits, offered us a glass of water, and then returned to his bed. The heat was the most torrid I had ever experienced. Why did the Arabs, Persians and Portuguese all choose this barren island without even water as the location for their capitals in the Persian Gulf?

Lorimer's description of Hormuz at the turn of the century could be used today: the population numbers the same; employment is the same, fishing, cargo transport by dhow and mining the red oxide (which is stored under a large, ugly metal shed next to the fort); five local cargo dhows were in the harbour when we made our visit; and, very likely, stones are still being removed from the fort from time to time to help out on new construction sites.

Walking through the village of Hormuz, Chryssee and I were slightly disappointed by the simplicity of the houses made of stone and mud bricks; few were taller than two storeys, but on the roofs of almost every one was a thatched shed underneath which a couple of beds were placed. At the time of our arrival, most of the people were sleeping on their roofs, trying to catch as much as possible of the sea breezes. Later, when they began to stir, they were shocked to see strangers in their midst. What were foreigners doing in Hormuz in June? We could not answer their questions as we could not speak Farsi or Arabic. In sympathy, many of the inhabitants offered us their scarce water which is still brought to them from the mainland by dhow. After ambling for a while through the dusty streets which, because of their past, intrigued us, we slowly made our way back to the fort.

Visiting the colossal Portuguese fort at Hormuz is in itself worth a trip to the Persian Gulf. Three of the four sides of it are in reasonably fine shape; the fourth, which is facing the sea, has almost completely disappeared, mainly due

A camel, one of the oldest means of land transport, next to the wreck of a dhow, the oldest form of long distance transport in the Indian Ocean; photographed at Khamir

to erosion from the sea, but also, I suspect, because this is the side from which stones have been removed for other building purposes. The huge, imposing wall facing the town is the most complete of all, and from the top of it one can get a spectacular view of what remains of the once mighty Hormuz and of the hills of the island in the background. There are still some old cannons lying about, and the many goats resident in the village enjoy perching upon them. Chryssee and I crawled over every nook and cranny of the fortification. The architect had certainly known his priorities and he had taken great care in erecting his first requirement, that gigantic wall surrounding the entire fort. His second requisite was the construction of numerous cisterns for the storage of enormous quantities of water. Even here aesthetics were not overlooked; the pillars around the smaller ones were elaborately decorated on top. We examined in great detail one of the largest, which was fifteen feet deep and had a roof designed to catch in its opening holes every drop of rainwater and was supported by massive stone pillars. This particular cistern was so big that it had a walkway around it just under the roof. There were many rooms inside the fort, some of which had vaulted arches connecting them one with another. I wished I could have spent days there.

In the early evening we returned to our dhow to begin the voyage back to Bandar Abbas. Unlike in the morning when the sea had been rough and the sky hazy, the sea had become calm and the visibility was excellent. On board, the young boy sang songs of the sea and of valiant and courageous heroes of the past. As the Portuguese fort slowly receded from our view, I thought back to the era when Hormuz had indeed been the jewel in the Indian Ocean. I remembered with a pang of regret the great Anglo-Persian siege of 1622, and in my mind's eye imagined the sea filled with hundreds of dhows transporting the 45,000 troops who came to destroy Portuguese power in Hormuz and left one of the world's great cities in smouldering ruins . . .

219

The Survival of the Dhow

The two thousand-year-old dhow trade, from the time of Christ until the arrival of the Europeans in the Indian Ocean in 1498, was a free trade. The dhow captains went where they pleased and carried whatever cargo they wished. However, when the Portuguese came into the Indian Ocean, they conquered many of the important trading centres: Kilwa, Mombasa, Muscat, Hormuz and Goa. Within only fifteen years, the Portuguese controlled most of the strategic towns of East Africa, Arabia and India, and at the same time tried to dominate the rich trade of this vast region. The Portuguese attempted to monopolize the gold and ivory trade of eastern Africa, the horse trade of Hormuz, the textiles of western India, and the spice trade of Malabar by enforcing a law requiring all non-Portuguese vessels to carry passports (*cartazes*). Not to do so risked forfeiture of life, ship and goods.[1] The Portuguese also introduced other restrictions on the dhows and their cargoes in order to raise revenue for the Portuguese Crown. They were not highly successful in their attempts to interfere with free trade: many of the dhow captains disregarded the regulations and did carry illegal (from the European point of view) commodities to ports where they were not allowed to go. This contraband trade was probably the beginning of large scale smuggling which has prevailed in the Indian Ocean ever since.

With the decline of Portuguese control in the Indian Ocean from the middle of the seventeenth century, the danger of being caught decreased because the Portuguese were unable to control the movement of dhows. But early in the nineteenth century, the British Government took over as the major outside power. By the end of the nineteenth century, the British politically controlled or had strong influence in East Africa, Arabia, the Persian Gulf and India. To

220

supervise the implementation of the Moresby Treaty of 1822 and other treaties which restricted the slave trade of the Indian Ocean, the British began actively patrolling the western Indian Ocean to ascertain whether dhow captains were transporting slaves illegally. They took very strong action against those they caught infringing their laws. Lieutenant Charles Smith of H.M.S. *London*, during a twenty-one-month period from 1880 to 1882, sighted 513 dhows off East Africa, boarded 420 of them and released 190 slaves.[2] Despite gallant efforts on the part of the British anti-slavery patrols, thousands of slaves were sent illegally to Arabia and the Persian Gulf, and many others were smuggled from Kilwa to various pick-up points along the East African coast in the late nineteenth century. Dhows were responsible for the movement of Africans as slaves to Arabia and the Persian Gulf.

There were other goods aside from slaves that dhow captains smuggled to and from Indian Ocean ports in the nineteenth century. Opium, which was produced in Persia in considerable quantities, was smuggled out of Bushire and Bandar Abbas on dhows destined for the west coast of India in the 1850s. The merchants of the Persian ports also at that time supplied legally by dhow 1,800 pounds of opium to Muscat, the main entrepôt for this drug. From there, the Hindu traders legally and illegally sent opium on dhows to Zanzibar, Karachi, Kutch and Malabar.[3] Arms constituted another clandestine cargo carried on dhows in the nineteenth century. In 1889, many *jahazis*, *mashuas* and even canoes carried arms illicitly from Zanzibar to German-occupied Tanganyika.[4] On a larger scale, guns and ammunition were supplied to the elite of Ethiopia throughout the nineteenth century by dhows from Yemen, Aden, Djibouti and Somali ports.

By the beginning of the twentieth century, the transportation of slaves by dhow from one port in East Africa to another and from East Africa to Arabia and the Persian Gulf had almost entirely stopped. There was one major exception, however, and that was the smuggling of Africans from Ethiopia in dhows to Yemen and Arabia. The last dhow caught carrying slaves from Ethiopia was captured in 1923, but this traffic undoubtedly continued longer, the dhows using secluded harbours protected by coral reefs.[5] Furthermore, there was still a demand for slaves in Saudi Arabia and some of the Trucial States until around 1960. In 1958 in Saudi Arabia, a male slave was worth $420 and an attractive female was valued at $2,000. The government of Saudi Arabia did not abolish the status of slavery until 1962,[6] and was one of the last countries in the world to do so.

With the decline of the slave trade, the dhow captains continued to carry people illegally. In the Arabian Gulf, thousands and thousands of Persians, Pakistanis, and Indians have been smuggled into the wealthy shaikhdoms since World War II, and this is still going on today. Some of the dhow owners take advantage of the poor immigrants, setting their human cargo ashore at night at low tide, on what looks like the mainland but is actually a sand spit or an island. In the morning, at high tide, the immigrants are either picked up by police boats or are forced to swim towards the shore in shark-infested waters to avoid drowning.[7] The numbers of people carried to the shaikhdoms illegally from the 1950s to the mid-1970s easily surpassed the total number of slaves imported into all of Arabia and the Gulf for the entire nineteenth century. Occasionally, there are human disasters in this lucrative business. In

September 1976, Reuter's News Agency reported that 1,000 illegal Pakistani immigrants were thrown overboard from two dhows off the United Arab Emirates when the dhow crews spotted the police; eleven of these unfortunate people drowned.[8] This horrifying story is similar to the drastic action sometimes taken by dhow crews a century earlier when British anti-slavery ships approached them.

During political upheavals, dhow captains help transport people illegally out of a country. After the Revolution in Zanzibar in 1964, many Arabs and Indians wished to leave Zanzibar and Pemba islands but were refused official permission. Therefore, some of the people simply hired a *ngalawa* or a *mashua* and sailed to Dar es Salaam. Again, early in the 1970s, when many Asians were dismissed from their jobs or had their shops in Zanzibar town confiscated from them and there was an acute shortage of all goods, especially food, many Asians left on dhows. To prevent the smuggling of people to the mainland, the Zanzibar Government prohibited all Indians from going out on boats to fish (a popular sport) and outlawed the movement of dhows at night. Despite restrictions, the Asians continued to hire *mashuas* for about Shs.50 to go to Dar es Salaam. When strict patrolling by the authorities began, the dhow captains charged up to Shs.1,000 for one trip. Most of these dhows departed from Zanzibar town because the majority of the Asians lived there, and detection was more difficult as there was always a large dhow fleet in the harbour. Hundreds of Asians and Arabs also escaped to the Tanzanian mainland at night, under cover of darkness, in small boats. The Asians satirically called this type of transport their V.C. 10 service.[9]

On Pemba island, dhow owners and captains have amassed small fortunes by smuggling cloves to Kenya. Before the Revolution, there was no clove smuggling because the farmers received a high percentage of the world market price. Afterwards, with living conditions becoming more difficult and the world market price of cloves rising steeply in 1967, the clove growers were less and less content to receive the Government's price for their cloves. In 1975, they were only paid by the Zanzibar Government eleven per cent of the world market price, and it is not surprising that they were willing to pay considerable sums of money to dhow captains who would take the risk of smuggling their cloves to the Tanzanian mainland and to Kenya. It was particularly advantageous to sell the cloves in Kenya for the Kenyan shilling was double the value of the Tanzanian shilling on the black market. When the dhows returned from Kenya to Pemba they often brought with them maize meal and sugar which they also moved clandestinely. From 1 July 1970 to 30 June 1971, the Zanzibar customs authorities captured $4,764,500 worth of cloves (roughly 1,400 tons) being smuggled out of the country. The Government, in fact, estimated that in 1975 about a third of the entire clove crop was successfully smuggled out of the country. Although the death penalty was mandatory for all those people convicted of smuggling cloves, this commerce continued to flourish through the mid 1970s. New laws, regulations and modern patrol boats have had little effect in trying to stop huge quantities of cloves illicitly leaving Zanzibar.[10]

Although there are not a great number of dhows registered in Zanzibar, many, if not most of them, have been involved with some type of illegal movement of goods since the Revolution. Perhaps the fundamental reason for this lies in the fact that there are so many restrictions on trade. Dhow crew even smuggle pineapples out of Zanzibar, where, in 1976, they sold for U.S. four cents each and took them to Dar es Salaam where they could get ten cents for one or to Mombasa where the price was seventeen cents per pineapple. Black pepper is another commodity grown on Zanzibar which sells for a higher price on the mainland and which, consequently, dhow crew also illegally move out of the country. Since the Revolution, in spite of more and more restrictions imposed on the movement of dhows and almost regardless of the severe penalties imposed on convicted smugglers, smuggling from Zanzibar has not declined; it may even be on the increase.

There is smuggling from mainland Tanzania as well. For many decades, foreign dhows have been taking out far more mangrove poles from the Rufiji than their licences from the Forest Department have allowed. Most foreign dhow crews that have come into the Rufiji Delta since the late 1930s have paid royalty on only about half of the poles that they have exported.[11] I wonder, had there been strict enforcement of the regulations by the Forest Department, whether so many foreign dhows would have sailed down into the mosquito-infested swamps during the rainy season to organize the cutting of mangrove poles for export. I seriously doubt it; I think, instead, the dhow captains would have paid slightly higher prices for the mangrove poles found in Kenya and would not have made the effort to go down into the swamps of the Rufiji.

During most of this century, the foreign dhows which have been coming into Kenya have, officially, been taking out much more produce than they have brought in. How are the dhow captains paying for this difference? There is not much evidence that they cash foreign travellers' cheques, and it is not legal for them to import Kenyan shillings, to which they probably do not have access anyway. Some of them coming into Mombasa illicitly bring in gold, foreign currencies and occasionally drugs, such as opium. Furthermore, I believe that some of the Kenyan businessmen use dhows as a method of avoiding exchange control. In other words, Mombasa merchants either hire dhows to take to Arabia and especially the Gulf shaikhdoms large quantities of ghee, cotton seed oil, grain, tea and coffee, or sell these products directly to the dhow captains. When the products are sold in the Gulf, the profit the businessmen make from them is paid in hard currency and does not come back into Kenya but is transferred to the foreign bank account of the Kenyan businessman.

There has been a lot of talk about foreign dhows smuggling ivory out of East Africa to Arabia and India. There is no doubt that ivory is taken out illegally. Ian Parker, one of the world authorities on the ivory trade writes:

> During the period 1959–73 the East African Customs record shows only .97 of a ton [of ivory] was shipped to the Persian Gulf. During these years Hong Kong imported 71 tons from the Gulf, a region with no known elephant populations! It seems probable that this ivory arrived there in the first instance aboard dhows sailing from the East African coast.[12]

The difficult question to answer is how did $840,000 worth of ivory get on to dhows and get transported out of East Africa without detection. Some of the tusks may have been collected from the Rufiji, an area which has thousands of elephants and is isolated from the Tanzanian government authorities.[13] Perhaps this ivory was loaded on to the bottom of the dhows and mangrove poles put on top to conceal the tusks. I have been told that this happens, but I have never actually seen it myself. As far as East African dhows are concerned, there is little evidence that Kenyan craft are involved in a big way in smuggled goods, though, of course, as earlier mentioned, Tanzanian craft regularly smuggle cloves, coconuts, pepper, seashells and food, particularly to and from the islands of Zanzibar, Pemba and Mafia.

In the wealthy shaikhdoms, dhows are the primary means of transport for the illegal importation of thousands and thousands of people especially to Kuwait, Qatar and the United Arab Emirates. Smuggling people has become an extremely lucrative business since the 1950s, and keeps many of the dhow captains busy plying from Iran, Pakistan and India, where they pick up the immigrants for the shaikhdoms, dumping them secretly at night.

Since the import duties in the Arabian shaikhdoms are extremely low, dhow captains have not generally found it profitable to bother with bringing in smuggled merchandise. However, hard drugs and hashish are imported illegally from Iran and Pakistan; and liquor, which is banned in Kuwait, is smuggled in on dhows from Iraq and Iran. On the other side of the Gulf, in Iran, where the taxes are very high, many dhow owners have made their fortunes by smuggling in manufactured goods such as radios, cars, record players and refrigerators. Without this two-way traffic whereby Iranian, Pakistani and Indian immigrants are smuggled into the shaikhdoms and in return manufactured goods from the shaikhdoms are smuggled into Iran, Pakistan and India, the number of dhows and the profits that the owners make would be small.

As far as smuggling commodities on dhows is concerned, Dubai takes the prize as the most important port from which goods are smuggled into other countries. Multiplying, as it does, many times the earnings made from smuggling to other Gulf ports and to Iran, Dubai's gold trade to India, which is legal as far as Dubai is concerned, is the most phenomenal in the world. From the mid-1960s until at least 1973, a minimum of $300,000,000 worth of gold was annually exported from there on Dubai and Indian dhows, to be smuggled into ports on the west coast of India. (In order to pay for this gold, the Indians illicitly exported silver, drugs and hard currencies.) I believe that most of the dhows that put into tiny Dubai, which has the greatest foreign dhow traffic in the Indian Ocean, are involved in purchasing goods there which they smuggle into other countries.

Conclusion

The dhow has survived. It has survived adverse regulations, apparently more efficient transport systems, modernization in both material and mind, and, because of its unique characteristics and the enterprise of owners and captains, the dhow shows promise of being able to cope with whatever the future may bring.

The dhows we now see sailing the western Indian Ocean are the descendants of the dhows of Ibn Battuta's time. Today's dhow is generally bigger (though its crew is not), certainly less elegant-looking, usually motorized, but still basically the same vessel it was even two thousand years ago. True it is that such types of dhows as the *mtepe*, with the planks of its hull sewn together with coconut fibre and its cumbersome matting sail, which plied the East African coastal waters until the 1920s, will never again be seen. The *mtepe* gave way to the nailed hull and cloth sail of the *jahazi*, just as other types of dhows long ago gave way to innovations, all of which were introduced to improve efficiency. The dhow's ability to respond to modernization has enabled it, amazingly enough, to compete with the steamship in certain conditions.

While the steamship requires a proper port for docking, the dhow can slip through little creeks and into harbours which perhaps do not even deserve the dignity of that name. The steamship, moreover, does not always arrive at the moment perishable produce is ready for shipping, and therefore costly refrigeration facilities are necessary for storage. Also, a port may not have enough produce to make a steamship trip profitable. But, the dhow is always readily available to transport lesser bulk at any desired time, except when the seas are too rough. For many smaller places, the dhow is, in fact, much better suited for transport purposes than, say, a schooner, which would additionally be more expensive to run and would entail maintenance problems.

One may suggest that the dhow is an outdated vessel and wonder who, in this modern age, is going to build a dhow. From my travels in western Indian Ocean ports I have seen everywhere a demand for dhows. I have found old men still teaching the younger generation in Kung, Kuwait, Bahrain, India, Zanzibar and Lamu their ageless craftsmanship. And, even if not so many dhows have been constructed over the past twenty years in East Africa, the ones that are there are being put to more frequent use than in the past.

It is not likely that one will again see the vast numbers of dhows from Arabia, the Gulf and India that came to East Africa during the 1950s because this long-distance trade no longer seems to be profitable. Even if Zanzibar opened up again, it is doubtful that many foreign dhows would return due to the radical changes that the economic infrastructure has undergone since the 1964 Revolution. Furthermore, it may well be that the local dhow trade in Kenya is doomed to extinction sometime in the not too distant future. The Kenyan dhow owners have not installed engines in their *jahazis* and *mashuas* to enable them to ply the Indian Ocean during the south-west monsoon. Trucks have had to be relied upon to transport goods from one port to another out of the dhow season, and now that there are excellent roads connecting most of the Kenyan ports, trucking has become more economical than shipping.

Such is not the case, however, in the Gulf ports, Pakistan and India. The dhow's special characteristics—the ability to enter small harbours where steamships cannot go, flexibility in use and the availability to sail at any time, lower costs of production and maintenance, and, especially, its advantages for smuggling—will enable the dhow to compete as a means of transport in the western India Ocean for many years to come.

We owe much to the ingenuity and resourcefulness of dhow captains and dhow owners for the survival of the dhow. Not only have they been willing to experiment with modifications to give commercial advantages to their craft, they have also, for the past five hundred years, risked their wealth and sometimes their lives to carry contraband. During this century, in particular, smuggling has become the most profitable and widespread business of the dhow. Quick to perceive which products are in demand, the men of the dhows will arrange for their transport, at a price, with few questions asked. Nefarious trading of cargoes in the east is not about to die.

Notes

CHAPTER ONE

1. East Africa refers to the present-day countries of Kenya, Uganda and Tanzania, while eastern Africa also includes Somalia, Ethiopia and Mozambique.
2. Wilfred H. Schoff (ed.), *The Periplus of the Erythraen Sea: Travel and Trade in the Indian Ocean by a Merchant of the First Century* (New York, 1912), pp. 28–9.
3. Schoff, pp. 27–8.
4. Schoff, p. 28.
5. H. C. Baxter, 'Pangani: The Trade Centre of Ancient History', *Tanganyika Notes and Records*, No. 17 (June 1944), pp. 17–18.
6. Neville Chittick, 'The Coast before the Arrival of the Portuguese', *Zamani, A Survey of East African History*, B. A. Ogot and J. A. Kieran (eds.), (Nairobi, 1968), p. 103.
7. Schoff, p. 28.
8. Marco Polo, *The Book of Ser Marco Polo, the Venetian, Concerning the Kingdoms and the Marvels of the East*, The Yule Edition (New York, 1969), pp. 49–50.
9. G. S. P. Freeman-Grenville, *The East African Coast: Select Documents from the First to the earlier Nineteenth Century* (Oxford, 1962), p. 4.
10. Neville Chittick, 'Discoveries in the Lamu Archipelago', *Azania*, Vol. II (1967), pp. 46 and 66.
11. The following paragraphs are adapted from Chryssee MacCasler Perry Martin and Esmond Bradley Martin, *Quest for the Past: An Historical Guide to the Lamu Archipelago* (Nairobi, 1973), pp. 1 and 2.
12. Freeman-Grenville, p. 15.
13. Freeman-Grenville, p. 16.
14. Freeman-Grenville, p. 14.
15. Friedrich Hirth and W. W. Rockhill (eds.), *Chao Jua-Kua on the Chinese and Arab Trade in the Twelfth and Thirteenth Centuries* (Amsterdam, 1966), pp. 126, 128, 131 and 237.
16. Paul Wheatley, 'A Corner of the Western Ocean, Additional Notes on Chinese Relations with East Africa', paper read at the conference 'East Africa and the Orient: Historical Problems of the Pre-Colonial Era', Nairobi, 1967.
17. J. H. Clive, 'A Short History of Lamu, Kenya', mimeographed paper, 1933.
18. M. Guillain, *Documents sur l'histoire, la géographie et le commerce de l'Afrique Orientale* (Paris, 1856), Vol. I, pp. 299–300.
19. Marco Polo, pp. 284–5.
20. See Neville Chittick, 'Kilwa: A Preliminary Report', *Azania*, Vol. I (1966), pp. 1–36.
21. J. V. G. Mills (ed.), *Ma Huan. Ying-Yai Sheng-Lan: The Overall Survey of the Ocean's Shores [1433]* (Cambridge, 1970), pp. 5–7.
22. J. J. L. Duyvendak, *China's Discovery of Africa* (London, 1949), p. 33.
23. Duyvendak, p. 33.
24. James S. Kirkman, *Men and Monuments on the East African Coast* (London, 1964), p. 89.
25. Mills, p. 10.
26. Duyvendak, p. 34.
27. Duyvendak, p. 35.

CHAPTER TWO

1. Edouard Barbuse, 'Description of the Situation, Customs and Produce of Various Places in Africa', *Documents on the Portuguese in Mozambique and Central Africa*, Vol. V (London, 1966), p. 379; Justus Strandes, *The Portuguese Period in East Africa*, trans. Jean F. Wallwork (Nairobi, 1961), pp. 27–8 and 30; Gaspar Correa, 'Lendas da India', *The Three Voyages of Vasco da Gama*, trans. Henry Stanley (London, 1869), pp. 120, 130 and 257–8; Armando Cortesao, *The Suma Oriental of Tomé Pires* (London, 1944), p. 47; William Brooks Greenlee, *The Voyage of Pedro Alvares Cabral to Brazil and India* (London, 1938), p. 67; and James Kirkman, *The Arab City of Gedi* (Oxford, 1954), pp. 95 and 151.
2. Gaspar Correa, pp. 291–306.
3. E. G. Ravenstein (ed.), *A Journal of the First Voyage of Vasco da Gama, 1497–1499* (London, 1898), pp. 42–3.

4. For a description of Swahili Culture, see: Esmond Bradley Martin, 'The Historic Coast: From Vanga to Mombasa', *Africana*, Vol. IV, No. 10 (July 1972), p. 33; James de Vere Allen, *Lamu* (Nairobi, 1972); and James de Vere Allen, *Lamu Town: A Guide* (Mombasa, 1974).

5. Friar Joao dos Santos in the 1590s observed that the people make 'many good silk and cotton cloths, especially in the island of Pate, where there are many weavers . . .' (Joao dos Santos, 'Aethiopian Oriental', *Hakluytus Posthumus or Purchas his Pigrimes*, Vol. IX, trans. Samuel Purchas, Glasgow, 1905, p. 244).

6. For a description of the traditional, aristocratic manner of taking meals, see Emily Ruete: *Memoirs of an Arabian Princess: An Autobiography* (New York, 1888), pp. 57–60. Emily Ruete was a daughter of Seyyid Said.

7. Kirkman, *Men and Monuments*, p. 119.

8. H. A. R. Gibb (ed.), *The Travels of Ibn Battuta A.D. 1225–1254* (Cambridge, 1962), Vol. II, p. 376.

9. Esmond Bradley Martin, *The History of Malindi: A Geographical Analysis of an East African Coastal Town from the Portuguese Period to the Present* (Nairobi, 1973), pp. 45–6.

10. Strandes, p. 64.

11. Strandes, p. 64.

12. F. J. Berg, 'The Coast from the Portuguese Invasion to the Rise of the Zanzibar Sultanate', *Zamani*, pp. 124–5; Edward A. Alpers, *Ivory and Slaves in East Central Africa* (London, 1975), pp. 49–52; C. R. Boxer and Carlos de Azevedo, *Fort Jesus and the Portuguese in Mombasa* (London, 1960), pp. 19–23; and Strandes, pp. 152–7.

13. Santos, p. 244.

14. John Gray, 'Portuguese Records Relating to the Wasegeju', *Tanganyika Notes and Records*, No. 29 (July 1950), p. 89.

15. The following description of the siege of Fort Jesus is based upon my article 'Fort Jesus, Past and Present', *Kenya Past and Present*, No. 6 (1975), pp. 31–5.

16. Although details may vary on the siege of Fort Jesus, I have relied upon the writings of Justus Strandes, James Kirkman and Charles Boxer, the foremost authorities on the history of Fort Jesus.

17. G. S. P. Freeman-Grenville, *The French at Kilwa Island: An Episode in Eighteenth-Century East African History* (Oxford, 1965), p. 58; and G. S. P. Freeman-Grenville, 'The Coast, 1498–1840' in *History of East Africa*, Roland Oliver and Gervase Mathew (eds.), (Oxford, 1966), Vol. I, p. 155.

CHAPTER THREE

1. Reginald Coupland, *The Exploitation of East Africa 1856–1890: The Slave Trade and the Scramble* (London, 1939), p. 134.

2. Freeman-Grenville, 'The Coast, 1498–1840', p. 152.

3. Gervase Mathew, 'The East African Coast until the Coming of the Portuguese', in *History of East Africa*, Vol. I, p. 101; James Kirkman, 'The History of the Coast of East Africa up to 1700', in *Prelude to East African History*, Merrick Posnansky (ed.), (London, 1966), p. 113; J. Spencer Trimingham, *Islam in East Africa* (Oxford, 1964), pp. 7 and 9; and Robert G. Gregory, *India and East Africa: A History of Race Relations within the British Empire, 1890–1939* (Oxford, 1971), p. 14.

4. Strandes, pp. 83, 152 and 210. Robert Gregory writes: 'During these centuries from 1500 to 1840, African slaves were brought to India in increasing numbers.' (Gregory, p. 17).

5. Freeman-Grenville, *Select Documents*, p. 162.

6. Alpers, p. 151; and Esmond B. Martin and T. C. I. Ryan, 'A Quantitative Assessment of the Arab Slave Trade of East Africa 1770–1896', *Kenya Historical Review*, Vol. 5, No. 1 (1977), pp. 77–79.

7. Crosson, in Freeman-Grenville, *Select Documents*, p. 196.

8. Freeman-Grenville, *The French at Kilwa Island*, pp. 106, 118, 119 and 123.

9. Freeman-Grenville, pp. 93, 106–7, 123–6 and 172.

10. Freeman-Grenville, pp. 149–50.

11. Freeman-Grenville, pp. 109, 119–20, 124 and 150.

12. Freeman-Grenville, pp. 108, 121, 163 and 164.

13. James Prior, *Voyage along the Eastern Coast of Africa* (London, 1819), pp. 66, 71 and 80.

14. Guillain, Vol. III, p. 305.

15. J. B. Emery writing to W. D. Cooley, 18 December 1835, Royal Geographical Society Archives, London.
16. Memo by Captain Thomas Smee, 6 March 1811, in Sir Joseph Banks Papers, Add 8958, British Museum.
17. Freeman-Grenville, *The French at Kilwa Island*, p. 221.
18. Hippo teeth, wart hog tusks and other large animal teeth are the poor man's ivory in India. Since at least the eighteenth century, hunters, mostly in Tanganyika, have killed hippos in the main rivers and removed the two main upper and lower incisors. A large hippo can produce sixteen pounds of ivory which was generally worth in the nineteenth century two-thirds of the value of elephant ivory. Although hippo teeth are very hard, they are excellent for carving. During the nineteenth century, most of the East African hippo teeth were brought to Zanzibar where the Indian traders made arrangements for their sale in India. Not all the teeth were made into ornaments; some people held on to them as a kind of currency (Guillain's Report in the Ministère d'Outremer, file Océan Indien 5/23, circa 1847; and personal communication from Ian Parker, Nairobi, November 1976, and Christine Nicholls, 12 September 1976).
19. Richard F. Burton, *Zanzibar; City, Island, and Coast* (London, 1872), Vol. II, pp. 45–6.
20. Thomas Smee, 'Observations during a Voyage of Research on the East Coast of Africa', *Transactions of the Bombay Geographical Society*, VI (September 1841 to May 1844), p. 44.
21. C. S. Nicholls, *The Swahili Coast: Politics, Diplomacy and Trade on the East African Littoral, 1793–1856* (London, 1971), p. 199.
22. Nicholls, p. 204.
23. Reginald Coupland, *East Africa and its Invaders, From the Earliest Times to the Death of Seyyid Said in 1856* (New York, 1965), p. 208.
24. Coupland, *East Africa and its Invaders*, p. 503.
25. Martin and Ryan, pp. 76–9.
26. The sources for these statistics are based upon Customs' returns in Zanzibar and Kilwa, various Consular reports, British Consuls in Zanzibar who made estimates, and observations made by various explorers and traders.
27. Burton, Vol. II, p. 347.
28. Burton, Vol. II, pp. 345–6.
29. David Livingstone, *The last Journals of David Livingstone in Central Africa from 1865 to his Death* Horace Waller (ed.), (London, 1874), Vol. I, p. 300.
30. Livingstone, Vol. I, p. 56.
31. *Hansard*, XV, 1826, p. 1034.
32. Notes written by Richard P. Waters (American Consul, Zanzibar), 18 October 1842 in *New England Merchants in Africa*, Norman Bennett and George F. Brooks, Jr (eds.), (Boston, 1965), p. 253.
33. Nicholls, p. 210.
34. Coupland, *The Exploitation of East Africa*, p. 147.
35. Burton, Vol. II, pp. 409–16.
36. Burton, Vol. II, p. 108.
37. Burton, Vol I, pp. 352–3.
38. Estimates implicit in Martin and Ryan, pp. 82–6.
39. British Parliamentary Papers, *Report by Sir A. Hardinge on the Condition and Progress of the East Africa Protectorate from Its Establishment to the 20th of July, 1897*, Africa No. 7 (1897). C. 8683, (London, 1897), p. 26.
40. Kirkman, *Men and Monuments*, pp. 42–3.
41. Estimates implicit in Martin and Ryan pp. 84–5.
42. Letter from Charles Gissing, British Vice-Consul, Mombasa, to Sir John Kirk, Zanzibar, 10 May 1884, Residency BB1, Zanzibar Archives.
43. Coupland, *East Africa and its Invaders*, p. 215.
44. letters from C. S. Smith, Vice-Consul, Kilwa Kivinje, to Sir John Kirk, 5 July 1884 and 29 November 1884, Residency BB1, Zanzibar Archives. C. S. Smith saw eleven slaves chained in a room at night ready for the march up the coast.
45. Letter from John Haggard, Vice-Consul, Lamu, to Sir John Kirk, 8 July 1884, Residency BB1, Zanzibar Archives.
46. Letter from John Haggard to Sir John Kirk, 9 September 1884, Residency BB1, Zanzibar Archives.

47. British Parliamentary Papers, *Africa No. 6* (1895), p. 36.
48. British Parliamentary Papers, *Africa No. 7* (1896), p. 35.
49. British Parliamentary Papers, *Slave Trade No. 1* (1888), p. 91; and British Parliamentary Papers, *Slave Trade No. 1* (1889).
50. British Parliamentary Papers, *Africa No. 6* (1891).
51. Letter from J. Bell Smith, District Superintendent, I.B.E.A., Malindi, 3 September 1892, to Ernest Berkeley, Administrator, Mombasa, Residency D5, Zanzibar Archives.

CHAPTER FOUR

1. F. J. Berg and B. J. Walter, 'Mosques, population and urban development in Mombasa,' in *Hadith I*, Bethwell A. Ogot (ed.), (Nairobi, 1968), p. 60.
2. Martin, 'The Historic Coast', p. 34.
3. J. L. Krapf, *Travels, Researches, and Missionary Labours during an Eighteen years' Residence in Eastern Africa* (London, 1865), p. 118; and Burton, Vol. II, p. 75.
4. Mombasa Dhow Registers, East African Customs and Excise Department, Old Port, Mombasa.
5. Mombasa Dhow Register, Old Port, Mombasa.
6. Letter from Mr Carver, District Commissioner Kilifi, to District Commissioner Lamu, 23 July 1938, Provincial Commissioner's Archives, Mombasa.
7. Dhow Statistics from *Blue Books*; and Mombasa Dhow Registers, Old Port, Mombasa.
8. Mombasa Dhow Registers, Old Port, Mombasa.
9. Mombasa Dhow Registers, Old Port, Mombasa.
10. Mombasa Dhow Registers, Old Port, Mombasa.
11. Coupland, *The Exploitation of East Africa*, p. 55.
12. Letter from J. G. Carter, Immigration Officer, Mombasa, to Principal Immigration Officer, Nairobi, 19 May 1945, Provincial Commissioner's Archives, Mombasa.
13. Interview with Khajamed, an Indian crew member, at Mombasa, 23 March 1973.
14. G. M. Wilson, A study of Prostitution in Mombasa, 'Mombasa Social Survey', mimeographed, Mombasa, 1957.
15. The statistics for the following paragraphs are from Mombasa Dhow Registers and Transire Notes.
16. One Iranian dhow arrived in Mombasa on 5 February 1970 with 158 'Arabian' chests, 200 carpets worth £1,650, fresh dates, dried shark and copper wire, the total value of the cargo being £6,540.
17. Interview with Ahmed Abeid, Persian captain of the *Jamil*, 29 March 1972.
18. Interviews with Shariff Mohamed Abdulla Shatry, 1971.
19. Interview with Ahmed Abeid, 29 March 1972.
20. Interview with Ahmed Rahman, 30 March 1972.
21. Mombasa Dhow Registers, Old Port, Mombasa.
22. Interview with Swaleh Ali, 1 April 1972.
23. Interviews with *nahodas* of Yemeni dhows, Mombasa, 1972–3.
24. Interviews with the captains of the Indian dhows, *Alimadat* and *Lakshmin*, Mombasa, 30 March 1973.
25. Interview with Rashid Abdulla, Under-Secretary, Ministry of Information, Abu Dhabi, 29 October 1972.
26. Interviews with Indian crew members in Dubai, October–November 1972.
27. The earnings given for the Arab and Iranian crews include any money made from profits at the end of the trip which are paid to the crew. However, on some dhows the profits are not shared amongst the crews. Information from interviews with crew members of Somali, Indian, Arab and Iranian dhows in 1972–3.
28. Hadi, who was born in Mukalla, Arabia, has been auctioning fish in Mombasa since 1945. He has an office in Old Town in which he has employed since 1970 a full-time clerk, Omar Nasser. Hadi's business includes helping dhow crew as well as auctioning fish. He lives in his own house near the Mwembe Tayari market. I estimate that he has net earnings of about £1,500 a year after expenses.
29. Interviews with the main fish and shark auctioneers: Rajab Garwan, Swaleh Sherman and Hadi Ahmed (and his clerk, Omar Nasser), 1972–4.
30. Interviews with Swaleh Sherman, Hadi Ahmed, Omar Nasser and Rajab Garwan, 1972–4.

31. Interviews with Mohammed Abdulla, former customs official, 1971–4.
32. Interview with Mohammed Ahmed Antar, February 1974.
33. Statistics for the year 1970 from the Fisheries Department, Mombasa.
34. For more details on traditional fishing on the coast of Kenya, see Martin, *The History of Malindi*, pp. 190–211.
35. Interviews with Abdulla Mohamed bin Ali, Kimosha Rihani, Mahfudh Salim and Amin Rijali, fishermen in Mombasa, February 1974.
36. Interview with Ali Kuppi, *nahoda* of the *Zaliha*, February 1974.
37. Interview with Mwalimu Shee, assistant *nahoda* of the *Ikbal-Alkheir*, February 1974.
38. Interviews with the assistant *nahoda* of the *Kole Kole*, Muhaji Omar, and with the engineer, Mohamed Said, February 1974.
39. Interviews carried out with various crew members of the *Kole Kole* and *Samaki*, February 1974.
40. Interviews with Mohammed Abdulla, 1974.
41. For a Swahili recipe, see: Esmond and Chryssee Martin, *Kuku na Ndizi na Nazi ya Lamu* (Lamu Chicken with Bananas in Coconut Cream), in Luther and Conda Douglas (eds.), *The Explorers' Cookbook, An International Potpourri of Recipes and Tales of World Adventurers* (Caldwell, Idaho, 1971), pp. 145–6.
42. Interviews with various dhow captains, February 1974.
43. The statistics for the following paragraphs were obtained from the Transire Notes and Mombasa Dhow Registers, Old Port, Mombasa.
44. Personal correspondence with John Jewell, 1975.
45. Dhow Registers, Old Port, Mombasa.
46. Dhow Registers and Transire Notes, Old Port, Mombasa.
47. For a discussion of the reasons for the general decline of the Kenyan foreign dhow trade from 1900 to 1940 see, P. A. Memon and Esmond B. Martin, 'The Kenya Coast: An Anomaly in the Development of an "Ideal Type" Colonial Spatial System', *Kenya Historical Review*, Vol. 4, No. 2 (1976), pp. 187–206.
48. Letter from J. G. Carter, Immigration Officer, Mombasa, to Principal Immigration Officer, Nairobi, 19 May 1945, Provincial Commissioner's Archives, Mombasa.
49. Information from Dhow Registers, Old Port, Mombasa.
50. Alan Villiers, *Sons of Sinbad*, New Edition (New York, 1969).
51. Marion Kaplan, 'Twilight of the Arab Dhow', *National Geographic*, Vol. 146, No. 3, (September 1974), pp. 330–351.

CHAPTER FIVE

1. Personal communication with O. M. Naaman, Officer in Charge of Customs, Malindi; and Dhow Registers, Malindi.
2. Forest Department Annual Report, Lamu, 1970.
3. Canada, Special Commonwealth Aid to Africa Program, *A Reconnaissance Inventory Survey of the Indigenous Forest Areas of Kenya*, R. W. Roberts, 'Lamu Mangrove Industry' (Ottawa, 1967).
4. Forest Department Annual Reports, Lamu, 1966–70.
5. Lamu District Annual Reports, 1916–40.
6. Lamu District Annual Reports, 1939–62; and Forest Department Annual Reports, Lamu, 1963–70.
7. Lamu Dhow Registers.
8. Information supplied by Terry Maginn, former Forest Officer, Lamu.
9. Lamu District Annual Report, 1959.
10. For further details on the Lamu *Maulidi*, see: Peter Lienhardt, 'The Mosque College of Lamu and its social background', *Tanganyika Notes and Records*, Number 53 (1959), pp. 228–242; and Chryssee and Esmond Bradley Martin, 'Maulidi Festivities at Lamu', *Kenya Past and Present*, Vol. I, No. 3 (July 1972), pp. 16–21.
11. *Daily Nation*, Nairobi, Kenya, 24 August 1971, p. 5.
12. *Daily Nation*, Nairobi, Kenya, 28 August 1971, p. 6.
13. Martin, *History of Malindi*, p. 215.
14. In 1973, the latest year for which I have statistics, there was no cargo carried by dhow from Malindi to Mombasa because the road by that time was tarmacked.

15. Malindi Dhow Registers.
16. Kilifi Dhow Registers.
17. Shimoni Dhow Registers.
18. Lamu Pass Notes, East African Customs and Excise Department, Lamu.
19. Malindi Pass Notes, East African Customs and Excise Department, Malindi.
20. A. H. J. Prins, *Sailing from Lamu* (Assen, 1965), p. 174.
21. Lamu Dhow Registers.
22. Lamu Dhow Registers.
23. Interview with Ahmed Bujra, 20 February 1974.
24. During the months of April to August when the traditional dhows do not sail due to bad weather, the 30-ton *jahazi, Ikbal*, with inboard engine earned Shs.1,800 a month for its owner (Interview with Mohammed Abdulla, 8 February 1974).
25. Dhows in Existence and out of Existence, Dhow Register, Lamu.
26. Interviews with Mohamed Usi, Ali Kuppi, Mwalimu Shee, Saidi Yusuf, Mohamed Seif Rogo, Said Seif, Said Hammed and Athman Ali, in Mombasa and Lamu, February 1974.
27. Interviews with captains and crew members of Kenyan dhows, 1974.
28. Lamu Dhow Register.
29. Typical passenger fares from Lamu to destinations in the archipelago in 1974 were: Matondoni (Shs.2), Siyu (Shs.3), Faza (Shs.4), and Ndau (Shs.6).
30. Interview with the Manager of Lamu Ginners, 2 July 1968.
31. Agricultural Annual Report, Lamu District, 1968.
32. Agricultural Annual Reports, Lamu District, 1966–1968.
33. Personal communication with James de Vere Allen, 11 August 1976.
34. J. Clive, 'The Mtepi', written 19 August 1933, Lamu Political Records, Volume II, DC/LAM/3/2, Kenya National Archives.
35. Letter from District Commissioner Lamu, 2 March 1943, to Provincial Commissioner Coast, Provincial Commissioner's Archives, Mombasa.
36. Lamu District Annual Report, 1959.
37. Information supplied by Omar Bwana, December 1976.
38. Information supplied by James de Vere Allen, Abdulla Kadara, Linda Donley and Omar Bwana, December 1976.

CHAPTER SIX

1. Examples of force used were recorded in the official newspaper, the *Daily News* during 1974 and 1975; see also Andrew Coulson, 'The Evolution of Rural Policies in Tanzania, or Can a Government Bureaucracy Bring about Development?', seminar paper presented to the Economic Research Bureau, University of Dar es Salaam, 21 January 1975, pp. 11, 14 and 15.
2. Coulson, p. 14.
3. In fact, the Government, in 1974, passed minimum acreage laws to compel farmers to cultivate individually (Coulson, p. 15).
4. See, for example, D. K. S. Grant, 'Mangrove Woods of Tanganyika Territory, their silviculture and dependent industries', *Tanganyika Notes and Records*, Number 5 (April 1938), pp. 5–16; and Alan Villiers, *Sons of Sinbad*.
5. *Blue Books 1921–1948*.
6. *Blue Book 1948*.
7. *Blue Books 1941–1948*.
8. *Blue Books 1921–1948*.
9. On 28 June 1975, an editorial in the *Daily News* warned: 'People to be repatriated should not be bundled into buses to be dumped at railway stations or bus stops. Doing that will only inconvenience the vagabonds temporarily; but they will soon find their way back to towns. And there must be follow-up supervision for those sent to *Ujamaa* villages . . . These people with reactionary ideas of town life can easily influence committed *Wajamaa* to follow their evil ways. This should not be allowed to happen at any cost.'
10. Since 1974, permission in writing must be received from the Bank of Tanzania for dhow owners to buy or sell goods (except food). About one week is needed to obtain the necessary permit (Interview with the main dhow agent in Dar es Salaam, Kidasi Zibe, 24 March 1975).

11. Interview with Visram Dhamji, a crew member of the *Keshri*, which has a tonnage of 158 and a crew of fourteen, on 8 March 1975, Dar es Salaam.
12. Transire Notes, East African Customs and Excise Department, Dar es Salaam.
13. Dhow Registers, East African Customs and Excise Department, Kwale.
14. I made these estimates at Kwale on 15 August 1975.
15. J. F. de S. Lewis-Barned, 'Kwale Island', in Kisarawe District Book I, MF 30, Tanzania National Archives.
16. Interview with Azani Juma, Salale, 3 February 1975.
17. Interview with Mr Mwanamwene, Simba Uranga, 3 February 1975.
18. There is not much of an opportunity for the people in the Rufiji to make a good living. The soil is poor and floods are a common hazard. Fishing is a possibility but the main centres of consumption are far away. Transport, except by dhow, is poor, and the entire delta is unhealthy for human beings and there is little for domestic animals to eat.
19. Neville Chittick, 'Report on Excavations at Kisimani Mafia and Kua', *Annual Report of the Antiquities Department [Tanganyika] for the year 1964*, pp. 15–16. An exception is Kisimani Mafia, not worth a special visit because the road to the site is poor and during the rainy season a four-wheel drive vehicle is imperative; the distance from the Mafia Island Lodge at Utende is twenty miles. Furthermore, most of the buildings at Kisimani Mafia have fallen into the sea, and thus there is little to see.
20. Statistics from Felix Sandi, Planning Officer, Department of Agriculture, Tanzania, 1975.
21. Ministry of Natural Resources and Tourism, Fisheries Division, *1973 Annual Report*, Dar es Salaam.
22. Neville Chittick, *Annual Report of the Department of Antiquities [Tanganyika] for the year 1958*, p. 25.
23. See: Mafia District Book I, Tanzania National Archives.
24. Statistics from the Department of Fisheries, Mafia.
25. Interview with Ali Amir, carpenter, Chole, January 1975.
26. Interview with Shomari Mfaume, carpenter, Jibondo island, 28 January 1975. A senior carpenter can earn as much as £100 per month.
27. The Bajuns are the only fishermen in East Africa to use a sucker fish, but this unusual method of catching turtles has been practiced in the past in north-west Madagascar and the Comoro islands (Personal communication from Jack Frazier).
28. Interview with Crispin Mbapila, District Development Director, Mafia, 26 January 1975.
29. Kilindoni Dhow Register, East African Customs and Excise Department, Kilindoni, Mafia.
30. Kilindoni Dhow Register.
31. Kilindoni Dhow Register.
32. Transire Notes, East African Customs and Excise Department, Kwale.
33. The population of Pangani in 1928 was about the same as today: 3,000 (Pangani District Book, Volume I, MF 7, Tanzanian National Archives).
34. Survey taken by the author in September 1975.
35. Tanga Dhow Registers, and Transire Notes, East African Customs and Excise Department, Tanga.
36. Walter T. Brown, 'Bagamoyo: An Historical Introduction', *Tanzania Notes and Records*, No. 71 (1970), pp. 69–83.
37. The retail businesses in 1975 in Bagamoyo consisted of twenty-six *dukas*, nine clothing and tailoring shops, five restaurants, four hotels, three petrol stations, two garages, two butchers, and one gold and silversmith, one carpenter, one laundry, one charcoal dealer, and one bank (Survey carried out by the author in February 1975).
38. As late as 1951, as much as six tons of gum copal was sold in Bagamoyo district (Bagamoyo District Book, Vol. I, MF 30, Tanzania National Archives).
39. From 1937 to 1953, the Bagamoyo Salt Works north of the township produced an average of 1,552 metric tons a year (Bagamoyo District Book, Vol. II, MF 30, Tanzania National Archives).
40. In 1973 there were 577 fishermen in Bagamoyo district; they caught 853 tons of fish worth £280,550 (Fisheries Division, *1973 Annual Report*).
41. *Blue Book 1925*.
42. Bagamoyo Dhow Registers, East African Customs and Excise Department, Bagamoyo.
43. Transire Notes, East African Customs and Excise Department, Dar es Salaam Dhow Wharf.

CHAPTER SEVEN

1. John Okello, *Revolution in Zanzibar* (Nairobi, 1967), p. 160.

2. In the official party publication, *The Afro-Shirazi Party Revolution 1964–1974* (Zanzibar, 1974), the authors write: 'Such revolutionary changes angered some teachers and reactionaries and drove them to flee the country, leaving our students in the lurch. Between 1964 and 1973 282 teachers ran away' (p. 132).

3. P. Selwyn and T. Y. Watson, *Report on the Economic Development of the Zanzibar Protectorate* (Zanzibar, 1962), p. 78.

4. The shell of the Hawksbill turtle, not the common green turtle's shell which is too fragile, has been in great demand by the upper class in the Occident and Orient for at least 2,000 years. The shell, or to be more exact, the individual plates are a natural plastic which craftsmen throughout the ages have used to make into luxury items, including Boulle furniture. The fishermen of the East African coast have been killing the Hawksbill for centuries; after the turtle is killed the fishermen either let it rot or pour boiling water on to it to remove the plates.

5. Hamerton received this information from separate sources: Mr Angelo, a long-term resident of Zanzibar, and Mr Blatisford, an American merchant (Hamerton to the Secretary of the Bombay Government, 1 July 1841, Secretariat E, Zanzibar Archives).

6. Rigby to the Secretary of the Bombay Government, 21 March 1860, Zanzibar Archives.

7. *Zanzibar Blue Book 1947*.

8. Later, the Zanzibar Government relented to some extent, and if prior permission was requested, the Government might agree to an Arab dhow coming in (Interview with the head of Customs from 1964–5, Zanzibar).

9. During the past ten years, the few foreign dhows which have put into Zanzibar brought mostly dried fish; one dhow arrived with twenty-four goats from Mogadishu (Dhow Registers, Zanzibar). Not even statistical distortions due to the definition of what constitutes an 'arrival' can explain the change shown in Table XIV.

10. Gomani has been a poor settlement for at least forty years; see: Ian Rolleston, 'The Watumbatu of Zanzibar', *Tanganyika Notes and Records*, No. 8 (December 1939), pp. 85–97.

11. I visited Tumbatu on 11 January 1976.

12. Information supplied by Ali Makame Nywali, Chairman of the Afro-Shirazi Party, Tumbatu Branch; Juma Hamisi; and Kombo Haji Kombo.

13. During the financial year of 1974–5, the main exports of Zanzibar and Pemba were: clove buds and oil (£9,428,000), coconut oil (£478,000), copra (£421,000), coir fibre (£67,400), seashells (£36,900), and seaweed (£26,000) (Statistics from the Department of Agriculture, Zanzibar).

14. Statistics from the Department of Agriculture, Zanzibar.

15. Information from Paul Strong, FAO Adviser in Zanzibar, January 1976.

16. Zanzibar Protectorate, 'Annual Report on the Port and Marine Department for the Year 1937', p. 6.

17. Zanzibar Government, *Annual Reports for 1909–10*, p. 86. In 1905, 6,027 passengers came into and went out of Chake Chake and Wete by dhow. Many people went down to Zanzibar after the clove season to purchase goods ('Report on the Administration of the Island of Pemba for the Year 1906').

18. Transire Notes, Mkoani, Chake Chake and Wete.

19. Zanzibar Protectorate, *Report of the Veterinary Adviser on Veterinary Matters in Zanzibar, 1922*.

20. Zanzibar Protectorate, *Annual Report of the Department of Agriculture, 1949*, p. 24.

21. Zanzibar Protectorate, *Annual Report of the Department of Agriculture, 1960*, pp. 7–9.

22. Statistics from Agriculture Department, Zanzibar.

23. Dhow Registers, Zanzibar; and Transire Notes, Zanzibar port.

24. Interviews with the following crew members: Ali Khamis, Ali Said Ali, Mwabadi Mwalim, Hija Ame, Saidi Shoka and Shaha Mohamed, Zanzibar, January 1976.

25. Dhow Registers, Zanzibar; and Transire notes, Zanzibar port.

26. These acreages are not absolute: many include double cropping and interplanting (Department of Agriculture, Zanzibar).

27. The piece-goods consisted primarily of *kangas*, large squares of cotton cloth, 6' 6" × 4' 6", in colour prints. The cloths were imported by German firms, though they were printed in Britain and Holland.

28. Zanzibar Protectorate, 'Report on the Administration of the Island of Pemba for the Year 1906'.

29. Kirkman, *Men and Monuments*, p. 182. Dr Kirkman now thinks that people from the Maldive islands probably did not build Pujini (Personal communication from James Kirkman, 1976).

30. In the 1967 Census, there were still 109 Asians in Chake Chake township, ninety-four in Wete, and fifteen in Mkoani (The United Republic of Tanzania, *1967 Population Census*, Vol. 2, Dar es Salaam, 1970, p. 161). In early 1976, there were thirty Asians—mostly Bohoras—in Kengeja, twenty-six in Chake Chake, seven in Wete, two in the rural areas, and one in Mkoani (Survey carried out by the author).

31. Of the twenty-six Asians who lived in Chake Chake, ten were Kumbaros, ten Bohoras, four Goans, and two Hindus (Survey carried out by the author in March 1976).

32. Survey taken by the author in March 1976.

33. Chake Chake and Wete Dhow Registers.

CHAPTER EIGHT

1. Geoffrey E. Ffrench and Allan Hill, *Kuwait: Urban and Medical Ecology* (New York, 1971), p. 20.

2. A. B. Kemball and Captain Hennell, 'Memoranda on the Resources, Locations and relations of the Tribes Inhabiting the Arabian Shores of the Persian Gulf' in *Selections from the Records of the Bombay Government*, No. XXIV, New Series (Bombay, 1856), p. 109.

3. Ffrench and Hill, p. 14.

4. J. G. Lorimer, *Persian Gulf Gazetteer (Geographical and Statistical)* (Calcutta, 1908–15), p. 1051.

5. Lorimer, pp. 1051 and 1053.

6. Lorimer pp. 1052–3 and 1056.

7. Lorimer, p. 1054.

8. Lorimer, p. 1054.

9. Villiers, pp. xix and xxii.

10. The kuwaiti-owned *booms* will employ non-Kuwaiti crews because they are cheaper.

11. I computed this figure by assuming that the number of cargo dhows I observed in Kuwait (137) bore the same proportion to the total cargo dhows coming into that port during the year as occurred in Dubai, where I had both figures.

12. Interviews with various dhow crew members, Kuwait, October 1972.

13. Interviews with various dhow crew members, Kuwait, October 1972.

14. Ffrench and Hill, pp. 22–4.

15. 'Law of Voyage for Kuwaiti Dhows', translated from the Arabic, circa 1913, probably written by Ahamed el-Jabiri es-Sabbah, a Moslem Judge in Kuwait, DC/MSA/8/5, Kenya National Archives.

16. Alan Villiers, 'Some Aspects of the Arab Dhow Trade', *The Middle East Journal* (October 1948), p. 399.

17. Information from Saddam A'ati and Abdulla Abboud, Kuwait, 19 October 1972.

CHAPTER NINE

1. Captain Burnes Brucks, 'Memoir Descriptive of the Navigation of the Gulf of Persia, 1819', in *Selections from the Records of the Bombay Government*, pp. 568–9.

2. A. B. Kemball and Captain Hennell, 'Memoranda on the Resources, Locations and Relations of the Tribes Inhabiting the Arabian Shores of the Persian Gulf' in *Selections from the Records of the Bombay Government*, pp. 105–6.

3. Kemball and Hennell, pp. 105–6.

4. Lorimer, p. 242.

5. Lorimer, p. 241.

6. Lorimer, pp. 238, 243 and 245.

7. Arnold T. Wilson, *The Persian Gulf: An Historical Sketch from the Earliest Times to the Beginning of the Twentieth Century* (Oxford, 1928), p. 30.

8. Richard LeBaron Bowen, Jr, 'The Pearl Fisheries of the Persian Gulf', *The Middle East Journal*, Vol. 5 (1951), p. 163.

9. Ffrench and Hill, p. 12

10. During the pearling season, the population of Indians expanded considerably in some of the Gulf towns. For example, in 1905, the number of Hindu traders in Bahrain rose from 69 to 175 (Lorimer, p. 240).

11. Colonel S. B. Miles, *The Countries and Tribes of the Persian Gulf* (London, 1919), Vol. II, pp. 414–16.

12. Bowen, pp. 176–77. For centuries pearls have also been in demand as an aphrodisiac. Cleopatra is said to have mixed powdered pearls with a drink before she met Antony. Today pearls are still purchased by Shaikhs, especially those with large harems (Ralph Hewins, *A Golden Dream: The Miracle of Kuwait*, London, 1963, p. 63).

13. Miles, pp. 414 and 415; Villiers, *Sons of Sinbad*, p. 351; and Charles Issawi (ed.), *Economic History of the Middle East 1800–1914* (Chicago, 1966), p. 312.

14. Bowen, pp. 168–169.

15. Information supplied by Bahraini dhow owners to the author, October 1972.

16. Bowen, p. 173.

17. The importation of large quantities of fresh vegetables and fruits has been common only since World War II because before this time the populations were quite small and these commodities were considered luxuries and were too expensive for the average Arab to purchase in Kuwait, Qatar, Abu Dhabi and Dubai (Interview with Rashid Abdulla, Under-Secretary, Ministry of Information, Abu Dhabi, 29 October 1972).

18. Bahraini *per capita* income in 1970 was $420, compared with $1,550 for Qatar, and $3,360 for Kuwait.

19. State of Bahrain, Ministry of Finance and National Economy, *Statistical Abstract 1972* (Bahrain, 1972), pp. 6, 7 and 17–19.

20. Bahrain, *Statistical Abstract 1972*, p. 17.

21. Interview with Khalil Aldoy, Muharraq, 23 October 1972.

CHAPTER TEN

1. Lorimer, pp. 1530–1533.

2. Lorimer, pp. 489–91.

3. Interview with Abdulla M. Al-Ghorairi, Assistant Director of Ports, Abu Dhabi, 25 October 1972.

4. Qatar Information Department, *Qatar into the Seventies* (Doha, 1971), p. 17.

5. Lorimer, p. 1754.

6. Richard Johns, *Abu Dhabi: Financial Times Survey*, 25 February 1970.

7. Donald Hawley, *The Trucial States* (London, 1970), pp. 241–2.

8. Hawley, p. 233.

9. Government of Abu Dhabi, Statistical Bureau, *Statistical Bulletin 1969 and 1970* (mimeographed).

10. Hawley, p. 241.

11. Hawley, pp. 212–13.

12. K. G. Fenelon, *Abu Dhabi: Financial Times Survey*.

13. *Statistical Bulletin 1969 and 1970*.

14. *Statistical Bulletin 1969 and 1970*.

15. Hawley, p. 233.

16. *Statistical Bulletin 1969 and 1970*.

17. Information supplied by Dr Merle Jensen, and Jack D. Yelf; the *Abu Dhabi News* 28 October 1972; and *Guide to Arid Lands Research Center* (Abu Dhabi, 1971).

CHAPTER ELEVEN

1. Anne Coles and Peter Jackson, 'A Windtower House in Dubai', *Art and Archaeology Research Papers* (London, June 1975), p. 2.

2. Lorimer, pp. 454–6.

3. Hawley, p. 19.

4. Hawley, p. 205.

5. Timothy Green, *The World of Gold Today* (London, 1974), p. 225.

6. Michael Tomkinson, *The United Arab Emirates* (London, 1975), p. 133.

236

7. Green, pp. 226–7.
8. Green, pp. 225–7.
9. These engines are usually installed in Dubai.
10. Information collected by the author in Dubai, November 1972.
11. Information supplied by a crew member involved in gold smuggling, Dubai.
12. Green, pp. 230–2; and information collected by the author in Dubai.
13. Green, pp. 231–2.
14. Hawley, pp. 206–8; and Green, p. 229.
15. Green, p. 229; and information collected by the author in Dubai.
16. Information collected by the author in Dubai.
17. In 1970, $2,513,000 worth of transistor radios, mostly made in Japan, were imported into Dubai (Government of Dubai, Statistics Section, *Statistics Report, 1970*, Dubai, 1971, p. 175).
18. In 1971, $259,000 of writing pens were imported into Dubai (Government of Dubai, Statistics Office, *Statistics Report, 1971*, Dubai, 1972, p. 311).
19. Hawley, p. 205.
20. Government of Dubai, Statistics Section, *Statistics Report, 1967* (Dubai, 1968), p. 39.
21. Government of Dubai, Statistics Section, *Statistics Report, 1968* (Dubai, 1969), p. 53; and *Statistics Report 1971*, p. 157.
22. Green, pp. 234–5.
23. Green, p. 233.
24. Green, p. 237.
25. Barry Wilson, as quoted in *The Standard* (Nairobi), 25 October 1974.
26. *Statistics Reports, 1966–1971*, Dubai.
27. *Statistics Report, 1967*, Dubai, p. 106.
28. *The Standard* (Nairobi), 7 November 1974.
29. *Statistics Report, 1971*, p. 97.

CHAPTER TWELVE

1. *Iran Almanac and Book of Facts 1972* (Tehran, 1973), pp. 665–6.
2. *The Encyclopedia of Islam*, New Edition (Leyden, 1960), Vol. I, p. 5.
3. *Nagel's Encyclopedia-Guide: Iran* (Geneva, 1972), p. 172.
4. Lorimer, pp. 129–31 and 1262–4.
5. Geographical Handbook Series, *Iraq and the Persian Gulf* (London, 1944), p. 511.
6. Interviews with dhow crew members in Khorramshahr, 5–8 June 1973.
7. *Iran Almanac*, p. 307.
8. Jahangir Amuzegar and M. Ali Fekrat, *Iran: Economic Development under Dualist Conditions* (Chicago, 1971), pp. 80–4.
9. *Iran Almanac*, pp. 307 and 543; and Amuzegar and Fekrat, pp. 91 and 123.
10. *Iran Almanac*, p. 543.
11. Wilson, *The Persian Gulf*, p. 176.
12. Brucks, pp. 584–5.
13. Lorimer, pp. 345–6.
14. Lorimer, pp. 345–6.
15. Roger Stevens, *The Land of the Great Sophy* (London, 1965), p. 257.
16. Lorimer, pp. 343–4.
17. Stevens, p. 257.
18. Interviews with various dhow captains, Bushire, 9–12 June 1973.
19. Survey carried out by the author, in Bushire, June 1973.
20. Wilson, *The Persian Gulf*, pp. 141–79.
21. Brucks, p. 604.
22. Lorimer, pp. 10–12.
23. Interview with the Shah of Iran, *Newsweek*, International Edition, 21 May 1973, pp. 20–1.
24. *Newsweek*, p. 19.
25. Interview with Mr Tehranshi, a long-term resident of Bandar Abbas, 23 June 1973.
26. Interviews with various crew members, Bandar Abbas, 20–24 June 1973.
27. Information supplied by residents of Tiyab, 21 June 1973.
28. Customs Department, Khamir.

29. Customs Department, Khamir.
30. Lorimer, pp. 1040–1.
31. Interview with Abed bin Bashir, Kung, 20 June 1973.
32. Lorimer, pp. 1088–1100.
33. Marco Polo, pp. 49–50.
34. Marco Polo, p. 258.
35. Wilson, *The Persian Gulf*, p. 104.
36. Abbé Raynal, in Wilson, *The Persian Gulf*, pp. 105–6.
37. H. A. R. Gibb, Vol. II, p. 400.
38. The trade in horses from the twelfth to the fifteenth centuries was an important one. Most of the horses came from Arabia and Persia and were sent on dhows to ports in western India (Hikoichi Yajima, *The Arab Dhow Trade in the Indian Ocean*, Tokyo, 1976, pp. 14–15).
39. Henry E. J. Stanley (ed.), *A Description of the Coast of East Africa and Malabar in the beginning of the Sixteenth Century by Duarte Barbosa* (reprinted New York, 1970), pp. 41–3.
40. Frederick C. Danvers, *The Portuguese in India* (London, 1894), Vol. I, pp. 161–8.
41. Wilson, *The Persian Gulf*, pp. 141–52.
42. G. N. Curzon, *Persia and the Persian Question* (London, 1892), Vol. II, p. 415.
43. Lorimer, p. 750.

CHAPTER THIRTEEN

1. Boxer and Azevedo, pp. 18–19.
2. John Gray, 'The British Vice-Consulate at Kilwa Kivinji, 1884–1885', *Tanganyika Notes and Records*, No. 51 (December 1958), p. 175.
3. Letter from Captain A. B. Kemball, Resident in the Persian Gulf, to H. E. Goldsmid, Bushire, 6 June 1853, Secretariat E 56, Zanzibar Archives.
4. Letter from British Consul Office, Zanzibar, 9 January 1889, Residency B 59, Zanzibar Archives.
5. Richard Pankhurst, *Economic History of Ethiopia: 1800–1935* (Addis Ababa, 1968), p. 123.
6. Suzanne Miers, *Britain and the Ending of the Slave Trade* (London, 1975), p. 295.
7. Tomkinson, p. 58.
8. *Daily Nation* (Nairobi), 21 September 1976.
9. Information obtained from various interviews with Zanzibaris, 1975 6.
10. *The Fifth Congress of Afro-Shirazi Party, 1st to 7th December, 1972, Book Four, Specific Problems* (Zanzibar, 1973), pp. 7–10.
11. Information supplied by Alan Villiers, Marion Kaplan and various authorities on the Tanzanian mangrove trade, 1973–5.
12. Ian Parker, 'Oh Quagga?' (mimeographed, Nairobi, 1976).
13. The Rufiji river runs through the Selous Game Reserve which contains one of the largest concentrations of elephants in the world; in early 1976, there were an estimated 80,000 elephants in the Selous (Iain Douglas-Hamilton, '80,000 Elephants Alive and Well in the Selous', *Africana*, Vol. 6, No. 3, October 1976, pp. 17–19). Some people believe that the poachers, when they have killed the elephants, load the tusks on to canoes and sail down the Rufiji to meet up with foreign dhows at Salale or Simba Uranga.

Index

major sellers of wooden chests, 53
Gulf shaikhdoms: characteristics of, 151–3,
  158–9; pearls as major source of wealth of,
  166–70
Guyucks, 198

Hadhramaut, 1, 47, 54, 103, 205
Hafun, 56, 68
Haji, Bakar bin Mohamed, 89
Haji, Haji, 137
Hamalis, 52, 61
Hamerton, Atkins, 28–9, 37
Hatshepsut, Queen, 7
Hatim, buyer of wooden chests, 53
Hawley, Donald, 178, 188; description of Dubai,
  182
Hennell, Captain, 153, 166: description of
  Kuwait, 153; description of Bahrain, 166
Herodotus, 7
Hodeidah, 55
Honey, Martha, 131; study of Asian communities
  of Tanzania by, 131
Hong Kong, 191
Hormuz, 6, 8, 12, 14, 16, 18, 193, 195, 205, 209,
  213–19, 220: Strait of, 213; Old, 214–15;
  reputation for magnificence, 215; looting of,
  218; fort at, 218–19

Ibn Battuta, 9, 17, 215, 225
Imperial British East Africa Company, 37
India, ix, xi, 2, 14, 23, 25, 27f., 30, 52, 59, 164,
  166, 170, 196, 226: appalling living conditions
  in, 158; payment for smuggled gold from
  Dubai, 186–7; illegal importation of watches
  by, 188; hoarding gold in, 188–9; amount of
  gold in, 189
Indicopleustes, Cosmos, 12
International African Institute, 2
Iran, x, 2, 47, 50, 52, 59, 72–3, 156, 170, 172,
  208: upsurge of dhow-building in, xi; export of
  gold to Dubai, 179; dhow trading with Dubai,
  189–90; most numerous foreign visitors to, 193;
  possesses largest fleet of operational hovercraft
  in world, 199; maldistribution of oil profits in,
  200; Shah of Iran's policy of protecting oil-
  producing areas of Gulf, 206–7
Iranians, smuggling by, 205
Isfahan, 193
Ivory smuggling, 223

Jahazis, 40f., 55, 61, 74, 76, 88ff., 92, 94ff., 137,
  141, 156, 185, 221, 225f.
Jask, 205
Java, 14
Jazir, 51, 55
Jazirat al-Hamra, 190
Jensen, Dr Merle, 180
Jibondo island, 116f., 119
Jomvu, 62
Juani island, 116
Juba River, 35

Kadara, Abdulla, 96
Kahe, 35
Kairouan, 82

Kamba people, 28
Kanzus, 64, 82
Kaplan, Marion, 2, 70, 72–3
Karachi, ixf., 1, 149, 151, 154, 158, 172, 175, 202,
  221; 'employment' agencies in, 191
Kareithi, Peter, 40
Karume, President Abeid, 124, 131, 135, 139,
  141–2: becomes Head of State in Zanzibar, 131;
  assassination of, 131
Karun River, 196, 198, 200
Kenya, 2, 33ff., 37, 67, 70, 223: number of slaves
  in, 35; abolition of slavery in, 35; Colony and
  Protectorate of, 37; charcoal production in, 91
Kenya Museum Society, 42
Kenya National Archives, 2, 43
Kerman, 210
Khajamed, Mr, 48
Khamir, 195, 210, 219
Kharg island, 202
Khartoum, 5
Khor, 176–7: as major fishing port for Qatar, 176
Khor Fakhan, 68
Khorramshahr, 52, 156f., 194, 196ff., 202, 207,
  226: highest percentage of Arabs living in
  Iranian city, 196, 198; chief exports of, 196; as
  largest Iranian port, 199; dhow trade of, 199
Khyber Pass, 151
Kianyagatwa, 114
Kikale, 109
Kikois, 54
Kilifi, 16, 35, 44, 86
Kilimanjaro, *see* Mount Kilimanjaro
K'i-lin, 14–15
Kilindini, 44, 54, 67; Harbour, 50
Kilindoni, 115f., 119, 121; major imports by
  dhow, 121–2
Kilwa, x, 12, 16f., 19, 22, 25, 27f., 30f., 37;
  French Slave Trading Station at, 25–7
Kilwa Kisiwani, 27, 30, 109
Kilwa Kivinje, 27, 30f., 33, 35
Kilwa Masoko, 122
Kimbo Creek, 75
Kipini, 37
Kipury, Ole, 40
Kirk, John, 37
Kirkman, Dr James, 14, 17, 38ff., 42, 144;
  personality, 38
Kisaware, 114, 118
Kish, 207
Kisiju, 101, 108f., 111, 122f.
Kisingitini, 61, 90, 95f.
Kismayu, 51, 56, 68, 70
Kiunga, 90
Kizimazki, 131
Klosser, A. J., 110, 114
Kofia, 64, 207
Koma island, 126
Konde, 144
Kotias, 54–5, 68, 107, 185
Kuala Lumpur, 147
Kung, 52, 55, 68f., 193f., 200, 207, 209ff.
Kuppi, Ali, 62
Kutch, 221
Kutch-Mandvi, India, 54ff., 107
Kuwait, xi, 1f., 6, 53, 59, 67f., 70, 103, 168, 170,

241

Tanganyika, 104; little dhow trade in, 122

Tanganyika, 2, 27, 33ff.: abolition of slavery in, 35; becomes German colony, 37; foreign dhow trade of, 102–4; imports, 103

Tanganyika African National Union (TANU), 101, 108

Tanzania, 1f., 27, 35, 67, 74, 78, 95, 97: becomes importer, 98; translocation of rural population to villages, 100; nationalization in, 100; local dhow trade of, 120–6; one way trade with Zanzibar, 126; formation of United Republic of Tanzania, 131; smuggling from, 223

Tanzania National Archives, 2, 104

Tanzanian Friendship Tourist Bureau, 142

Taru desert, 35

Tehran, 72, 193f., 201, 209, 213

Temacine, 78

Tiyab, 195, 200, 208f.

Tongoni, 16

Trucial Coast, 168

Trucial States, 174, 177, 221

Tsavo National Park, 91

Tudor Creek, 62

Tumbatu island, 131, 135–6, 141; as centre of dhow building in Zanzibar archipelago, 135

Tungi Bay, 27

Uganda, 67

Ujamaa villages, 97–8, 100, 118f.

Utende, 110, 115, 117

Utete, 109

Uzi island, 136

Vanga, 37

Vasco da Gama, 15, 17–18, 79

Vienna, Alfred, 40

Villiers, Captain Alan, 2, 70, 155; works, *Sons of Sinbad*, 70q., 155q.

Wasini, 34

Wete, 132, 138, 144, 146

Wilson, Dr Gordon M., 48–50; survey on prostitution conducted by, 48–9

Wishwa, 88

Yaos, 27

Yelf, Jack, 180

Yemen, 26, 50, 59; dhows from, 55, 221

Yung Lo, Emperor, 12

Zaid, Shaikh, 178f.

Zaire, 51, 67, 82

Zambia, 101

Zanzibar, xf., 1f., 6, 12, 16, 20, 26ff., 31, 33ff., 46f., 59, 70, 78, 82, 93, 102f., 107, 116, 122, 124, 126, 156, 202, 210, 221, 224, 226: as most important slave exporting town on East African coast, 27; importation of slaves into, 29; most important exports, 33; abolition of slavery in, 35; island, 126; as world's largest producer of cloves, 127f., 137–8; Revolution, 1964, 130–1, 135ff., 144f., 222f., 226; foreign policy of, 131; overseas dhow trade of, 132–5; life in, 134; coastal dhow trade, 137–41; involvement in illegal movement of dhows, 222–3

Zanzibar Archives, 2

Zimba cannibals, 19–20

Zinj, ix., 9, 11f.